Democracy Despite Itself

Democracy Despite Itself: Why a System That Shouldn't Work at All Works So Well

Danny Oppenheimer and Mike Edwards

The MIT Press
Cambridge, Massachusetts
London, England

MIT Press books may be purchased at special quantity discounts for business or sales promotional use. For information, please email special_sales@mitpress.mit.edu or write to Special Sales Department, The MIT Press, 55 Hayward Street, Cambridge, MA 02142.

This book was set in Stone Sans and Stone Serif by Toppan Best-set Premedia Limited. Printed and bound in the United States of America.

Library of Congress Cataloging-in-Publication Data

Oppenheimer, Danny.
Democracy despite itself: why a system that shouldn't work at all works so well / Danny Oppenheimer and Mike Edwards.
    p.   cm.
Includes bibliographical references and index.
ISBN 978-0-262-01723-7 (hardcover: alk. paper)
1. Democracy—Psychological aspects. 2. Voting—Psychological aspects.
I. Edwards, Mike, 1978–. II. Title.
JC423.O67   2012
321.8—dc23
                                                          2011031504

10 9 8 7 6 5 4 3 2

To our parents
Phil and Teri Oppenheimer
Bob and Karen Edwards

Like democracy, you're totally crazy.
But like democracy, you're the best.

Contents

Acknowledgments

First and foremost, we would like to thank Sarah Edwards. She gave helpful feedback on every version of every chapter, and kept us organized, motivated, and on task. Without her, this book would still be just an idea that we wistfully chat about while playing video games.

Our editor, Phil Laughlin, could not have been more fantastic. Thank you for giving us the freedom to tell our story, and the guidance to tell it right. Thanks also to everyone else at the MIT Press who helped make this book a reality.

Thanks to our agents, Jim Levine, Kerry Sparks, and the entire Levine/Greenberg team. There were times that it seemed like the project was headed toward a dead end, and your support was essential in keeping us on the right track.

We are grateful to all the people who read parts or all of the manuscript and gave us constructive criticism. In particular, thanks to Liv Coleman, Alaine Fay Coppin, Delores Edwards, Karen Edwards, Robert Edwards, Sara Etchison, Rachel Mackenzie, Rebekah O'Donnell, Teri Oppenheimer, Andy Rotering, Maren Stone, Pam Strickland, and Richard Strickland. Thanks also to Chas Ballew and Stephen Morrow for their feedback on how to frame our arguments back when the book was just a proposal.

A number of people lent us their expertise on various topics covered in the book. Our appreciation goes to Sara Etchison, John Darley, Debbie Prentice, Donna Shestowsky, David Schkade, and Ido Leviatan. And thank you to the Opplab, and particularly to research assistants David Mackenzie and Ani Momjian, for all the grunt work that goes on behind the scenes.

And last, but not least, thanks to ice cream, the ultimate motivator.

I   Democracy Is Crazy

The will of the people is the only legitimate foundation of any government, and to protect its free expression should be our first object.

—Thomas Jefferson

Merlin's Beard

Democracy is rife with stories of inept, corrupt, unqualified, or just plain bizarre politicians. One of our favorites is the story of State Senator Duncan Scott of Albuquerque, New Mexico. In 1995, Scott introduced the following bill for consideration by the New Mexico State Senate:

> When a psychologist or psychiatrist testifies during a defendant's competency hearing, the psychologist or psychiatrist shall wear a cone-shaped hat that is not less than two feet tall. The surface of the hat shall be imprinted with stars and lightning bolts.
>
> Additionally, a psychologist or psychiatrist shall be required to don a white beard that is not less than 18 inches in length, and shall punctuate crucial elements of his testimony by stabbing the air with a wand. Whenever a psychologist or psychiatrist provides expert testimony regarding a defendant's competency, the bailiff shall contemporaneously dim the courtroom lights and administer two strikes to a Chinese gong.

This bill actually passed the New Mexico State Senate, although fortunately for New Mexico's psychiatric community it never became law. But our favorite part about this example, other than the question of how vigorously the psychiatrist must stab the air when making a crucial point, is this: Only two New Mexico state senators were voted out of office in the following election. It would seem that the people of New Mexico thought so much of the representatives who passed this bill that they reelected them.

Democracy relies on ordinary people—people like you and us—regularly voting in meaningful elections for politicians who are supposed to follow our will. That's a scary thought. As you will see in the pages that follow, ordinary people don't know the first thing about most of the laws that govern their daily lives. Ordinary people stick to their first impressions well after they have plenty of evidence that those first impressions are wrong. Ordinary people are driven to make important decisions based on completely meaningless factors. Moreover, the ignorance and irrationality of ordinary people is only part of the problem. The elections that we use to determine our leaders are riddled with biases and opportunities for error. And, of course, once those leaders do get into office, it is extremely difficult for them to accurately interpret what the people truly want, even if they are trying to pay attention.

As a result, we elect officials who want to put psychiatrists in wizard's hats.

It's not as though the problem here is a simple lack of voter education. After all, in the United States there exist thousands of small, reasonably well-educated communities that hold frequent elections for their leadership positions. These communities have at most a couple thousand people and everyone knows basically everyone else. Most of them have 100 percent literacy rates. People are active and engaged; they participate in sports, the arts, and various social clubs. These are communities where virtually everyone has read Shakespeare, taken algebra, and studied the causes of the American Civil War. But do these communities yield particularly good elected officials—leaders who engage in lively issues-driven debates that result in policies that make those societies substantially better places?

Well, *our* high school elections were certainly nothing like that.

Winning elections in high school isn't about having the best policies; it's about being liked by the most people. Find the kid in the popular clique who gets along well with the geeks, goths, and jocks, and chances are you've just identified the class president, irrespective of his or her ideas—that is, unless someone else can come along and give a particularly funny speech on Election Day.

"Real" elections aren't that much different. Sure, presidential elections are much larger, more diverse, and more complicated than choosing a student council—but the more things change, the more they stay the same.

Just like in high school, presidents win elections by building broad coalitions of voters—only this time, those coalitions might be made up of churchgoers, small business owners, and suburban housewives, instead of geeks, goths, and jocks. Just like in high school, being broadly liked by those groups is much more important than having the best ideas.

A Tale of Two Citizens

Danny Oppenheimer is a psychologist at Princeton University. He has devoted his career to studying how people make decisions, and the results typically aren't pretty. In one study, Oppenheimer and his colleagues biased people's estimates of the length of the Mississippi River by nearly 500 miles just by having them draw three short lines before making their guess. In another study, the font on the survey influenced people's decisions about whether or not to disclose personal and embarrassing information to a stranger. "We the People"—the folks who get to decide who our leaders are and what direction our country goes in—regularly make bad decisions for bad reasons. When Oppenheimer talks about his findings, listeners often come away worried that democracy must be hopeless.

But Mike Edwards has a different take on things. Edwards has studied political science extensively and knows that democracy isn't doomed—quite the opposite, in fact. Relative to people in other countries, the citizens of democracies live longer, are better educated, have more freedom, and have better access to basic public services. By almost any measure, democracy is a tremendously successful form of government. When Edwards thinks about democracy, he thinks about a form of government that is uniquely suited to guaranteeing the lives, liberty, and prosperity of its citizens.

These two contrasting perspectives lead to a riddle: Given that voters make irrational and biased choices, how can democracies produce such well-functioning societies? We call this the paradox of democracy: Democracy shouldn't work—but it does.

This book is structured around that basic dilemma. In Part I, we will address exactly why democracy is so flawed. Voters are ignorant of even the most basic knowledge about political candidates and issues. All voters, no matter how educated or politically astute, are prone to make snap judgments about candidates based on superficial factors and to then irrationally hold on to those beliefs. Elections will always favor certain candidates over others, for reasons that have nothing to do with which candidate has the best ideas or is the best leader. And even well-meaning political leaders usually cannot understand what the true will of the people is, even if they are trying to follow it.

In Part II, we will explore why democracy works so well anyway. Democracy works because mass participation in contested elections creates psychological pressures for individuals to be better citizens and for politicians to be better leaders. It works because regularly alternating power between different factions helps to avoid political instability. It works because of the many ways that individuals and crowds can overcome their ignorance and make informed decisions. And it works because people will occasionally punish politicians, thereby helping to curb the worst abuses of the public trust.

Part I is about the craziness inherent in any democracy; Part II is about the sanity that makes democracy the greatest form of government humankind has ever devised.

Foundations of Government

If democracy works so well, what is the point of including Part I at all? Why talk about all the problems, if we're just going to turn right around and conclude that democracy is actually quite successful?

Well, in order to really understand something, you have to know about its strengths *and* its weaknesses. For instance, before you buy a house, the property will usually have to undergo a thorough inspection. The inspection will detail all of a house's flaws, from leaky pipes to cracked foundations. Of course, many fundamentally sound houses have water leaks. But just because you are buying a good, well-built house doesn't mean that you can ignore the leak. Nor can you fix a leak without first understanding where the water is coming from.

This book is like an inspection report for democracy. Like a well-built house, democracy is a strong and structurally sound system of government. But it also has its flaws. The purpose of Part I is to pinpoint the weaknesses of democracy so that we can fix them; the purpose of Part II is to identify the strengths of democracy so that we can bolster them.

Of course, before we can analyze the strengths and weaknesses of democracy, we first have to know what democracy means. Unfortunately, *democracy* is a surprisingly difficult concept to define, but for the purposes of this book, we will consider a country to be democratic if it regularly holds free, fair, and meaningful elections. There's not a word in the previous sentence that isn't controversial or hard to define, but let's give it a go, anyway.

Elections are *free* if there are few restrictions on who can run for election and who can vote in those elections. In France, all citizens are automatically registered to vote when they turn 18, and any citizen over the age of 23 is eligible to run for office so long as they have fulfilled their required military obligations. By contrast, in South Africa under apartheid the vast majority of adults were forbidden from participating in national elections because they were black.

Elections are *fair* if they are untainted by bribery, intimidation, or corruption, and if the outcome is not predetermined by the leadership. In Great Britain, Parliamentary elections are regularly held with little or no controversy, and small political parties frequently claim unexpected victories in various districts. In Cuba, the Castro regime has regularly been reelected every couple of years, but those elections have always been rigged so that it was impossible for there to be any other outcome than a landslide victory for Castro.

Elections are *meaningful* if the winners of those elections are put into positions of real power and authority. In Japan, the winners of the parliamentary elections become legislators, capable of creating the laws of the land. By contrast, in Iran the president is elected democratically, but once in power all of his decisions can be vetoed by an unelected council of religious leaders.

This definition of democracy is not without its faults. In particular, it is purposefully vague. For instance, we never say exactly what percentage of the population needs to be eligible to vote in order for a country to be a democracy. In the early days of American government, only white men who owned property were allowed to vote. While the property restrictions were lifted over the next sixty years or so, African Americans were, for the most part, not legally allowed to vote until after the Civil War, and restrictions existed for most black voters until the 1960s. Women were not guaranteed the right to vote until 1919, 18-year-olds were not allowed to vote until 1971, and many convicted felons are barred from voting even today. So when did the United States become a democracy?

Similar debates can be had about many countries, but they are not especially relevant for this book. We can quibble over the details of how free, fair, or meaningful a given election is, but some countries are clearly more democratic than others. When we talk about democracy, we are mainly referring to the set of least controversial democracies in the world, places like the United States, Brazil, Germany, South Korea, and Botswana. By nondemocracies, we mean countries with transparent violations of the above criteria, such as Syria, Zimbabwe, Cuba, Belarus, and Vietnam.

The paradox of democracy applies to all democracies. All people are irrational and uninformed, and all electoral systems are flawed. Yet democracy is an extraordinarily successful form of government, and has proven successful in almost every region of the globe, despite whatever local forms of craziness plague any given country. That being said, we have chosen to focus our attention on the particular brand of American craziness for the sake of simplicity and familiarity.

One last caveat before we begin: Throughout this book we will talk about how "crazy" or "irrational" people are. If you were to call your friend "crazy," it would mean he's "not all there" or he's "acting emotionally." But in the social sciences, *irrational* refers to people making inconsistent or imperfect decisions. We all do this; so, according to social scientists, we are all irrational. So when we say that the voters are "crazy," we don't mean that voters are insane—certainly not in a talking to trees or eating your neighbors sort of way. We simply mean that voters are human.

So we implore you not to take any of this personally. At times during this book, it's going to seem like voters are ignorant and foolish pawns of a political system they don't understand. To be honest, that's actually a fairly accurate description: Voters often are ignorant and foolish pawns of a system they don't understand. But we would include ourselves in that category too. Our purpose is to inform, not to insult.

In short, people may be irrational but democracies are quite sane. The sum is greater than its chaotic parts. The late columnist Molly Ivins once said that democracy "requires a certain relish for confusion." In other words: Democracy is crazy—but maybe that's not so bad.

References

Quotes

Ivins, M. N.d. Great-Quotes.com. Retrieved March 23, 2011, from http://www .great-quotes.com/quote/1429619.

Jefferson, Thomas. 1801. Letter to Benjamin Watson. Retrieved March 23, 2011, from http://www.famguardian.org/Subjects/Politics/ThomasJefferson/jeff0500.htm.

Wizard Hats

Albuquerque Journal. 1996. Pg. C2. Retrieved April 16, 2011, from Lexus-Nexus.

Oswald, M. 1995. Polls show legislators don't have many fans. *The Santa Fe New Mexican*, March 6, p. B1.

Wizard of id. 1995. *Harper's Magazine* 291 (1742), p. 16.

Definition of Democracy

Don't expect reforms, Khatami says. *Boston Globe*, March 18, 2004. Reprinted from the Associated Press. Retrieved April 17, 2011, from http://articles.boston.com/2004-03-18/news/29207277_1_guardian-council-hard-liners-liberal-publications.

EdGate.com. 2000. Copernicus election watch: History of the vote. *USA Today*. Retrieved April 17, 2011, from http://www.edgate.com/elections/inactive/history _of_the_vote/.

FOX News. January 20, 2008. Cuban elections could shed light on Castro's future. Reprinted from the Associated Press. Retrieved April 17, 2011, from http://www .foxnews.com/story/0,2933,324147,00.html.

Ministère des Affaires étrangères. 2007. French Presidential Election. French Embassy to the United Kingdom. Retrieved April 16, 2011, from http://www.ambafrance-uk .org/The-presidential-election.html.

Overcoming Apartheid. N.d. Unit 2 colonialism and segregation: The origins of apartheid. In association with Michigan State University. Retrieved April 17, 2011, from http://overcomingapartheid.msu.edu/unit.php?id=12&page=1.

Parliament.UK. 2011. Current state of the parties. Retrieved April 17, 2011, from http://www.parliament.uk/mps-lords-and-offices/mps/state-of-the-parties/.

Saeki, Y. 2008. Japan's parliament okays extra budget for econ steps. Forbes.com, October 16, reprinted from Thompson Financial News. Retrieved April 17, 2011, from http://www.forbes.com/feeds/afx/2008/10/16/afx5561867.html.

1 Don't Know Much About . . . Well, Anything, Really

The best argument against democracy is a five-minute conversation with the average voter.

—Winston Churchill

Here's a fun experiment you can try out on a friend before the next election. First, ask your friend what the most important issue will be in that election. Then find out which candidate your friend is supporting. Next, ask your friend how well he understands his candidate's position on the aforementioned issue. Your friend will undoubtedly tell you that he understands it quite well—it is, after all, what he considers the most important issue.

Now ask your friend to explain his candidate's stance on that issue. Depending on how much you enjoy poking fun at your friends, the results will either be humorous or disturbing. (Just make sure that *you* actually know the answers, otherwise you will only embarrass yourself.)

No, we don't think that the readers of this book have remarkably ignorant friends; ignorance is the rule rather than the exception. New York University Business School professor Adam Alter and his colleagues ran this study on a group of New Jersey voters in the week following the 2008 presidential primaries. At the time, Barack Obama and Hillary Clinton were in a heated contest for the Democratic nomination, and John McCain, Mike Huckabee, and Mitt Romney were fighting for the Republican nomination. Passions were running high and partisans were fervent in their beliefs that their favored candidate was the best for the position. However, when asked to describe their candidates' positions on their self-described "most important issue," people were dumbfounded.

Although most people could give at least cursory answers (e.g., "she wants to improve health care"), very few could explain anything substantive about the specifics of the candidate's plans. And despite strong differences in opinion about who would be the best candidate, almost nobody could explain how the candidates differed on any issue. In fact, after attempting to describe a candidate's policy position, the vast majority of people in this study acknowledged that they didn't know as much as they had initially believed. This pattern held true of both Republicans and Democrats across all issues. It was even true for people who claimed that the primary factor influencing their choice of whom to support was the candidate's policy positions. In other words, while people believe that they understand the policy positions of their candidates, this belief is not supported by their actual knowledge.

Modern democratic theory is based on the notion that people vote in line with their interests and principles. To be able to do this, people need to understand the key issues, the important facts relevant to those issues, and the positions of the candidates on those issues. However, voters are rarely so well informed. What we know about the issues is often biased, incomplete, lacking, or downright false. We lack the information and expertise needed to make good decisions about issues and candidates, we have trouble finding that information, and we can't even remember it once we've found it. There's an old saying that knowledge is power; but in democracies, the people have the power, but are largely missing the knowledge.

Facts of the Matter

Pop quiz: For every 1 million babies born in the United States, how many legal abortions are there? Stop and think about it for a second. How high would that number have to be to surprise you? How low would it have to be to surprise you? When University of California, Berkeley, professor Michael Ranney and his colleagues asked this question of college students, the average estimate was 10,000. Does that seem high to you? Low? About right? The correct answer is 335,000, more than 30 times larger than the average estimate.

Ranney and his colleagues have been running estimation surveys for over a decade. They've looked at such diverse issues as immigration, education, crime, and the environment. They've taken surveys from a broad range of people: liberals and conservatives, students, the general population, and even professional journalists who cover these issues. Across it all, estimates are typically woefully inaccurate. (See table 1.1.)

These aren't just "gotcha" questions about useless trivia. People need this information to make informed policy decisions. A person who thinks the immigration rate is 150 times the true rate is going to have uninformed opinions on immigration policy. Somebody who thinks there are 65 times more people in jail than are actually incarcerated is likely to support different policies on crime and punishment than if he had accurate information. And indeed, there is evidence that people are strongly influenced by their incorrect beliefs about the facts.

For example, over 60 percent of Americans believe that the United States spends too much on foreign aid. The average voter believes that we spend 20 percent of the federal budget on foreign aid and that we should only be spending half that much—about 10 percent. But in reality, less than 1 percent of the U.S. budget goes to foreign aid! If the U.S. government were to spend as much as the average American seems to desire, then that would be a tremendous *increase* in spending on foreign aid. Yet most Americans want to dramatically *decrease* the foreign aid budget. It isn't necessarily the case that increased foreign aid is the correct policy. The important point is that when "We the People" do not evaluate policies with correct information, our desires and our policy preferences may not match up.

Similarly, our ignorance of the truth can have a dramatic impact on Election Day. In October 2004, a month before the U.S. presidential

Table 1.1

Examples of estimates of policy-relevant facts.

Issue	Median Estimate	True Value
Legal annual immigration per 1,000 residents	460	3
Garbage production per day per U.S. resident	25 lbs.	4.5 lbs.
Incarceration rate per 1,000 residents	450	7
College degrees per 1,000 adults	418	275
Executions per 1,000 murders	99	4

The data in this table are consolidated from a series of studies done by Michael Ranney and colleagues between 2003 and 2005. See reference list for full citations. Note that the specific numbers might fluctuate over time.

elections, the Program on International Policy Attitudes surveyed the electorate about their knowledge of issues, policies, and candidates. The results were disturbing. For example, even though there was no credible evidence that Iraq provided significant support to Al Qaeda, nearly 40 percent of voters believed that clear evidence of support had been found. Importantly, this (false) belief was highly related to people's political attitudes. Nearly two-thirds of Bush supporters believed that a link between Iraq and Al Qaeda had been found, but only 15 percent of Kerry supporters held this belief. Similarly, a majority of Bush supporters believed that Iraq did actually have weapons of mass destruction (WMDs), when in reality both the Senate Intelligence Committee and Chief Weapons Inspector Charles Duelfer had concluded the exact opposite. Voters who correctly believed that no WMDs had been found were much more likely to support Kerry. It may very well be that Bush was the better candidate in this election—there were certainly other valid reasons one could have had to vote for him. But voters who based their votes on the mistaken impression that WMDs had been found were not expressing their true preferences.

Democracy is supposed to work because voters will choose the candidates with the best ideas. But how can we vote for the candidate with the best ideas if we don't have the information necessary to evaluate those ideas?

The Devil Is in the Details

Regardless of your political affiliation, you probably believe that having nuclear missiles landing on your house is a bad thing and would prefer government policies that reduce the odds of such an occurrence. Of course, you can't support those policies unless you know what those policies are.

So, in an effort to help you be more informed, we humbly ask that you do your best to understand the following policy analysis from John Pendleton, the Director of Defense Capabilities and Management, in his report to the Strategic Forces Subcommittee of the House Committee on Armed Services describing important policy challenges regarding the Missile Defense Agency (MDA):

> Oversight of MDA is executed by the Under Secretary of Defense for Acquisition, Technology, and Logistics. Because MDA is not subject to DOD's [Department of

Defense's] traditional joint requirements determination and acquisition process, DOD developed alternative oversight mechanisms. For example, in 2007 the Deputy Secretary of Defense established the Missile Defense for Acquisition, Technology, and Logistics, or Deputy Secretary of Defense, as necessary, with a recommended ballistic missile defense strategic plan and feasible funding strategy for approval. In September 2008, the Deputy Secretary of Defense also established a life cycle management process for the Ballistic Missile Defense System. The Deputy Secretary of Defense directed the Board to use the process to oversee the annual preparation of a required capabilities portfolio and develop a program plan to meet the requirements with Research, Development, Test, and Evaluation; procurement; operations and maintenance; and military construction in defensewide accounts.

So, what do you think? Is this an appropriate policy for oversight of the MDA budgeting and acquisition process? Would you vote in favor of a policy like this? Did it even make sense to you? If it did, you're either an expert on defense procurement processes or extremely focused and persistent—much more so than we are.

We know that we want to be secure against a nuclear missile attack as safely, efficiently, and cost-effectively as possible. But the specifics are not nearly so clear or straightforward. It turns out that most of the issues that society faces are complex and nuanced. To really understand the likelihood and effects of climate change, you need to have a fair grasp of atmospheric chemistry. To reduce the appeal of gangs to underprivileged teenagers, it is useful to have a background in sociology. To develop a solid financial regulatory policy, you'd best study up on your economics. These are critically important issues, and yet most of us don't have the time, inclination, or ability to master even one of these disciplines. So if "We the People" don't really understand the issues, how can we express our will about associated policies?

Of course, even having a solid mastery of the facts surrounding an issue still may not be enough to truly understand that issue. Alan Greenspan is one of the world's foremost experts on the effect of regulation on macroeconomic systems. He holds a Ph.D. in economics from New York University, served as the Chairman of the Federal Reserve for nearly twenty years, and was a trusted advisor to both Democrats and Republicans on economic issues. And yet, in late October 2008 after the collapse of the stock market and bankruptcy of several iconic corporations, Greenspan conceded before Congress that he had failed to understand the situation.

In other words, even the world's most accomplished experts have trouble successfully navigating the intricacies of the complex systems of policymaking. What chance do the rest of us have?

To add insult to injury, there are a vast number of issues, many more than any single person could effectively become an expert on. As of the writing of this book, there are 192 nations recognized by the United Nations. For each of those nations, we need to have trade agreements, defense arrangements, and extradition treaties, among many other issues. So here's a question for all of you budding foreign policy buffs out there: What are your thoughts on the appropriate amount to tariff Guinean bauxite?

Or maybe the environment is more your cup of tea. There are nearly 100 categories for toxins and pollutants listed on the Environmental Protection Agency's website. Each of these requires policy for its regulation and cleanup. So what is your policy preference regarding the maximum allowable levels of dicholorethylene in drinking water?

There are equally minute and complex issues involving poverty, education, public health, defense, race relations, the economy, communications, taxation, crime, drugs, natural disasters, natural resources, energy, the arts, agriculture, abortion, civil liberties, firearms . . . we could go on. And those are just the federal issues. Don't forget that we're also supposed to be informed about what's going on in our states, our counties, and our local city councils. There are so many issues that it would be impossible to be even moderately informed about more than a small fraction of them.

Some might argue that we don't need to be informed on all the issues. Maybe democracy really means expressing our will on only the most important ones. Maybe we don't need to know the specifics of the policies or the underlying science and history; as long as we understand the gist of the policies, we should be able to have basic preferences that we can pass along to our leaders—right?

Unfortunately, many voters do not have even that basic level of knowledge. In the early 1960s, political scientist Phil Converse surveyed the American electorate about their belief systems. He found that over 20 percent of the population had an understanding of issues and the political scene that had, in his words, "no shred of policy significance whatsoever." Nearly half of the respondents could not reliably label policies as being "liberal" or "conservative" or identify which party (Democrat or Republican) holds which stance in major policy debates. Indeed, a third of the people surveyed "could supply no meaning for the liberal-conservative distinction" whatsoever. These sorts of findings have been replicated dozens of times. For example, in the mid-1980s when political scientists Milton Lodge and Ruth Hamill asked people to categorize policy items as either associated with Republicans or Democrats, more than a third of the respondents seemed to be randomly guessing.

Part of this is understandable. The meanings of *Democrat* and *Republican* are constantly changing. The North American Free Trade Agreement (NAFTA) was championed by a Democrat, Bill Clinton, in 1994, and then 14 years later was strongly criticized by a Democrat, Hillary Clinton, in the 2008 presidential primaries. Mandatory health insurance was endorsed by Richard Nixon in the 1970s, the conservative Heritage Foundation in the 1990s, and as recently as 2006 by Mitt Romney, who would two years later run in the GOP presidential primary. But in 2010, conservative talk show hosts, think tanks (including the Heritage Foundation), and politicians (including Mitt Romney) were decrying this provision of the Obama Health Care Reform Bill as a violation of basic rights.

So some confusion is only to be expected. Politics is, after all, extremely volatile. However, the extent of our ignorance on policies that we claim to care deeply about is disconcerting. For example, the Annenberg Public Policy Center noted that on the eve of the House vote on the 2010 Health Care Reform Bill, a surprisingly large number of people believed that it involved a federally run health care plan (i.e., a public option), even though that element had never been passed in the Senate. Town Hall Meetings were flooded with people furious about the provision of "death panels," despite the fact that the bill didn't include anything that even remotely met that description. In short, while there are often understandable reasons for our ignorance, the fact remains that the average voter knows depressingly little about the important issues of the day.

Knowing Where They Stand

Radio shock jock Howard Stern is perhaps better known for his dirty jokes than for his research in political science. But he also has an interest in politics, even going so far as to run for the Governor of New York in 1994. Fourteen years later, less than a month before Barack Obama defeated John

McCain for U.S. president, Stern and his staff ran an impromptu survey on the streets of New York.

One of Stern's colleagues approached Obama backers in Harlem and asked them whether they supported Obama more "because he's pro-life or because he thinks our troops should stay in Iraq and finish this war?" Astute readers may note that Obama is pro-choice and that one of the pillars of his campaign was his promise to end the war in Iraq. In other words, the question made no sense whatsoever. Unfortunately, this did not seem to matter to the people being interviewed. As one respondent confidently replied, "I think because our troops should stay in Iraq and finish this war, I'm really firm with that." The reporter followed up:

> Reporter: And if he wins would you have any problem with Sarah Palin [McCain's running mate] being vice president?
> Respondent: No I wouldn't, not at all.
> Reporter: Obama says that he's anti stem-cell research, how do you feel about that.
> Respondent: I believe that's [pause] I wouldn't do that either, I'm anti stem-cell.

Not only did people seem to have no idea that these were not Obama's policies (or his choice of vice president), but they seemed to adopt their policy stance on the spot in support of their candidate rather than choosing who to support based on the candidate's positions. Lest we think that this kind of reasoning is unique to Democrats, the reporter also found a McCain supporter:

> Respondent: I think he wants to get away from the war thing, I know that for sure.
> Reporter: McCain wants out of the war?
> Respondent: He wants out of the war.

Of course, McCain had repeatedly expressed the opposite position.

It would be tempting to believe that interviews like these are just a publicity stunt by a shock jock looking to stir up some controversy. After all, it is a radio show, and it's much more entertaining and provocative to show people who are uninformed. You might think that they had to approach dozens of people just to get a few good sound bites of people sounding ignorant. Fortunately for Stern's producers, but unfortunately for the rest of us, scientifically rigorous surveys have concluded that the results of Stern's interviews are depressingly common.

A survey conducted by the Program on International Policy found that in the month before the 2004 presidential elections, a majority of George

Bush's supporters believed that he supported bans on land mines and nuclear testing, wanted the United States to participate in the International Criminal Courts, and endorsed U.S. participation in the Kyoto accords. President Bush actually opposed all of those things. Inaccurate perceptions of a candidate's positions were not by any means unique to Republicans. For example, the same survey revealed that more than half of John Kerry's supporters misunderstood his position on defense spending. Nor was this lack of knowledge limited to the 2004 election.

In the 2008 presidential elections, a surprisingly large number of voters believed that Barack Obama was a Muslim (he wasn't), and that John McCain had an affair with a lobbyist (he didn't). And this misinformation can be long-lasting: Based on the 2000 campaign, many voters still believe that Al Gore claimed to have invented the Internet (a claim he never made[1]).

Of course, our belief in untruths is not just limited to presidential candidates. For example, a survey in 2004 showed that in states where both senators voted against a nuclear test ban treaty, 65 percent of their constituents believed that the senators were in favor of the treaty. In that same year, Congress passed a bill supporting compliance with World Trade Organization (WTO) rulings. Only 52 percent of people in districts with pro-WTO congressmen accurately believed that their congressmen supported the bill, whereas 62 percent of people with anti-WTO congressmen thought their congressmen supported the bill. That is, people were 10 percent more likely to believe that their congressmen had supported the bill if, in fact, their congressmen had not.

Defense spending increased by over 30 percent between 2001 and 2004, and yet a full 65 percent of Americans thought that Congress wanted to simply keep defense spending at a constant level. In fact, a survey by the Program on International Policy revealed that from land mine treaties to nuclear testing to environmental regulation to missile defense, a majority of Americans misperceived the positions of their representatives in Congress.

How do people come to believe these untrue things about candidates?

One problem is that we simply assume that our favored candidate agrees with us. Most people generally think that others share their beliefs—a

---

1. The actual quote was: "During my service in the United States Congress, I took the initiative in creating the Internet," referring specifically to his early advocacy of the research that would eventually lead to the Internet.

phenomenon that psychologists refer to as the *false consensus effect*. For example, one study interviewed Canadians immediately prior to a 1992 referendum to rewrite the Canadian Constitution. People who supported the referendum believed that the referendum was significantly more popular than it actually was, while people who opposed it believed that it was less popular than it actually was. Another study looked at the 1980 U.S. presidential election and found that the supporters of Jimmy Carter tended to overestimate the amount of national support for Carter, while the supporters of Ronald Reagan tended to overestimate the national support for Reagan. In the same way that we overestimate how much other voters agree with us, we also assume our favored politicians agree with us. The aforementioned Program on International Policy Attitudes surveys showed that when voters make errors about politicians' stances on the issues, those errors almost always align with the voters' personal policy preference.

In short, we don't know the necessary facts to make policy, don't know what actual government policies are, and don't know where the various candidates stand on the issues. That's disturbing, but at least it's solvable, right? If voters don't have the necessary information to express their will, then maybe we can fix that by giving them the information. Unfortunately, the problem is not so easily fixed.

Forgive and Forget

Without looking back, what was the name of the researcher who studied people's estimates of abortion rates that we talked about earlier in the chapter? Don't worry if you can't recall. Unless you happen to be that researcher or one of his friends or close relations, it's very unlikely you remembered. In fact, our memories are quite fallible, which is one of the reasons that our knowledge of the facts is so poor.

For those of you who didn't flip back to check, the estimation guru's name is Michael Ranney, and this next study was done in his lab as well. Ranney asked people to guess the United States' legal immigration rate, its incarceration rate, and fourteen other facts that are relevant to current policy debates. As usual, people didn't do very well. Ranney then briefly told them the correct answers. It was hoped that the feedback would make them more informed about the facts related to their policy preferences.

Eight days later, Ranney tested half of the facts, and people's memories were strong. However, twelve weeks later, he asked them for estimates about the other half of the facts. The results were less encouraging. People's estimates at that point were typically closer to their initial estimates than to the true values. Indeed, the median estimate for the inflation rate after twelve weeks was even identical to what it had been before feedback. That is, although in the short term people had learned the information, in the long term they mostly forgot what they had learned.

This finding has been replicated several times. In 2002, Princeton professors Alex Todorov and Eldar Shafir were teaching a class to students studying to earn a Master in Public Affairs degree. As a demonstration, they asked students to estimate the percentage of the U.S. budget that goes to foreign aid. As you may recall (if you read the first half of the chapter within the past few weeks, anyway), the average American estimates about 20 percent, while the true number is less than 1 percent. The median estimate of the students was 5 percent—perhaps unsurprisingly, students who are studying public affairs have a better sense of the U.S. budget than the general population—but they still guessed more than five times too high. The students were then given the correct answer. Four weeks later, the students again estimated the percentage of the budget going to foreign aid. This time, the estimate was 3 percent. Although better than their original guess, this is still off by a factor of three. Even people who know a great deal and care deeply about policy cannot retain the correct answer for a mere four weeks. Our guess is that a year later their estimates would have reverted back to 5 percent.

Forgetfulness isn't limited solely to simple facts; it extends to our knowledge of politician's positions as well. For example, Milton Lodge from State University of New York, Stony Brook, and his colleagues gave voters fictional biographies of a hypothetical "Congressman Lucas." Half of the voters were told that Lucas was a Republican; the others were told that he was a Democrat. The voters read a series of forty policy statements that were attributed to "Congressman Lucas" and then took a ten-minute vocabulary task to distract them. Finally, they were given a surprise memory task where they looked at a long list of policy statements, and were asked to identify which ones Lucas had espoused.

The voters were divided into thirds on the basis of their political knowledge and sophistication. The "uninformed" and "average" voters each got

basically half of the answers correct. They would have been just as successful at identifying which policy statements "Congressman Lucas" had
expressed had they flipped a coin to determine their answers. That is, two-
thirds of the population cannot remember what a politician's policy positions are after a mere ten minutes of distraction. Even the most sophisticated
voters only had slightly better than 60 percent accuracy, which is still
unimpressive.

Of course, we do remember some things. For example, although most
people don't know how much the United States spends on foreign aid,
many people can recall having heard that the Great Wall of China is the
only human-made object visible from space. The only problem is that it's
not true. Consider this: The Great Wall's width is, at its widest, approxi-
mately 25 feet. Compare that to Toronto's Highway 401, which is over 180
feet at its widest. At any height from space that the Great Wall is visible,
so would be Highway 401 and any number of other highway systems
around the world.

Whether or not we remember something bears little relationship to
whether or not that something is true. Stanford professor Chip Heath and
his colleagues have spent the last decade exploring why we remember and
believe urban legends. It turns out that whether something is emotional,
surprising, concrete, and/or simple will matter a lot more for whether we'll
remember it than whether it is true. And the truth about candidates and
policies is often not nearly as emotional, surprising, concrete, or simple as
some of the rumors that propagate through the electorate. In other words,
what we learn about our candidates during an election isn't necessarily the
truth. One reason why people have such poor knowledge about facts, policies, and candidates is that it's very hard to remember accurate, factual
information.

Of course, we don't necessarily need long-term memories to be informed
voters. If we can just remind ourselves of the relevant facts on or about
Election Day then we'll be fine, even if we forget those facts immediately
after we vote. Unfortunately, our ability to locate and gather the necessary
information is deeply flawed.

Ignorant of Ignorance

Think back to the last time you disagreed with somebody and turned out
to be wrong. It happens to us all the time. Not long ago, one of the authors

of this book was so confident that the plural of "octopus" was "octopodi" that he lost a bet on it. In retrospect it seems like a crazy belief, but at the time he was sure of it. (Acceptable plurals of "octopus" are "octopuses," "octopi," or "octopodes," in case you were wondering.) We take, and lose, these kinds of bets because when we "know" a piece of false information, it feels the same as when we know a piece of true information. Being wrong doesn't come with a warning label.

In fact, the people who know the least are often in the worst position to evaluate their knowledge. The less you know, the less you know what you don't know. Or, as more eloquently put by Charles Darwin, "ignorance more frequently begets confidence than does knowledge." Psychologists call this ability (or inability) to critically reflect on our own knowledge or thinking *metacognition*.

It turns out that there are several reasons that we overestimate how much we know. For example, most things can be thought of in both abstract and concrete ways—just typically not at the same time. Take a moment and think about how a bicycle works. Be precise. Now try and draw a bicycle, including the gears and brakes, and explain how the parts work together to cause it to move. On one level, we are very familiar with bicycles; and yet, unless you've actually worked on bicycles for a living, that task was probably not easy for you. We know what they are and what they are used for. We know what they look like. We know how to ride one. We even know that there are gears and pedals. But we don't know exactly how those parts interact with the wheels.

The problem is that people have a tendency to confuse their knowledge of the abstract with their knowledge of the concrete. When we asked you to draw a bicycle you probably thought "that's not hard, I know a lot about bicycles!" Of course, if you actually sat down to do it you probably ended up with a lot of parts that you knew needed to be there—but didn't really know how they connected. Yale psychologist Frank Keil and his colleagues have demonstrated that our belief that we know things more deeply than we really do applies to a wide variety of common things, from toilets to earthquakes.

These same principles apply to politics, as demonstrated by the studies by Adam Alter and his colleagues described in the opening example of this chapter. When a voter thinks of a favored candidate, he has a lot of knowledge in the abstract. He knows what the candidate looks like and knows that the candidate would like to reduce crime, improve education, and keep the economy strong. When he evaluates how much he knows about that candidate, he can rightly say "a lot." But when it comes to the nitty-gritty of the policy details, voters are pretty ignorant, as we've demonstrated.

People don't realize how little they actually know. So how can they possibly seek out enough information to develop fully informed policy preferences?

Hide and Go Seek

In 2006, the liberal political action committee Votevets.org put out an ad claiming that Senator Elizabeth Dole voted to deny body armor to U.S. troops serving in Iraq. However, funding for body armor was never explicitly raised as an issue in the Senate during her tenure. In truth, Dole voted against a bill for $1 billion dollars of unspecified "equipment," a vote that had nothing to do with the body armor shortage. The lack of sufficient body armor was due to a shortage of the Kevlar fabric used to make armor, not to a lack of funds, and certainly not to Dole's vote. The ad was downright deceptive; the goal was to mislead voters into thinking that Dole didn't care about the safety of U.S. troops.

That ad is hardly unique. The nonpartisan FactCheck.org has cataloged thousands of inaccurate claims being put forth by politicians and interest groups. For example, in the 2008 presidential campaign, John McCain repeatedly stated in ads and speeches that the Obama tax plan would increase taxes on families making over $42,000 a year. In reality, Obama's plan would only raise taxes on families making over $200,000 a year, nearly five times what McCain claimed. Not to be outdone, Obama's campaign put out an ad suggesting that McCain was opposed to stem cell research, the opposite of McCain's actual position.

Not all misinformation is as blatant as the above examples. Sometimes it involves framing a story out of context. For example, consider the 2008 Higher Education Act, which changed the process for applying for federal financial aid and created stricter regulation of the private student loan industry. Several amendments were considered for this bill, including one proposing new regulations on greenhouse gas emissions and another proposing the designation of federal funds to programs aimed at reducing gang violence. While environmental protection and reducing violence are laudable goals, they are totally unrelated to the central purpose of the bill. Imagine that a senator opposes the changes to financial aid. If she votes against it, you can be sure that when the time for reelection comes around her opponent will say that she voted against a bill that would have protected the environment and helped stem gang violence. While it is a true statement, it's also misleading—the intention of the vote had much more to do with student aid policy. You can't really learn about the senator's view on crime or the environment from her vote on an education bill.

Other misleading information comes from differences in assumptions. Imagine that a candidate proposes changes to school lunches that involve providing healthier options to kids. How much will such a change cost? Well, it depends. Economist 1 might look at the number of kids currently eating in school cafeterias, multiply that number by the additional cost per lunch, and project that total as the cost of the new law. Economist 2 might believe that if lunches were healthier, more parents would take advantage of them. And so Economist 2 might predict that 20 percent more school lunches would be sold, and provide a 20 percent higher cost projection than Economist 1. Undoubtedly politicians in favor of the plan would use Economist 1's estimate in attempting to rally public support, while opponents would use Economist 2's estimate to try and argue against the bill.[2] It isn't always obvious which estimate is better, so this isn't inherently deceptive. With so much conflicting information coming in, it's no wonder that voters are confused.

Another way of misleading the public is by hiding certain information. Presidents in particular have wide latitude to label embarrassing information as "classified" or to claim "executive privilege." While these techniques have often been used for legitimate reasons, it is also true that they have been abused. For instance, it is only in the last few years that the

---

2. Of course, this example only scratches the surface of the problem, because there are limitless numbers of economic factors that one could consider. For example, Economist 3 might note that if kids eat healthier today, they will be healthier in the long run and thus have fewer costly hospital visits in the future. Or he might argue that healthier lunches will lead kids to have more energy and be able to pay more attention in school, thus improving their educational outcomes and future productivity in the workplace. Not to mention the economic impacts on the U.S. vegetable farmers and food producers. The problem of which factors to take into account means that it is often possible to make legitimate arguments for any number of cost estimates, making the problem more or less intractable.

government declassified the records of the 1971 FBI surveillance of former Beatle John Lennon. Previously this information, including meetings between Lennon and various 1960s radicals, was classified because it might lead to "military retaliation against the United States." More likely, it was considered embarrassing to the FBI to have bothered to keep one of the most recognizable men on the planet under constant surveillance.

More recently, President George W. Bush's administration effectively sued to prevent the release of information about meetings between Vice President Dick Cheney and top oil executives, including even the White House visitor logs of the days on which those meetings took place. While we cannot know for certain what was said at those meetings, it is highly doubtful that the oil executives were consulting with Vice President Cheney about anything that needed to be kept secret. More likely, the administration thought that the details of these meetings might be politically embarrassing, and so they fought against their release.

Even when they don't actively hide information, politicians are often simply conveniently coy. It turns out that there's no such thing as a perfect policy; every policy has strengths and weaknesses. Policies that do more good typically have a higher price tag. Policies that make some people better off typically make others worse off. Policies that increase our safety typically decrease our civil liberties. If you actually know the details of a politician's policies, then you'll know the flaws. And if you know the flaws, you'll be much less motivated to go out and vote. So politicians tend to oversimplify their own positions in most of their speeches and campaign releases, and only release the specifics in long inscrutable documents. As a result, if you ever try to find the specific details of a candidate's plan, or his or her position on a more obscure policy issue (e.g., water rights in the Southwest), good luck to you. Even if you do find a "plan" on their website, it is usually boiled down to a small number of vague talking points that hide as much as they reveal.

Politicians distort, obscure, and conceal the information the public needs to be informed. So how can we possibly find enough accurate and detailed information to develop fully informed policy preferences? This problem is made even worse by the fact that our information gathering is inherently biased. We tend to seek out information that supports what we already believe, and actively avoid information that contradicts our current opinions.

The Gathering Storm

In a classic study, Iowa State psychologist Aaron Lowin asked voters during the 1964 presidential election between Lyndon Johnson and Barry Goldwater to look through various brochures that either supported or opposed their preferred candidate. Some of the brochures contained strong arguments; others were substantially less convincing. He found that when the arguments in the brochures were strong, voters much preferred to read positive arguments about their favored candidate than about the rival candidate. Similarly, people much preferred to read strong negative arguments about the opposing candidate than about their own candidate. In other words, they preferred information that reinforced their current opinion, and they tended to ignore information that was counter to it. Interestingly, if the arguments in the brochure were weak, voters were happy to read arguments that went against their own opinions—presumably because the weak arguments were easily discounted. This tendency to seek out information in line with what we already believe is called a *confirmation bias*.

Back in the 1960s, the implications were mostly theoretical. There was no cable news and no Internet, which meant that the average voter had little choice in the media he or she could consume. These days, however, it is easy for people to selectively acquire political information in line with their prior beliefs. Indeed, the 2007 Zogby/Lear Survey on Politics and Entertainment found that whereas 70 percent of conservatives reported that they frequently watched Fox News, only 12 percent of moderates and liberals did. Similarly, whereas nearly 70 percent of liberals reported frequent viewing of NBC, the numbers were considerably lower for conservatives and moderates. Americans are getting only a subset of the relevant information, and are not learning the facts, policies, and arguments that are being espoused by their political opponents.

Of course, even when people get objectively the same information, they are often pretty biased about the interpretations of that information. This phenomenon was observed in the early 1950s by Dartmouth professor Al Hastorf and Princeton Professor Hadley Cantrel regarding a football game between the two schools. The game was quite rough, with a number of penalties, injuries, and accusations of dirty play. Princeton and Dartmouth students all saw the same game, but as you can guess the interpretations differed greatly. Nearly 90 percent of Princeton students believed that it was the Dartmouth team that had played dirty and instigated the conflict, but less than 40 percent of Dartmouth students had the same belief. On the other hand, over 50 percent of Dartmouth students claimed that both sides were equally at fault, while only 11 percent of Princeton students believed the same thing. Despite being exposed to the same evidence, different interpretations were reached depending on the observer's affiliation. Princeton students believed a pro-Princeton interpretation; Dartmouth students believed a pro-Dartmouth interpretation.

Nearly thirty years later, Stanford researchers Charles Lord, Lee Ross, and Mark Lepper found that people have similarly biased ways of interpreting political information. Both proponents and opponents of the death penalty were asked to read two fictitious studies: one providing evidence that the death penalty was an effective crime deterrent and the other providing evidence that the death penalty was not an effective crime deterrent. The subjects were then asked to rate how convincing they found the different studies. Death penalty proponents found the pro-deterrence study to be over 35 percent *more* convincing than the anti-deterrence study, whereas opponents of the death penalty regarded the pro-deterrence study to be 25 percent *less* convincing than the anti-deterrence study. Remember that they read the exact same materials. More disturbingly, the subjects used their biased interpretations of the studies to inform their policy preferences. Proponents became even more convinced in the rightness of the death penalty, while opponents became even more convinced of its wrongness. Greater information led to greater polarization.

When learning about policies and candidates, we will disproportionately search out information that is in line with what we already believe. Even when we are exposed to relevant facts and arguments from the opposing viewpoint, we will tend not to believe them.

To solve this problem, in most democracies there are many professional journalists working for virtually all major media outlets who strive to present unbiased coverage of the important events of the day. These journalists help to form that initial impression through which people will filter future information. So, in theory, they should be able to ensure that people are forming correct opinions. Unfortunately, reality fails to measure up to the theory, even among professional, skilled, and well-meaning journalists.

News You Can Trust?

Between 2004 and 2008, 207,574 people were killed in traffic accidents in the United States. The most dangerous highway was I-15 in San Bernardino, California, which connects Las Vegas and Los Angeles. During that five-year period, 346 people were killed in car accidents on that one stretch of highway alone. How many of those fatalities were reported in the *New York Times*, widely considered the most prestigious newspaper in the country? In our fairly extensive archive searches, we could find none.

In that same time period, there were a total of 159 airplane accidents in the United States recorded by the National Transportation Safety Board, which resulted in the combined deaths of 90 people. Although we cannot definitely say that the *New York Times* reported every single one of those accidents or deaths, a brief search certainly turned up extensive reporting of the vast majority of those accidents.

There were more than three times as many people killed on that one stretch of highway as died in all plane crashes in the country. But imagine that Congress was considering diverting money from the air traffic control system to pay for highway improvements in California. Many voters would surely be outraged; after all, they read about airplane accidents all the time, and they've never even heard of California having dangerous highways. From a standpoint of saving lives, such a policy move might make perfect sense. But because of biased media coverage, it would surely meet with substantial resistance.

When people hear about media bias, they tend to immediately think of political biases: either the "liberal bias of the mainstream news media" or alternatively the "conservative bias of Fox News." Certainly political bias does exist, but we would argue that political bias is not nearly as detrimental as the simpler biases that pervade every aspect of media coverage.

Often, as in the case of car accidents versus airplane accidents, the bias is in favor of the rare and spectacular over the common and mundane. Car accidents happen all the time. We know this and we see it in our daily lives. A car accident, even one that kills somebody, is not really "news" in that sense. Crash landings of airplanes, however, are very rare things. When an airplane crashes, it taps into commonly held fears and fascinations about flying. There is also the potential for even greater tragedy, as airplanes can hold hundreds of passengers and can potentially crash in populated areas. This "disaster averted" element gives airplane crashes an additional element of intrigue that car crashes tend to lack. The end result is that the media tend to ignore car crashes, while giving extensive coverage to airplane crashes.

Of course, that bias is not really the media's fault. First of all, there is a general tendency for people to overestimate the likelihood and frequency of improbable events. Journalists are people and hence susceptible to the same psychological biases. We can't expect journalists to be more than human. However, these biases are exacerbated by the fact that the media are also responding to public demand. Newspapers, television shows, magazines, and Internet news sites all receive the majority of their revenue from advertising. Advertisers want large audiences; therefore the news media want large audiences.

In other words, the media aren't trying to deceive us intentionally. It just so happens that snowstorms are more interesting when they happen in May than when they happen in December. Or to put it another way, which story would you rather hear about: the small private jet that crashed into an Atlanta neighborhood and came twenty feet from plowing into a house, or any one of a hundred stories about a drunk driver who was killed by driving his car into a tree?

In the same way, the media tend to focus on local stories over distant ones, stories that involve celebrities over those that don't, stories that involve great disaster and tragedy over stories where everything pretty much worked out okay for all parties involved. From the perspective of maximizing viewership, those decisions make perfect sense. But from the perspective of educating voters about the true state of the nation—well, suddenly those decisions look much less appealing.

For example, back in 1999, National Public Radio ran a poll asking people to grade the schools in their own communities on an A through F scale, and then asked them to do the same for the United States' public school system in general. You can see the results in figure 1.1.

Notice that most people thought that their own schools were doing a fine job; most of the respondents gave the schools in their own communities (the lighter bars) either an A or a B. But when asked about the nation's schools in general (the darker bars), people were much more pessimistic: Over half of people gave the nation's schools a C, and the number of Ds jumped by 6 percent.

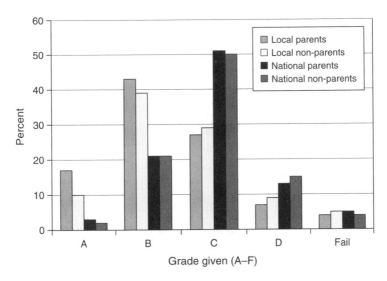

Figure 1.1

What's going on here? People with kids who go to school or who live in the same communities as a school have a lot of experience with those schools. But when people talk about schools around the country in general, they have very little experience; they are mostly going by general trends they hear in the news.

When people have experience with a school, they generally believe the schools are pretty good. Not necessarily perfect; those Bs could always be As, of course, but Bs are nothing to be too concerned about. Unfortunately, B schools and B students aren't newsworthy. It's the F schools and F students that make the news the most often (although the As do occasionally break through with a fluff piece about spelling bee champions or science fairs). The news focuses on the extreme and mostly negative cases, because those make for the most interesting articles and the most compelling shows. But the result of this focus on negatives and extremes is that people believe that schools in general are failing; even parents with lots of experience conclude that their own flawed but reasonable schools must be the exception and not the rule.

A bias for sensationalism isn't the only problem with the news media. There's also a variant of a problem we discussed previously: It is impossible for anyone to be an expert at everything. When reporters tell the audience what is happening in the world, the reporters are usually relaying information that other people have told them. The actual information originates with either sources or experts. Unfortunately, those sources and experts are just people too—people with their own flaws, biases, and agendas.

On September 8, 2002, Michael Gordon and Judith Miller of the *New York Times* published an article detailing Iraqi attempts to purchase high-grade aluminum tubes on the international black market. Citing "high profile Bush administration sources"—which turned out to mostly be the Vice President's Chief of Staff Scooter Libby—Gordon and Miller wrote that these tubes were likely intended for use in uranium enrichment and were strong evidence that Saddam Hussein's Iraqi regime was trying to develop nuclear weapons. That same weekend, the Bush administration's foreign policy team made a broad public relations appeal to encourage public support for a war with Iraq, prominently citing that *New York Times* article. Of course, once the United States and its allies invaded Iraq, no such nuclear weapons program was discovered; the aluminum tubes were probably intended to be used in building conventional rocket launchers. Moreover, it turned out that there had been significant disagreement within the executive branch about the intended usage of the tubes, disagreement that was never reported in the *New York Times* article.

What happened? To put it simply, the *New York Times* was used. The White House sources had an agenda: to promote a war with Iraq. By leaking select bits of information to the *New York Times*, these sources were able to further that agenda. What the *Times* published was true, as far as it went: Iraq had actually attempted to purchase aluminum tubes and those tubes could have conceivably been used to make nuclear weapons. But the conclusion that both the Bush administration and the *New York Times* article jumped to—that Iraq had an active nuclear weapons development program—was false. A true story with a misleading conclusion may sound somewhat benign, but in this case the result was to nudge the American people toward supporting a war.

The run-up to the Iraq War has become somewhat notorious, but the fact of the matter is that all reporters rely on their sources and that reliance can leave them open to mistakes. After all, the *New York Times* editorial board does not include numerous experts on the construction of uranium centrifuges who could have spotted the holes in the story. Newspapers have to rely on sources to get information; and sometimes that information is false or misleading.

Reporters often try to get around this problem by consulting experts, but even that solution is flawed. After all, how is a reporter supposed to know who is an expert, or which expert to bring in? Often, news agencies rely on obvious credentials: employment at prominent universities, affiliation with prominent think-tanks, and so on. But identifying the appropriate expert can be trickier than it seems. An economics professor at the local university may be able to answer general questions about international trade, but is unlikely to know the details of a particular new trade agreement between China and the United States. He might be able to give a more informed opinion than the journalist, yet he still isn't a true expert. Instead, most people with detailed knowledge of a new treaty are likely either involved in writing the treaty, or have studied it extensively because it affects their business. In other words, the people who are truly expert on that trade agreement probably have an agenda that they want to promote, which makes it very difficult for journalists to provide accurate and unbiased analysis.

Misinformation can also persist because of common human error—even after the perpetrators of that error have long since tried to correct the story. On March 29, 2009, in response to a suicide that had gained national attention, a district attorney in Massachusetts charged six teenagers in conjunction with the prolonged harassment of the suicide victim. Because of a miscommunication at a press conference, however, it was widely reported that nine teenagers, instead of six, were being charged. When the error was identified, a correction was reported in the *New York Times* and on the cable news networks on April 8. And yet, despite the correction, blogs were still reporting the incorrect figure a week later, presumably because the bloggers hadn't read the correction. The charges were a front-page story. The correction, if it was mentioned at all, was mentioned as an afterthought.

Actually, the *New York Times* is religious about its corrections. For instance, on April 14, 2010, the *New York Times* reported errors in stories about the Chinese president's support for sanctions against Iran, on Sweden's unemployment rate, and on Tiger Woods's golf score at the Masters. None of those were malicious mistakes, but all of them made their way into the paper. The corrections themselves tend to get buried, and it is often unclear from reading the corrections page exactly how important the original error was. More importantly, often the corrections are a week old or more; there is a good chance that the readers of the original article never even see the corrections page.

The *New York Times* is one of the most thorough newspapers in the business. Most media outlets don't even bother to print or announce corrections unless the errors are particularly egregious. Again, it's not because they are trying to deceive the public. If you give a producer at CNN the choice between correcting an error in a week-old story that most of his audience won't even remember, or spending another two minutes on the latest breaking news—it doesn't take an expert in television ratings to figure out which story is going to help generate the larger audience. The result is a misled public.

Finally, there is no way to present a truly balanced and accurate perspective of an issue when opinions on that issue are not equally prevalent. To give unequal time is to favor one side over the other. To give equal time is to give a misleading impression about the state of the world. The dilemma exists with issues like global warming, where the scientific consensus is challenged by popularly held beliefs. The dilemma exists when trying to relay information about small political parties or third-party candidates. And it exists when trying to cover new ideas that are slowly gaining traction in a particular realm, whether it's a new philosophy of public education, new tactics in crime fighting, or a new dieting fad. In other words, the problem exists for basically every major issue of the day. There is simply no way to give balanced coverage of an imbalanced world.

Biases and errors occur because reporters are fallibly human. Finding truly expert and unbiased analysts is extremely challenging. Giving a balanced perspective on contentious issues is impossible. Add to all of that an incentive structure that rewards reporting negative, extreme, and emotional stories and it becomes clear why the media is unable to educate voters successfully in a modern democracy.

Summary

So where does that leave us? Voters don't know very much, aren't aware of how little they know, aren't particularly proficient at getting the information they need, and can't remember the information once they've learned it. The problem is made even worse by politicians and interest groups that actively hide information, by issues that are often complex enough to stymie even the experts, and by the vast number of important issues. Plus, the media that we use to get our information have their own biases and prejudices; no matter how hard reporters strive for neutrality, they too are only human and thus susceptible to the same foibles of information processing as the rest of us. The reporters' sources of information are biased too, which means that a lot of the information that we use to make our decisions is flawed from the beginning. Even if we were good at gathering accurate information (which we're not) it would be an almost insurmountable challenge to have enough information to make properly informed decisions. How can democracy possibly be successful when it relies on the choices of voters who know so little?

References

Lead Quote
Churchill, W. N.d. Great-Quotes.com. Retrieved December 15, 2011, from http://www.great-quotes.com/quote/39874.

Ignorance about Facts
B.B.C. News. 2005. US closes book on Iraq WMD hunt. April 26, 2005. Retrieved April 15, 2011, from http://news.bbc.co.uk/2/hi/4484237.stm

Garcia de Osuna, J. M., M. A. Ranney, and J. M. Nelson. 2004. Qualitative and quantitative effects of surprise: (Mis)estimates, rationales, and feedback-induced preference changes while considering abortion. In *Proceedings of the 26th Annual Conference of the Cognitive Science Society*, ed. K. Forbus, D. Gentner, and T. Regier, pp. 422–427. Mahwah, NJ: Lawrence Erlbaum.

Munnich, E. L., M. A. Ranney, and M. L. N. Bachman. 2005. The Longevities of policy-shifts and memories due to single feedback numbers. In *Proceedings of the Twenty-seventh Annual Conference of the Cognitive Science Society*, ed. B.G. Bara, L. Barsalou, and M. Buciarelli, pp. 1553–1558. Mahwah, NJ: Erlbaum.

Munnich, E. L., M. A. Ranney, J. M. Nelson, J. M. Garcia de Osuna, and N. B. Brazil. 2003. Policy shift through numerically-driven inferencing: An EPIC experiment about when base rates matter. In *Proceedings of the Twenty-fifth Annual Conference of the Cognitive Science Society*, ed. Richard Alterman and David Kirsh, pp. 834–839. Mahwah, NJ: Lawrence Erlbaum.

Pincus, W., and D. Milbrook. 2004. Al Qaeda–Hussein link is dismissed. *Washington Post*, June 17, p. A01.

Senate Committee on Intelligence. 2006. Postwar Finding About Iraq's WMD programs and links to terrorism and how they compare with prewar assessments. 109th Congress, September 8. Retrieved from http://intelligence.senate.gov/phaseiiaccuracy.pdf.

The Chicago Council on Foreign Relations and the Program on International Policy Attitudes. 2004. Hall of mirrors: Perceptions and misperceptions in the Congressional foreign policy process. October 1. Retrieved April 15, 2011, from http://www.worldpublicopinion.org/pipa/articles/governance_bt/88.php?nid=&id=&pnt=88&lb=btgov.

Infinite Expertise Required

Butler, S. M. 1992. A policy maker's guide to the health care crisis, Part II: The Heritage Consumer Choice Health Plan. March 5. Retrieved April 15, 2011 from http://healthcarereform.procon.org/view.resource.php?resourceID=004182.

Converse, P. 1964. The nature of belief systems in mass publics. In *Ideology and Discontent*, ed. D. Apter, 206–261. Glencoe, IL: Free Press.

Darling, B. 2009. Is there a constitutional basis for mandatory health insurance? From The Foundry Blog at The Heritage Foundation, November 12. Retrieved April 15, 2011, from http://blog.heritage.org/2009/11/12/is-there-a-constitutional-basis-for-mandatory-health-insurance.

Echoes of Kennedy's Battle with Nixon in Health-Care Debate. 2009. *Newsweek*, August 26. Retrieved April 15, 2011, from http://www.newsweek.com/blogs/the-gaggle/2009/08/26/echoes-of-kennedy-s-battle-with-nixon-in-health-care-debate.html.

Knowlton, B., and M. Grynbaum. 2008. Greenspan "shocked" that free markets are flawed. *New York Times*, October 23. Retrieved April 15, 2011, from http://www.nytimes.com/2008/10/23/business/worldbusiness/23iht-gspan.4.17206624.html.

Lodge, M., and R. Hamil. 1986. A partisan schema for political information processing. *American Political Science Review* 80:505–515.

Page, S. 2007. Clinton seeks to reevaluate NAFTA. *USA Today*, October 9. Retrieved April 15, 2011, from http://abcnews.go.com/Politics/story?id=3705441&page=1.

Pendleton, J. H. 2009. Key challenges should be addressed when considering changes to missile defense agency's roles and missions. Testimony before the Strategic Forces Subcommittee, Committee on Armed Services, and House of Representatives, March 26. Released by the Government Accountability Office. Retrieved April 15, 2011, from http://www.gao.gov/new.items/d09466t.pdf.

Robertson, L. 2010. A final weekend of whoppers? Annenberg Public Policy Center, March 19. Retrieved April 15, 2011, from http://www.factcheck.org/2010/03/a-final-weekend-of-whoppers.

Stephanopoulos, G. 2011. Mitt Romney: No apology for health care mandate. From George's Bottom Line blog at ABCNews.com, February 1. Retrieved April 15, 2011, from http://blogs.abcnews.com/george/2011/02/mitt-romney-no-apology-for-individual-health-care-mandate.html.

Ignorance about Candidates

Alter, A. L., D. M. Oppenheimer, and J. C. Zemla. 2010. Missing the trees for the forest: A construal level account of the illusion of explanatory depth. *Journal of Personality and Social Psychology* 99 (3):436–451.

Brown, C. E. 1982. A false consensus bias in 1980 presidential preferences. *Journal of Social Psychology* 118 (1):137–138.

Dimock, M. 2008. Belief that Obama is Muslim is durable, bipartisan—but most likely to sway Democratic voters. Pew Research Center, July 15. Retrieved April 15, 2011, from http://pewresearch.org/pubs/898/belief-that-obama-is-muslim-is-bipartisan-but-most-likely-to-sway-democrats.

Koestner, R., G. F. Losier, N. M. Worren, L. Baker, and R. J. Vallerand. 1995. False consensus effects for the 1992 Canadian referendum. *Canadian Journal of Behavioural Science/Revue canadienne des sciences du comportement* 27 (2):214–225.

Perez-Pena, R. 2009. Libel suit against the *Times* ends. *New York Times*, February 19. Retrieved April 15, 2011, from http://www.nytimes.com/2009/02/20/business/media/20lawsuit.html?_r=2&ref=media.

Ross, L., D. Greene, and P. House. 1977. The false consensus effect: An egocentric bias in social perception and attribution processes. *Journal of Experimental Social Psychology* 13:279–301.

Snopes.com. 2005. Internet of lies. May 5. Retrieved April 15, 2011, from http://www.snopes.com/quotes/internet.asp.

Stern, H. 2008. Sal Interviews Obama Supporters in Harlem. *The Howard Stern Show*, October 1. New York: Sirius Radio. Retrieved April 15, 2011, from http://www.youtube.com/watch?v=b5p3OB6roAg.

Memory, Metacognition, and Misleading Information

Annenberg Public Policy Center. N.d. FactCheck.org.

Brooks, J., and J. Bank. 2008. Body armor claim: Still false and nasty. Annenberg Public Policy Center. October 24. Retrieved April 15, 2011, from http://www.factcheck.org/2008/10/body-armor-claim-still-false-and-nasty.

Clymer, A. 2003. Agency ends pursuit of Cheney energy panel data. *New York Times*, February 8. Retrieved April 16, 2011 from http://query.nytimes.com/gst/fullpage.html?res=9B06E5DE123BF93BA35751C0A9659C8B63.

Gillens, M. 2001. Political ignorance and collective policy preferences. *American Political Science Review* 95:379–396.

Heath, C., and D. Heath. 2007. *Made to Stick*. New York: Random House.

Keil, F. C. 2003. *Folkscience*: Coarse interpretations of a complex reality. *Trends in Cognitive Sciences* 7:368–373.

Kruger, J., and D. Dunning. 1999. Unskilled and unaware of It: How difficulties in recognizing one's own *incompetence* lead to inflated self-assessments. *Journal of Personality and Social Psychology* 77 (6):1121–1134.

Library of Congress. N.d. Amendments for H.R. 4137. Retrieved August 5, 2011, from http://www.govtrack.us/congress/bill.xpd?bill=h110-4137&tab=amendments.

Lodge, M., and C. Taber. 2000. Three steps toward a theory of motivated political reasoning. In *Elements of Reason Cognition Choice and the Bounds of Rationality*, ed. A. Lupia, M. McCubbins, and S. Popkin, pp. 183–213. Cambridge: Cambridge University Press.

MSNBC. 2006. FBI releases final Lennon surveillance files. December 20. Reprinted from the Associated Press. Retrieved April 16, 2011, from http://today.msnbc.msn.com/id/16296929/ns/today-entertainment.

Todorov, A. 2006. Public opinion. Lecture given at Princeton University, Princeton, NJ, May 30.

Biased Interpretations

Hastorf, A. H., and H. Cantril. 1952. They saw a game: A case study. *Journal of Abnormal and Social Psychology* 49:129–134.

Lord, C., L. Ross, and M. Lepper. 1979. Biased assimilation and attitude polarization: The effects of prior theories on subsequently considered evidence. *Journal of Personality and Social Psychology* 37 (11):2098–2109.

Lowin, A. 1967. Approach and avoidance: Alternative modes of selective exposure to information. *Journal of Personality and Social Psychology* 6:1–9.

Zogby International and Norman Lear Center. 2007. Zogby/Lear Center Poll, November 12. Retrieved April 16, 2011. from http://www.learcenter.org/pdf/Politics SurveyRelease.pdf.

Media Bias

Eckholm, E., and K. Zezima. 2010. 6 teenagers are charged after classmate's suicide. *New York Times*, March 29. Retrieved March 26, 2011, from http://www.nytimes.com/2010/03/30/us/30bully.html.

Gordon, M. R., and J. Miller. 2002. Threats and responses: The Iraqis; U.S. says Hussein *intensifies* quest for A-bomb parts. *New York Times*, September 8. Retrieved March 26, 2011, from http://www.nytimes.com/2002/09/08/international/middleeast/08IRAQ.html?pagewanted=1.

Government Printing Office. 2004. Report of the Select Committee on Intelligence on the U.S. Intelligence Community's Prewar Intelligence Assessments on Iraq together with Additional Views. Senate Report 108-301, July 9. Chapter X: White Paper on Iraq's Weapons of Mass Destruction Program.

Lott, M. 2009. Top ten deadliest stretches of road in America. FOX News, February 11. Retrieved March 26, 2011, from http://www.foxnews.com/story/0,2933,490940,00 .html.

MSNBC. 2010. Brutal bullies: What makes kids cruel? MSNBC.com, April 9. Reprinted from Livescience.com. Retrieved March 26, 2011, from http://www.msnbc.msn .com/id/36335617/ns/health-kids_and_parenting/.

National Public Radio. 1999. NPR/Kaiser/Kennedy School Education Survey. Retrieved March 26, 2011, from http://www.npr.org/programs/specials/poll/ education/education.results.html.

National Transportation Safety Board. 2010. Aviation accident statistics, table 5: Accidents, fatalities, and rates, 1990–2008, 14 CFR 121, Schedules and Nonscheduled Service. Retrieved March 26, 2011, from http://www.ntsb.gov/aviation/Stats .htm.

2 "We the People" Are Irrational

A government can be no better than the public opinion that sustains it.
—Franklin Delano Roosevelt

Speed Dating for Senator

One hundred milliseconds. One-tenth of a second. Think about how fast that is: It's twice as fast as you can snap, three times as fast as the shortest recorded time between human heartbeats. It is, quite literally, a blink of an eye. One hundred milliseconds isn't enough time to identify a candidate's party affiliation, let alone his or her views on taxes or civil rights. But it may be long enough for you to decide who will win your vote.

There's a lot of evidence that it doesn't take people long to form lasting impressions about others. Nalini Ambady from Tufts University has offered several compelling demonstrations that people infer all sorts of things from very brief observations. People form impressions about status hierarchy, teaching ability, and even romantic involvement very, very quickly. This insight forms the theoretical foundation of speed dating: If people can form a lasting impression so quickly, then why waste a full evening on a first date? Recently, psychologists have started to investigate whether these first impressions can influence political decision making as well.

Princeton University researcher Alex Todorov and his colleagues gave people pictures of unfamiliar politicians' faces from the 2000, 2002, and 2004 Congressional elections. People were asked how competent the candidate looked in the photo. These ratings correctly predicted more than 70 percent of United States Senate races, and two-thirds of the House races. In fact, the more competent that a candidate appeared in his or her photo, the larger his or her margin of victory. First impressions were important for young candidates and old candidates, for incumbents and challengers. If first impressions didn't matter at all, then ratings about how competent somebody appears in a photo would only predict elections about 50 percent of the time—no better than a coin flip. But 70 percent? Even the most knowledgeable experts would be hard pressed to predict where Americans stand on an issue with 70 percent accuracy, aside from ridiculous issues like "not setting puppies on fire." Our first impression of a candidate plays a huge role in whether she'll ultimately receive our vote.

Two years later, Todorov and his collaborators followed up on this study by looking at how quickly people made these competence judgments, this time using pictures of gubernatorial candidates. As before, Todorov asked people to judge how competent each candidate looked. Critically, while some people were given unlimited time to look at the faces, others saw each face flashed briefly on the computer screen for 250 milliseconds or even 100 milliseconds. And yet, it didn't matter how little time the photo was on the screen—whether they saw it for only a brief moment or stared at it for as long as they wanted to, the basic pattern of results was the same. Impressions formed in the first 100 milliseconds of seeing a politician's face will go a long way toward deciding whom we vote for.

Predictions made on brief impressions of competence can even be more accurate than pundits who make forecasts based on issues, political trends, and polling data. For example, in October 2007 *USA Today* reported that there was broad consensus across the political spectrum about the state of the 2008 presidential primaries, noting that Hillary Clinton "dominates the Democratic nomination battle," while Giuliani and Romney were "atop the race" for the Republican nomination. Former President Bill Clinton and former Speaker of the House Newt Gingrich, bitter archrivals from the mid-1990s, were both actually in agreement about this state of the race. These two authorities on American politics were certainly not alone in their assessment, as pundits from across the political spectrum agreed with them. Obviously the experts were wrong.

At around the same time, J. Scott Armstrong, a professor at the University of Pennsylvania, wanted to see if Todorov's findings would also work in presidential elections. The problem was, in the United States most people already knew what the candidates looked like, and so it was too late to get unbiased ratings of how competent each face looked. To get

around this problem, Armstrong went to a population not typically con-
sulted for predictions about American politics: New Zealand schoolgirls.
Despite the fact that they had no idea who any of the candidates were,
these children from the other side of the globe thought that Barack Obama
and John McCain looked the most competent—correctly predicting who
would win the primaries. The greatest minds in American punditry were
beaten by a group of completely uninformed children.

The studies we have discussed so far have focused on candidates whose
faces appear more competent. That makes sense most of the time: For
voters who care about foreign policy or fiscal discipline, the primary
trait they want in a leader is competence. But in some cases, other facial
characteristics might affect someone's vote. For instance, it turns out that
the features that make somebody look competent are different from the
features that make a person look compassionate. If the most important
issue in an election is race relations or family values, then a candidate's
most important trait might be compassion. In other words, depending
on what issue is the most important, different facial structures might have
an edge.

Danny Oppenheimer teamed up with Alex Todorov to test this possibility. They surveyed people to find issues that called for a competent leader,
and issues that called for a caring leader. Then they had people rate faces
on both how competent and caring they looked. They took faces that
looked competent but not caring, and paired them with faces that looked
caring, but not competent. They then asked people to vote in hypothetical
elections between these pairs. Half the people were asked to think about
the issues that called for a caring leader, and the other half considered the
issues that demanded a competent leader. Sure enough, when the issue
called for caring, the person who looked caring won; when the issue called
for competence, the person who looked competent won.

Another set of studies used complex computer algorithms to create faces
that were unrecognizable, but had the defining elements of George W.
Bush or John Kerry's face. Even though they didn't recognize the faces,
people preferred the Bush-like face in a time of war, but preferred the
Kerry-like face in a time of peace. It goes without saying that at the time
of the 2004 presidential election when Bush defeated Kerry, the United
States was engaged in two wars—one in Iraq and one in Afghanistan. These
studies suggest that issues might actually matter in an election, just not in

the way we normally think that they do. The candidates' stances are still irrelevant, but the issues of the day do seem to affect which facial features the voters prefer in their politicians.

Of course, we don't base our decision of who to vote for entirely on whether a candidate has the appropriate facial features. The candidate's height matters too. From 1900 to 1980 the taller candidate won nearly 80 percent of presidential elections in the United States, and the average height of male senators and governors is above six feet tall—well above the national average of five feet, ten inches.

And let's not forget the importance of perspiration: Richard Nixon's defeat by John F. Kennedy in 1960 is widely attributed to Nixon's profuse sweating under the bright lights of the first ever televised presidential debate. Concerned about the possibility of looking too feminine, Nixon refused to wear makeup and ended up looking sickly and pale. It didn't help his cause that his opponent was younger, better looking, and more charismatic. People who listened to the debate and had to base their evaluations on the content of what was said believed Nixon was the winner, but those who observed the debates on television believed Kennedy had won.

Ultimately we would like to think that people desire more from their leaders than a chiseled jaw and an impressive physical stature. We should care about a candidate's integrity, experience, and stance on the issues— and we do care about those things. They just get overshadowed by other factors that have little to do with a candidate's qualifications for the job. As renowned television talk show host and blogger Dick Cavett astutely observed regarding the 2008 presidential election: "Laughs aside, unfortunately, I realized during the last debate that watching the two of them together on the screen I would think anyone, even a non-lip-reading, non-English-speaking viewer with the sound off, could see at a glance which man is presidential."

There are more idiosyncratic ways that a candidate's appearance can influence voters as well. Consider the well-established finding that people tend to like others who share incidental similarities (e.g., have the same favorite color or both owned a parakeet as a child). Jeremy Bailenson from Stanford University and his colleagues wondered if this would extend to visual similarity and would influence political preferences. In an ingenious set of studies, Bailenson acquired people's photos and visually morphed those pictures with photos of politicians. In doing so, he created a set of faces that were hybrids of the politician's face and the face of an experimental participant. The examples shown in figure 2.1 are from the 2006 Florida gubernatorial race between Charlie Crist and Jim Davis.

Although none of the participants noticed that the hybrid face was modified to look more like their own, the morphing had a large effect on their political attitudes. People had much more positive evaluations of and expressed greater willingness to vote for politicians who were made to look more like them. Our preference for candidates who look like us is true both for unfamiliar candidates and for familiar candidates such as Bush and Kerry (although in the latter case, the effect was greatly diminished for people who already had strong preferences before viewing the morphed photos).

Figure 2.1
From Jeremy Bailenson, Shanto Iyengar, Nick Yee, and Nathan A. Collins (2008), "Facial Similarity between Voters and Candidates Causes Influence," *Public Opinion Quarterly* 72 (5). By permission of Oxford University Press.

Fortunately, at this point we don't know of any politicians who are sending personalized and morphed campaign photos to increase their vote share. However, even without such obvious manipulation from the campaigns, some candidates will naturally share features with some voters. Those similarities can affect our votes.

The fact that our votes are so influenced by the physical features of the candidates is disturbing, but it only scratches the surface. Our preferences are inconsistent, fickle, and swayed by things that are totally irrelevant to what matters in a leader. In the rest of this chapter we will explore a subset of these irrational tendencies and look at what that means for the will of the people. The peculiarities of human reasoning lead to a whole host of biases that often prevent us from even knowing our true opinions on issues. How can the people possibly express their will if they don't even know what that will is?

Prime Real Estate

What's the first word that comes to mind when you read the word *cat*? Odds are that you came up with the word *dog, mouse,* or *kitten*—the vast majority of people do when they're asked this sort of question. Dogs and cats are strongly associated, so that when you think of one, the other automatically comes to mind. This so-called *associative priming* means that when you see a cat, you are quicker to read the word *dog*, recognize a picture of a dog, and are generally more likely to think about dogs. Priming is a good thing; it allows people to be much more efficient at processing information. For instance, "hit me" means something quite different at a blackjack table than in a boxing ring, and it is important to quickly understand the difference between the two commands.

Priming has implications beyond avoiding brawls in casinos. Primes change what information we think about, and in so doing can shape who we vote for. Consider a hypothetical school bond measure—the local school board would like to purchase and install a new educational technology that will improve the schools but also raise your taxes. If, as you deliberate on whether or not to support this initiative, you happen to glance at your bank statement and notice your rapidly dwindling savings account, it will prime you to think of finances and the burden that the additional taxes will place on you. If instead you happen to glance out the window at your neighbor's children playing next door, it will prime you to think of our nation's youth and the importance of education. If you're thinking mostly about finances you're likely to oppose the bill, but you may support it if you're thinking about children.

Jonah Berger from the University of Pennsylvania and his colleagues tested this logic about how priming could influence voters. They showed people photographs and had them engage in a decoy task—rating how bright each picture appeared. Critically, for half of the people, the set of pictures contained school-related images that primed the notion of education (e.g., a locker) while the other half saw images unrelated to education (e.g., a fire hydrant). All of the participants later read a description of an education initiative taken from an actual Arizona ballot, and indicated how they would like to vote. People who had seen the pictures of schools were 7 percent more likely to vote for the bill—a larger margin than the proposition actually passed by. Moreover, having been primed by images of schools made people more likely to vote for the proposition even if they had no children or were extremely opposed to higher taxes.

One might protest that findings like these would only occur in a lab. Surely people wouldn't be influenced by such obviously irrelevant factors during a real election, where real taxes and real educational outcomes were riding on the result. To test this, Berger and his colleagues looked precinct by precinct at electoral results from the actual Arizona election where the proposition had been considered. As is typical during elections, people are assigned to various voting locations; some vote in churches, some vote in schools, some in firehouses, and so on. The researchers found that people who voted in schools, and therefore were primed with education, were more likely to vote for the education initiative than people who voted in other locations. This tendency was true in both liberal and conservative districts.

You're more likely to think about education issues when you're voting in a school, making it more likely that you'll vote for an education bond or for a candidate with a (supposedly) stronger record on education. Meanwhile, public safety comes to mind when you're voting in a fire station and moral issues are prominent when you're voting in a church. In other words, how you vote depends on where you vote.

Of course, location isn't the only prime we're exposed to during political campaigns. Have you ever noticed that American political candidates almost always give speeches in front of a red, white, and blue backdrop? These flags are meant to prime you with the concept of patriotism, and make you think more highly of the candidate's dedication to America. Similarly, the lyrics of the background music when a candidate walks to the podium are meant to prime you with notions consistent with campaign messages. For example, in the 2008 presidential primary campaign, John McCain began playing ABBA's "Take a Chance on Me" when he was looking to make a comeback after having slipped in the polls. McCain probably wasn't trying to appeal to the legions of ABBA fans. More likely, he was trying to reinforce the notion that he was a "maverick" who took risks, and to ask his voters to do the same.

The media can also prime various issues. Stanford professor Jon Krosnick and his colleagues found that voters tend to place more importance on issues immediately after they receive media coverage. Of course, this tendency could be the result of the media responding to voter interest in the topic, rather than the other way around. Therefore Krosnick randomly exposed some people to stories about crime, others to stories about pollution, and still others to stories about unemployment. When people later evaluated presidential candidates, they tended to care more about the issues that they had been exposed to during the study. In theory, this tendency allows the news media to encourage certain election results through their choice of headlines and stories in the days leading up to an election. An election about increased spending on education may actually hinge on whether the local paper leads with stories about the deficit or stories about failing schools.

Priming can influence our political decision making in subtler ways, too. Consider the common political metaphor that the liberals are on the left and the conservatives are on the right. The metaphor originated back in 1791 when the French Legislative Assembly was organized with the commoners (who wanted radical social change) on the left side of the chamber. This historical trivia may have done more than produce an imaginative way of describing the political spectrum. It might actually influence the way we think about politics. Just as hearing the word *cat* makes us think about a dog, hearing the word *left* primes the notion of liberal. And this priming can change our judgments and attitudes about candidates.

Caterina Suitner and her colleagues considered the possibility that politicians facing to the right would be thought of as more conservative than those facing to the left. They showed Italian students photos of purported politicians and had the students guess the political party of the candidates. For each photo, a mirror image was digitally created (i.e., the image was horizontally flipped), which resulted in two versions of each photo, one with the candidate facing left, and one with the candidate facing right. When students saw the left-facing version, they were more likely to believe the politician was from a liberal party, and when they saw the right facing version they were more likely to assign him or her to a conservative party. That is, merely facing left or right can serve as a prime that influences our beliefs about how conservative or liberal a candidate is. Which way the candidates turn could change who gets your vote.

The left–right metaphor can have more direct effects on political attitudes as well. Oppenheimer and his colleague Tom Trail investigated whether people's political attitudes might shift in the direction of their spatial orientation. Half of the participants squeezed a handgrip in their left hand for five seconds while the other half used their right hand, thus orienting them to the left or right side of their bodies. People who had used their left hand reported more agreement with the Democrats on political issues than people who had used their right.

While the fact that people's political attitudes can be influenced by which hand they use to squeeze a handgrip is disconcerting, the effect could be caused by something other than priming of the left–right political spectrum. For example, most people are right handed, and thus might have found it easier to squeeze the handgrip in their right hand. So the differences that result from using different hands could be due to confidence, or feelings of dominance, or any number of other things. To rule this out, Oppenheimer and Trail had people sit in a chair that tilted slightly to the left or the right. Thus, people who sat in the chair were literally forced to lean to the left or right as they completed a political attitudes survey. The researchers found that people who leaned to the left physically also leaned to the left politically—people were more than 15 percent more liberal when leaning to the left than to the right, and nearly 9 percent more conservative when leaning to the right than to the left. Leaning to the left will not turn Dick Cheney into Nancy Pelosi, nor will leaning to the right turn

Michael Moore into Ann Coulter. But it can move people more toward the center, or alternatively make them more extreme.[1]

Priming can influence our political attitudes even when the prime is something that we may not consciously associate with politics. For example, most people find the concept of death quite scary. When we are scared we seek out things that feel safe and familiar—sort of the psychological equivalent of comfort food. This makes people more supportive of the status quo, more likely to adopt relatively traditional stances, and less open to change or risk.

Following this logic, New York University professor John Jost has demonstrated that thinking about death leads people to become more conservative—at least temporarily. In one study, he and his colleagues exposed people to death-related words and images (e.g., a hearse, the grim reaper, a chalk outline) to prime them with the notion of death. Participants were then surveyed about their political attitudes on a host of issues ranging from immigration to affirmative action to same-sex marriage. On average, people who were exposed to death-related primes were nearly 13 percent more conservative on the political attitudes survey than people who had been exposed to non-death-related primes. Importantly, this trend occurred across the political spectrum: for liberals, moderates, and conservatives. Walking by a cemetery or hearing about a murder on the news makes everybody temporarily more conservative.

Studies from other labs have shown that priming people with death changes our attitudes not just toward individual policies, but toward

---

1. Another metaphor, besides the left–right spectrum, that has received widespread attention is the nation-as-family metaphor, initially proposed by University of California, Berkeley, linguist George Lakoff. Just as we speak of liberals as on the left and conservatives as on the right, we tend to use family-based metaphors when describing nations as a whole. Germans refer to the fatherland, Russians talk about Mother Russia, and in the United States we hear about Uncle Sam, the founding fathers, and occasionally Big Brother. Importantly, Lakoff noted that although both conservatives and liberals tend to use the nation-as-family metaphor, the nature of the metaphor is very different depending on one's political attitudes. According to Lakoff, conservatives tend to think that parents' primary role is that of a disciplinarian, whereas liberals tend to think of parents in a more nurturing role. This has led some researchers to speculate that using different family metaphors to talk about politics will change people's political attitudes, but as of the writing of this book, the evidence for this notion is decidedly mixed.

politicians as well. For example, in a study by Florette Cohen and her colleagues in 2004, the researchers asked moderate-to-liberal voters questions about either death or television, and then asked them if they would vote for George Bush or John Kerry for president in the upcoming election. While these voters tended to prefer Kerry to Bush by a 4:1 margin when asked about television, that margin dropped to 2:1 when voters were talking about death!

Voters' thoughts and opinions are constantly being influenced by sights, sounds, and other environmental factors. How can voters express their will when that will changes based on random things they encounter while driving to the voting booth?

Frame of Mind

Think about mad cow disease. It's scary. A cow unable to stand, flailing her legs as her eyes roll back in their sockets—and it could possibly spread to humans. Now think about bovine spongiform encephalopathy. It's a clinical condition: a neuro-degenerative disease affecting the brains and spinal cords of cattle. Of course, bovine spongiform encephalopathy is just the scientific name for mad cow disease. They're the same thing. Nonetheless, INSEAD business school professor Marwan Sinaceur and his colleagues showed that people find the descriptor "mad cow disease" more emotional—so much so that they will eat less beef than if they hear its scientific alternative. Language, it turns out, can matter as much as content.

Back in the early 1980s, Nobel Laureate Danny Kahneman and Amos Tversky first identified what they called *framing effects*. They gave people a hypothetical scenario describing preparations for a new disease that was expected to kill 600 people. Two programs were proposed to combat the virus. Half of the participants were told that if Program A were adopted, 200 people would be saved, and if Program B were adopted, there was a chance that everybody would be saved, and also a chance that nobody would be saved. The other half of the participants were told that if Program A were adopted 400 people would die, and if Program B was adopted there was a chance that nobody would die, and also a chance that everybody would die. Of course, Programs A and B were logically the same in both studies: when 600 deaths are expected, 200 saved is the same outcome as 400 dying. It's just a different description of an identical outcome.

Nonetheless, whereas nearly 3 in 4 people preferred Program A when it was described in terms of lives saved, fewer than 1 in 4 opted for Program A when it was described as lives lost.

Think about the implications of this finding. It means that slight differences in descriptions can lead to huge swings in public support. This has not escaped the attention of marketers—you'll note that products are typically described as 95 percent fat free rather than 5 percent fat. Sometimes, they give it another name entirely, such as "whole milk," to avoid having to mention the fat content at all. Framing has also come to the attention of political players. To take an example from politics, conservative strategist Frank Luntz, author of the strategy memo "The Language of the 21st Century," identified that even though majorities of Americans were in favor of an "inheritance tax" or an "estate tax," the logically equivalent but negatively framed "death tax" led to strong opposition. By reframing the debate as a death tax, conservative politicians were able to undermine public support for what had previously been an uncontroversial source of government revenue.

Of course, it is not just the conservatives who have influenced public perception of policies through language. The credibility of President Reagan's "Strategic Defense Initiative," a program intended to create antiballistic-missile technology, was undermined when Senator Ted Kennedy successfully relabeled it "Star Wars," suggesting that the idea was so implausible that it was best described as science fiction. Later, proponents of the program renamed it the "Ballistic Missile Defense Organization" in an attempt to regain some support for the plan, but the new name never gained traction among the public or media.

There is far more support among Americans for increasing spending on "aid for the poor" than on "welfare," even though the phrases generally refer to the same programs. People are happy to endorse policies for "dealing with drug addiction" but shy away from policies for "drug rehabilitation." The notion of "global warming" riles people up, which is why you'll hear liberals and environmental advocates using that terminology, while the less emotionally evocative "climate change" tends to be more common in conservative and pro-business circles. And if you want to increase spending on "law enforcement," you're much more likely to be successful if you describe your policy as "halting the rising crime rate."

Certain words or phrases evoke common responses regardless of how relevant they are to the issue at hand. Harvard psychologist Ellen Langer and her colleagues examined the effectiveness of different reasons people could give when asking for a small favor, such as cutting in line to use a copy machine. She found that when given a reason, people allow others to cut in line, even when that reason is entirely vacuous (e.g., "May I cut in line because I need to make copies"—obviously you need to make copies, that's why you're in line for the machine, but it doesn't explain why I should let you cut in). The word *because* leads people to think that a reason is being given; we don't always think through what follows. Rather, our behavior (allowing the person to cut in line) is based on the mere presence of that word.

In another strategic memo for conservatives, Frank Luntz took this notion to its logical conclusion: "Women consistently respond to the phrase *for the children* regardless of the context. From balancing the budget to welfare reform, *for the children* scores highest of all arguments offered. Therefore, rather than creating a 'Compassion Agenda,' Republicans need to create a communication framework that involves children." In other words, how we say something can matter more than what we say.

Indeed, psychologist Natalia Engavatov ran a study testing how a communication framework could influence attitudes. Two hundred fifty participants across a broad spectrum of political beliefs read speech excerpts advocating either traditionally liberal (e.g., unemployment benefits) or traditionally conservative (e.g., tax cuts to stimulate jobs) policies. Importantly, for half of the participants, the speech talked about how this policy would help workers. For the other half of the participants, the word "workers" was replaced with "families." Other than that simple change, the speech was the same for all of the participants. But this change was enough to sway liberals to increase their willingness to vote for conservative policies by nearly 5 percent, and lead conservatives to be more favorable toward the liberal policies by about 4.5 percent. In other words, the communication framework can make a real difference.

This sort of reasoning has led to such colorful policy names as George W. Bush's "Healthy Forest Initiative" (which allowed companies to thin certain forests in the hopes of preventing forest fires), Barack Obama's "American Recovery and Reinvestment Act" (also known as the 2009 stimulus package), and the bipartisan "No Child Left Behind" (a Bush-era education law). After all, nobody wants to leave children behind, and everybody likes healthy forests and investing in America. As noted in chapter 1, very few people have any idea about the specifics of these policies and what they actually do aside from what the names suggest. This strategy has also been used to help garner support for military operations, such as Operation Enduring Freedom (also known as the War in Afghanistan). It is very hard for people to oppose the idea of enduring freedom.

Even seemingly trivial changes to the grammatical structure of a press release can influence our attitude toward a politician. In a recent paper, University of California, Merced, cognitive scientist Teenie Matlock and her colleagues provocatively asked "Can grammar win elections?" They gave people descriptions of political candidates and then had people indicate how favorable or unfavorable they found the candidates being described. It turned out that very subtle changes in the grammatical structure of the descriptions had significant changes in how favorably or unfavorably people viewed the different candidates. For instance, a candidate that "was collecting" money for charity was viewed more favorably than if the same candidate "collected" money for charity.

The names of policies. The metaphors that are used to describe those policies. Even the grammar that might be used in referencing those policies. None of these should matter to voters. What should matter is the content of the policies. But unfortunately, although function is all well and good, form matters quite a bit as well.

Easy Does It

Which would you rather read: A book written in this font (9 pt. Stone Serif), *or a book written in this font (9 pt. French Script MS)*? If you chose the former your preferences align with the vast majority of readers. That makes perfect sense; Stone Serif is easy to read, while French Script would be generously described as challenging. Things can be easy or difficult to mentally process for all sorts of reasons. French Script is hard to read because it is visually complex and fairly small. Tongue twisters are hard to pronounce, as are words that are particularly long, rare, or with unusual combinations of letters (e.g., coccyx or electroencephalography). Events that occurred a long time ago are hard to remember, whereas things that we've seen recently or frequently are easier to bring to mind. People generally have a preference for things that are easy, or, in psychology jargon, *fluent*. And it turns out that this preference extends well beyond choosing a book based on its cover (or font).

For example, New York University researcher Adam Alter and his colleagues have found that fluency increases perceptions of value. The researchers showed that people prefer stocks of companies with easy-to-pronounce names—enough to drive up the prices of those companies' stocks immediately after their initial public offering (IPO). Even when controlling for the size of the company, the country of origin, and the industry of the company, this trend emerged. In fact, even the pronounce-ability of the stocks' three-letter ticker code influenced stock prices. Companies with pronounceable tickers (e.g., VUG) tended to have inflated stock prices compared to companies with unpronounceable tickers (e.g., VDG). It's not just ease of pronunciation of stocks that matters. Alter also showed that familiar currency is judged as more valuable than less familiar currency. Susan B. Anthony dollars, $2 bills, and even dollar bills subtly altered to be less familiar were undervalued compared to their more fluent counterparts.

Fluency also increases perceptions of truth. Rolf Reber from the University of Bergen and his colleagues asked people to determine whether or not various statements such as "Lima is in Peru" were true. Sometimes the statements were written in dark font, to maximize the contrast between the text and the background. Other times, the statements were in a lighter font, which made them harder to read. People were much more likely to believe that the statements were true when they were easy to read. Matthew McGlone from the University of Texas and his colleagues showed people phrases that either easily rolled off the tongue because they rhymed (e.g., "Woes unite foes") or subtly altered versions that didn't rhyme (e.g., "Woes unite enemies"). People rated the statements as being truer when they rhymed. "Birds of a feather flock together" seems more plausible than "Birds of a feather flock conjointly."

Moreover, fluency can affect our opinions about the intelligence of an author or speaker. For instance, Oppenheimer found that easier-to-read texts are perceived as coming from smarter authors. He took essays and either increased or decreased the average word length with a thesaurus. People reliably rated the authors of the essays with shorter, easier-to-read words as more intelligent. People even thought that the author of an essay presented in an easy-to-read font was smarter than when the exact same essay was presented in a hard-to-read font.

Let's recap for a second. When statements are easier to process, people like them more, judge them as more valuable, think they are truer, and think the authors are more intelligent. These trends explain a lot of common behavior in political debates. Have you ever wondered why politicians repeat the same catch phrases over and over ad nauseam? Repetition is a way of priming the audience that makes the message seem truer, more likeable, more valuable, and can even improve the public's view of the politician. And why do politicians often avoid the nuances, specifics, and complexities of their proposals and instead use easy-to-understand more general descriptions? Adding the complexities might inform voters, but they simultaneously make the arguments harder to understand, which undermines the credibility and likeability of the candidate.

Consider research done by Mike Norton and his colleagues at Harvard. The researchers showed people video clips from a simulated political debate. The clips came in one of three forms. In one version, the candidate answered a question about health care policy. The second version was substantively the same, except that the speech was made harder to process. The candidate paused several times while answering, and his answer was slowed by "uhs" and "ums" between phrases. In the final version, the candidate was asked the same question about health care, but answered on the topic of illegal drugs. In other words, the candidate dodged the question, but did so in smooth, easy-to-process speech.

Norton and his colleagues showed people one of these three video clips and asked people to evaluate the candidate. People gave equally positive evaluations to the fluent answers, regardless of whether or not the answer was on topic. However, less fluent answers were penalized; participants gave evaluations that were more than 10 percent lower when the candidate paused and fumbled for words. In other words, it was the delivery that mattered rather than the content. An on-topic mumbled answer did worse than an off-topic fluent answer. Is it any wonder that politicians memorize their talking points and stick to the script during debates? They know they won't be hurt if they are slightly off topic, but will be if their answer isn't delivered smoothly.

The impact of fluency on political decisions doesn't end with debates. Even cursory features of the candidates, like how easy it is to pronounce their names, can impact electability. Oppenheimer and his colleague Anuj Shah collected the names of candidates from contested primary elections for seats in the U.S. House of Representatives. They asked people to evaluate how easy or difficult each name was to pronounce, and compared these pronounceability ratings with how well each candidate did in the actual election. There was a nontrivial correlation between name pronounceability and electoral success. Candidates with names that were hard to pronounce received, on average, 5 percent fewer votes than candidates with easier names. So although Dennis Kucinich, Rod Blagojevich, and Ted Kulongoski did all manage to get elected, they have a built-in disadvantage compared to George Bush, Al Gore, and Bob Dole.[2] As surprising as it may seem that a person's name could make a difference, politicians have been aware of this for years. In fact, so many politicians were legally changing their names to try and get an electoral advantage that in 2007 Illinois passed a law expressly designed to counter that strategy.

Making a statement easier to read doesn't change how true it is, but it can change how true we think it is. And unfortunately, that means that voters often reward form over substance.

Summary

If the candidate's pet dog is cute. If the candidate has a pleasant-sounding voice. If the candidate shares your birthday, or comes from your home town, or has similar hobbies to yours. None of these things should influence which candidate we support. But they do (even if we don't believe that they do, or admit that they do). In this chapter, we've explored only a few of the many surprising findings about voter behavior. When we talk about policies reflecting the will of the people, we're typically referring to the content of those policies, not the context in which they were presented or the specific words used to describe them. And yet context, presentation,

---

2. It's worth noting that Kucinich, Blagojevich, and Kulongoski were running in local elections, not national ones. Having the name Kucinich or Blagojevich is probably less of a handicap in cities like Cleveland and Chicago, where there are significant Polish and Eastern European populations and the names are more fluent.

and first impressions all contribute to our voting decisions. How can democracy possibly be successful when voters are driven by such absurd considerations?

References

Lead Quote
Roosevelt, F. D. 1936. Jackson Day Dinner Address, Washington, D.C., January 8.

First Impressions
Ambady, N., F. J. Bernieri, and J. A. Richeson. 2000. Toward a histology of social behavior: Judgmental accuracy from thin slices of the behavioral stream. In *Advances in Experimental Social Psychology, 32*, ed. M. P. Zanna, 201–272. Waltham, MA: Academic Press.

Ambady, N., and R. Rosenthal. 1993. Half a minute: Predicting teacher evaluations from thin slices of nonverbal behavior and physical attractiveness. *Journal of Personality and Social Psychology* 64 (3):431–441.

Ballew, C. C., and A. Todorov. 2007. Predicting political elections from rapid and unreflective face judgments. *Proceedings of the National Academy of Sciences of the United States of America* 104:17948–17953.

Willis, J., and A. Todorov. 2006. First impressions: Making up your mind after a 100-ms exposure to a face. *Psychological Science* 17 (7):592–598.

Wolf, R. 2007. Gingrich, Bill Clinton agree on who's ahead: Hillary, Romney, Giuliani. *USA Today*, October 1, p. 7a.

Importance of Appearance
Armstrong, J. S., C. Kesten, R. Green, J. Jones, Jr., and M. J. Wright. 2010. Predicting elections from politicians' faces. *International Journal of Public Opinion Research* 22 (4):511–522.

Bailenson, J. N., S. Iyengar, N. Yee, and N. Collins. 2008. Facial similarity between voters and candidates causes influence. *Public Opinion Quarterly* 72 (5):935–961.

Cavett, D. 2008. Anger mismanagement. From The Opinionator blog at NYTimes.com, October 17. Retrieved April 17, 2011 from http://opinionator.blogs.nytimes.com/2008/10/17/anger-mismanagement.

James, S. D. 2010. TV Debate makes JFK superstar, Nixon a loser. ABC News, September 25. Retrieved April 17, 2011, from http://abcnews.go.com/Politics/50th-anniversary-1960-presidential-debate-made-kennedy-star/story?id=11694525&page=1.

Kristof, N. 2008. Did Clinton campaign darken Obama's complexion? From On the Ground blog at NYTimes.com, March 6. Retrieved April 17, 2011, from http://kristof .blogs.nytimes.com/2008/03/06/did-the-clinton-campaign-darken-obamas -complexion.

Little, A. C., R. P. Burriss, B. C. Jones, and S. C. Roberts. 2007. Facial appearance affects voting decisions. *Evolution and Human Behavior* 28:18–27.

Open, N. Y. 2008. The measure of a president. *New York Times*, October 6. Retrieved April 17, 2011, from http://www.nytimes.com/interactive/2008/10/06/opinion/ 06opchart.html.

Oppenheimer, D. M., and A. Todorov. N.d. Issues and traits (unpublished dataset, collected August 2006).

Priming

Berger, J., M. Meredith, and S. C. Wheeler. 2008. Contextual priming: Where people vote affects how they vote. *Proceedings of the National Academy of Sciences of the United States of America* 105 (26):8846–8849.

Cohen, F., Ogilvie, D., Solomon, S., Greenberg, J, and Pyszczynski, T. 2005. American roulette: The effect of reminders of death on support for George W. Bush in the 2004 presidential election. *Analyses of Social Issues and Public Policy* 5 (1):177–187.

Cox, A. M. 2008. S.C. takes a chance on McCain. *Time*, January 20. Retrieved April 17, 2011, from http://www.time.com/time/politics/article/0,8599,1705446,00 .html.

Jost, J. T., G. Fitzsimons, and A. C. Kay. 2004. The ideological animal: A system justification view. In *Handbook of Experimental Existential Psychology*, ed. J. Greenberg, S. L. Koole, and T. Pyszczynski, 263–282. New York: Guilford Press.

Lakoff, G. 1996. *Moral Politics*. Chicago: University of Chicago Press.

Miller, J. M., and J. A. Krosnick. 2000. News media impact on the ingredients of presidential evaluations: Politically knowledgeable citizens are guided by a trusted source. *American Journal of Political Science* 44 (2):301–315.

Mislavskaya, N. 2006. Political framing: Testing the impact of the society-as-family metaphor. Doctoral dissertation, Stanford University Department of Psychology.

Oppenheimer, D. M., and T. Trail. 2010. When leaning to the left makes you lean to the left: Spatial metaphor and political attitudes. *Social Cognition* 28:651–661.

Suitner, C. 2009. Where to place social targets: Stereotyping and spatial agency bias. Doctoral dissertation, University of Padua. Retrieved April 17, 2011, from http:// paduaresearch.cab.unipd.it/1756/1/tesi_suitner.pdf.

Framing

Fausey, C. M., and T. Matlock. 2011. Can grammar win elections? *Political Psychology* 32:563–574.

General Social Survey, 1972–1994. 2010. Survey documentation and analysis dataset. University of California, Berkeley. Retrieved April 17, 2011, from http://sda.berkeley .edu/GSS/Doc/gss004.html.

James, R. 2009. Pollster Frank Luntz, warrior with words. *Time*, September 21. Retrieved April 17, 2011, from http://www.time.com/time/nation/article/ 0,8599,1925066,00.html.

Lang, S. W. 2007. Where do we get "Star Wars"? *Eagle*, March, p. 9. Retrieved April 17, 2011, from http://www.smdc.army.mil/2008/EagleArchives.asp.

Langer, E., A. Blank, and B. Chanowitz. 1978. The mindlessness of ostensibly thoughtful action: The role of "placebic" information in interpersonal interaction. *Journal of Personality and Social Psychology* 36 (6):635–642.

Lee, J. 2003. A call for softer, greener language. *New York Times*, March 2. Retrieved June 23, 2011, from http://www.nytimes.com/2003/03/02/us/a-call-for-softer-greener -language.html.

Sinaceur, M., C. Heath, and S. Cole. 2005. Emotional and deliberative reactions to a public crisis: Mad cow disease in France. *Psychological Science* 16 (3):247–254.

Tannen, D. 2003. Let them eat words: Linguistic lessons from Republican master strategist Frank Luntz. *The American Prospect*, August 31. Retrieved April 17, 2011, from http://prospect.org/cs/articles?article=let_them_eat_words#.

Tversky, A., and D. Kahneman. 1981. The framing of decisions and the psychology of choice. *Science: New Series* 211 (4481):453–458.

Fluency

Alter, A. L., and D. M. Oppenheimer. 2006. Predicting short-term stock fluctuations by using processing fluency. *Proceedings of the National Academy of Sciences of the United States of America* 103 (24):9369–9372.

Alter, A. L., and D. M. Oppenheimer. 2008. Easy on the mind, easy on the wallet: The effects of familiarity and fluency on currency valuation. *Psychonomic Bulletin & Review* 15:985–990.

McGlone, M., and J. Tofighbakhsh. 1999. The Keats heuristic: Rhyme as reason in aphorism interpretation. *Poetics* 26 (4):235–244.

Oppenheimer, D. M. 2005. Consequences of erudite vernacular utilized irrespective of necessity: Problems with using long words needlessly. *Applied Cognitive Psychology* 20 (2):139–156.

Reber, R., and N. Schwarz. 1999. Effects of perceptual fluency on judgments of truth. *Consciousness and Cognition* 8:338–342.

Reeder, S. 2007. Illinois politicians can't play "name game." *Quad-Cities Dispatch*, February 10. Retrieved April 17, 2011, from http://qconline.com/archives/qco/display.php?id=326484.

Rogers, T., and M. Norton. 2008. The Artful Dodger: Answering the wrong question the right way. Harvard Business School Working Paper. Retrieved April 17, 2011, from http://www.hbs.edu/research/pdf/09-048.pdf.

Shah, A. K., and D. M. Oppenheimer. N.d. Fluency and political names (unpublished dataset, collected August 2006).

3 Electoral Madness

A citizen of America will cross the ocean to fight for democracy, but won't cross the street to vote in a national election.

—Bill Vaughan

Beacon Hill is a beautiful old Boston neighborhood. The narrow streets are lined with brownstones. Many buildings are marked with historical plaques indicating the famous people who once lived there, including many of America's first abolitionists. To the north sits Charlestown, site of the famous battle of Bunker Hill. To the south lies the old Boston Commons and Chinatown. To the east is the historic North End, where Paul Revere lived. To the west of Beacon Hill the Charles River runs past the Massachusetts Institute of Technology and Harvard University. All of those places—Cambridge, Charlestown, the North End, and Chinatown, north, south, east, and west—are part of U.S. Congressional District 8. Beacon Hill, however, is part of U.S. Congressional District 9. The rest of District 9 stretches through the old Southie neighborhood and continues to include a wide swath of suburbs south and southwest of Boston. So why is Beacon Hill part of District 9 and not the more geographically and culturally similar District 8?

Because after the 2000 census, Massachusetts state lawmakers decided that the Democratic Party was more likely to maintain control of both Districts 8 and 9 if Beacon Hill were placed in District 9. That process is called *gerrymandering*, or drawing district lines to maximize electoral success. Political parties do street-by-street analyses of the voting trends so that they can draw district lines in ideal ways and thereby guarantee that they will win the most seats in the legislature. The result is districts that look like strangled amoebas.

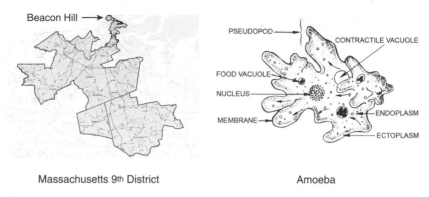

Massachusetts 9th District   Amoeba

Figure 3.1

In chapters 1 and 2, we talked about how voters are largely irrational and uninformed, and how this can affect which candidates they prefer. But even those flawed preferences do not necessarily translate directly into electoral outcomes. In this chapter, we will review many of the ways that the will of the people—already irrational and uninformed—can be further distorted by the electoral process itself. Voters consistently fail to vote for their preferred candidates because of confusing ballots, simple errors, or strategic voting concerns. Vote-counting processes are often biased, thanks to election officials with partisan loyalties. Seemingly benign choices about how to count the ballots, when to schedule elections, who can vote in a primary, and how to draw district lines can change the outcome of any given election. All of these factors contribute to elections in which the most popular candidate is in danger of losing and the most popular political party can find itself shut out of power.

How to Lose a Vote and Win an Election

Dissecting the Amoebas

In the 2004 U.S. House of Representative elections, there were 403 Representatives elected from states other than Texas. In those 403 races, 27 incumbents chose not to run for reelection, while 7 incumbents who ran for reelection lost. That means that outside of Texas, 92 percent of incumbents were returned to office. Meanwhile in Texas in 2004, only 72 percent (23 out of the 32) of incumbents were returned to Congress. As you can see in figure 3.2, only 3 of the 403 non-Texas Congressional races shifted

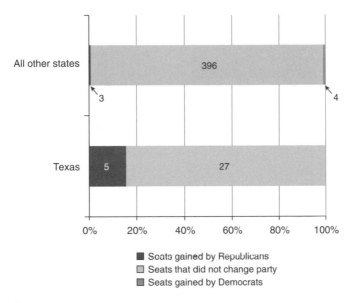

Figure 3.2
Changes in Party composition of the U.S. House of Representatives as a result of the 2004 election.

from being controlled by the Democratic Party to being controlled by the Republican Party. In Texas, 5 seats out of 32 shifted from Democrat to Republican.

Why this difference? It had nothing to do with a drastic change in voting patterns in Texas between 2002 and 2004. Texas voters hadn't changed: the Texas Congressional district map had.

When the results came back from the 2000 census, the Texas state legislature had been controlled by the Democrats, and those Democrats had the constitutionally mandated task of drawing district lines for the House of Representatives. Unsurprisingly, those Democrats drew district lines that were favorable to their own party; this favoritism helped the Democrats win 16 of the 32 seats. But the GOP gained control of the Texas legislature after 2002, and they decided they didn't like the way that the Democrats had drawn the House district lines. So the Republicans took the very unusual step of redrawing those lines in the middle of a decade. In 2004 the first election was held with the new district map, and obviously the GOP's strategy paid off.

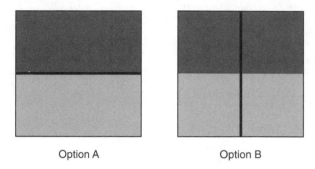

Option A   Option B

Figure 3.3
Two districts.

It would be tempting at this point to attribute gerrymandering to rampant partisanship. But before we attack either party too much, let's look a bit more carefully at the process of drawing district lines. Imagine that you're in charge of drawing the district map in your state. To make it simple, we'll say that you're from a perfectly square state with a perfectly even population density and only two districts. Moreover, in your state all of the Republicans live in the northern half of the state (the dark section in figure 3.3), and all of the Democrats live in the southern half of the state (the light section). So this should be easy, right? In fact, we can boil your choices down to one of two options (the black line denotes the district boundaries).

Option A creates one Democrat district and one Republican district. The benefit of this option is that voters are all guaranteed a member of Congress who agrees with them. Democrats are represented by a Democrat while Republicans are represented by a Republican. The problem, however, is that neither party's voters are given a real choice on Election Day, which effectively means that each party gets to choose the member of Congress from that district. Although it is true that no one is forced to vote for his or her own party, in reality party loyalty is strong enough that most Republicans will vote for their own party the vast majority of the time, as will most Democrats.

In fact, even trying to get a half-decent Democratic candidate to run in a Republican-dominated district (or vice versa) can be difficult. For instance, in heavily Democratic Massachusetts in 2008, the Republican Party contested only 58 of the state's 200 legislative seats. If they had won each and every race in which they put a nominee on the ballot, they would have controlled only 29 percent of the state's legislature. The GOP tried, but it is hard to convince candidates to run for races that they are almost guaranteed to lose. In short, districts that are heavily stacked in favor of one political party will reduce the likelihood of a competitive election, effectively giving voters less choice.

Option B, of course, gives voters plenty of choice on Election Day, as each district contains Democrats and Republicans in equal proportion. The problem here is that all too often, both members of Congress from your state will be from the same party. When that happens, your state's Congressional delegation will not accurately reflect the population of your state. Your state could send a radically liberal delegation to Congress one election, and two years later elect a pair of extreme conservatives. In neither case does the representation reflect the moderate nature of your state.

So which option will you choose: better elections, or more accurate representation? Even when you are trying to make that decision in a partisan-free manner, there is no clearly correct answer; and yet your decision will have major consequences on who represents your state. There is no such thing as a district map that both guarantees accurate representation of the people's beliefs and also allows for meaningful competition on Election Day.

In fact, the problems with drawing fair district lines only get worse as the districts become larger and more complex. So now imagine that your state is still square, still has a perfectly even population density, and is still evenly divided along geographic lines between Republicans (dark) and Democrats (light). But this time, you are given four congressional districts to draw (fig. 3.4). Here are your options.

Option A gives your state two Republican districts and two Democratic ones. Just like with two districts, this ensures accurate representation in Congress, but denies voters real choice on Election Day.

Option B gives your state four equally divided districts. Once again, this gives your voters choice, but leaves open the possibility that one party will dominate the elections and give half of your state's citizens poor representation in Congress. In fact, it even allows for a party to "win" your state without winning a majority of votes. For instance, let's say that in the far left district, some enthusiastic Republican goes door-to-door throughout the entire Republican area of that district, encouraging people to go vote

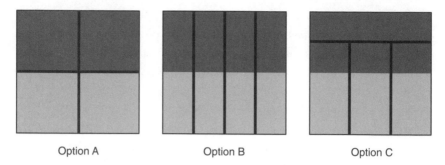

Option A   Option B   Option C

Figure 3.4
Four districts.

on Election Day. The volunteer does a tremendous job, and so in the left district the Republican wins by 5,000 votes. Meanwhile, in each of the other three districts, a Democrat prevails in tight races, in each case winning by 500 votes. In that election, more people in your state voted Republican than voted Democrat—and yet, your Congressional delegation includes three Democrats and one Republican. Choosing Option B is not an attempt to gerrymander, and yet the end result can still give control of the government over to a minority party.

Both Grover Cleveland in 1888 and Al Gore in 2000 lost the presidency for this basic reason. Both candidates received more votes in their respective elections than their opponent, and yet both lost the presidency. Why? Because their votes were not spread evenly across enough different states to win in the Electoral College. This was not the fault of gerrymandering or conspiracy. No one adjusted the Florida–Georgia state line to deny Al Gore the presidency. Instead, his loss was simply due to a common flaw of any system that determines winners based on their performance in multiple different districts.

By gerrymandering district maps, a political party can exploit this flaw to its own advantage; hence Option C. Consider Option C from the perspective of a Democrat. This option gives the Republicans 100 percent representation in one district. Why would Democrats want to give the GOP a guaranteed win? Because every other district is now 67 percent Democrat and 33 percent Republican. The GOP has one guaranteed win; the Democrats have three. So, if you're a Democrat who strongly believes that Democrats are better at governing the country than Republicans, which option will you choose? Probably Option C. Although this same result (three Democrats, one Republican) can happen through Option B, skillful gerrymandering guarantees that outcome.

Of course, real states are not square, they don't have uniform population densities, and Democrats and Republicans are not evenly divided along easily defined geographic lines. This makes the issues more complex, the "best" districting strategy more elusive, and the outcomes more distorted. Gerrymandering in the real world requires block-by-block decisions about where to draw different district lines, based on voting patterns and demographic trends; hence the strangled amoebas. It's a hard job, and the parties often make mistakes, but when done successfully it can have the kind of dramatic impact that the Republicans saw in Texas in 2004.

So while parties can take advantage of districting to their own ends, the fact remains that there is no way to draw district lines in a way that both accurately represents voter preferences and still gives voters meaningful choices. While some district maps are certainly better than others, this basic problem is unsolvable. The mere existence of districts will necessarily distort the will of the people.

The Incumbency Advantage

You might have noticed in the Texas redistricting example that over 90 percent of incumbents nationwide were returned to the U.S. House of Representatives in 2004. That success rate is common for incumbents. In 2008, 92 percent of incumbents were returned to office. In 2006, a year in which the Democrats had a major victory and took back control of the House of Representatives, 87 percent of incumbents were returned to office. Even in the legendary 1994 "Republican Revolution," when the GOP took control of the House of Representatives for the first time in decades, over 80 percent of incumbents were returned to office, and in the massive Republican victory of 2010, 77 percent of incumbents kept their seats. The results for Senate elections are not quite as biased in favor of incumbents, although you only need to look at the prolonged careers of people like Ted Stevens (41 years in the Senate), Ted Kennedy (47 years), Strom Thurmond (47 years), and Robert Byrd (51 years) to see how hard it can be to unseat a well-entrenched senator.

It is commonly assumed that the incumbency advantage results from gerrymandering. But according to statistical analysis done by political scientists Gary Cox and Jonathan Katz, gerrymandering has only a small effect on the incumbency advantage. Just look at what happened in that Texas example: Redistricting there actually contributed to the losses of several incumbents. Cox and Katz found that the biggest reason that incumbents tend to get reelected is the inherent characteristics of the candidates. The same name, facial features, speaking style, and ideology that attracted voters to a particular candidate in 2002 probably also existed in 2004 and 2006. If you're the kind of candidate who can win an election once, then there is a good chance that you will continue to do so.

Of course, there are other reasons for the incumbency advantage that have less to do with voter choice. In particular, it is easier to solicit campaign donations and receive publicity if you are already in office.

The money is easy to understand: Corporations, unions, and well-connected individuals give campaign contributions to sitting members of Congress as part of their lobbying efforts. Of course, it is illegal to explicitly buy votes, but there is still the widely held belief that candidates are more likely to listen to someone who has given them money. Candidates can use that money to help themselves win elections.

The name recognition advantage is often more subtle, but equally powerful. Psychologist Robert Zajonc ran a number of experiments in which he demonstrated the *mere exposure effect*: merely being exposed to people, ideas, or objects can make you like them. For instance, he repeatedly showed people pictures of symbols that looked like Chinese characters. Each time he showed a particular symbol, he asked the respondents what they thought the character might mean. It turned out that the more someone saw a picture, the more likely that person was to identify it with a positive characteristic (good, beautiful, etc.) and the less likely that person was to identify it with a negative characteristic (bad, ugly, etc.). Simply put, familiarity breeds attraction. Even if people know nothing about their member of Congress, simply by the fact that she gets her name in the news occasionally will cause more people to view her favorably.

Name recognition also feeds back on itself, creating free advertising. For instance, local news loves to cover natural disasters; when the president shows up at a disaster site with the local congressmen in tow, the event gets plenty of media attention. For that matter, when any celebrity or widely recognized public figure visits the site, there will be plenty of cameras on hand to record the visit. On the other hand, what about a potential challenger to a high-profile incumbent? If you are thinking about running for office but haven't yet declared, you can expect to receive no such coverage. You may have worked long hours clearing debris, but no one would know that you were there unless he or she were wielding a shovel next to you.

Of course, as voters we have the power to change our minds and vote incumbents out of office. Every election cycle, some well-entrenched representative, senator, or governor is unseated in favor of a long-shot, no-name candidate. But these events are relatively uncommon. People can change their minds about candidates; but they rarely do, for reasons that have very little to do with manipulation by insidious politicians.

Some things just cannot be made perfectly fair. There is no way to guarantee challengers and incumbents equal name recognition, just like there is no way to draw "perfect" district lines. And in general, challengers have a difficult time winning elections against incumbents—even when the challenger would otherwise be preferred by a majority of voters.

The Little Things That Matter

The First Tuesday after the First Monday in November

In 1845, Congress decreed that Congressional elections should always be held on the first Tuesday after the first Monday of November. They wanted to set a date after the fall harvest, so that the largely agrarian population could reasonably take the time off to go to the polls, but before the weather turned excessively cold; hence early November. They didn't want Election Day ever falling on the Sabbath (which eliminated Saturday and Sunday), or on Market Day, which in most places at the time was Wednesday. So they settled on Tuesday. Finally, they didn't want Election Day to fall on the first of the month, both because many farmers and businessmen balanced their books on the first of the month, and also because November 1 is All Saints Day, a Catholic holiday. All of that was very reasonable logic in 1845.

Of course, it is no longer 1845, and the United States is no longer an agrarian nation. But the tradition of voting on a Tuesday has become so entrenched that many states now even schedule primaries and other state and local elections on Tuesdays. Yet in the twenty-first century, voting for president on the first Tuesday after the first Monday of November seems pretty arbitrary, which is why there have been many proposals to move Election Day. The problem is that no matter on which day the election is held, that date will favor some voters over others.

Let's look at the day of the week. Most Americans work on Tuesdays, and taking off work to go vote is not always a possibility. Federal law states that an employee cannot be fired for missing work to vote in a federal election, but for state and local elections only 30 states mandate that employers allow employees to take time off to vote. Only 20 of those states actually mandate punishments for employers who violate those laws, and in many cases those punishments amount to a trivial monetary penalty. The penalty in Arkansas is probably the silliest: Employers found in violation of the law are fined a whopping $25. But even if your employer is willing to give you time off, the pressures and distractions of a busy work day make it a real problem for some people to get out and vote. Teachers have classes, doctors have appointments with patients, lawyers have deadlines for filing paperwork; many voters can't reasonably leave work to vote even when they don't face the threat of official sanctions for missing time.

As a result, some people have suggested either making Election Day a federal holiday or moving Election Day to the weekend. But according to one study by economist Henry Farber, such a change might not lead to an increase in voting—and could actually cause fewer people to go vote. He compared voter turnout among people who worked for state governments in different states, some in states that give their employees time off on Election Day and some that don't. He found no evidence to suggest that an Election Day holiday would increase voter turnout.

Why wouldn't more people vote if they didn't have to go to work? Well, most managers do actually give people time off to vote, whether it is official policy or not. As a result, by voting you get to leave work a few hours early; an appealing option to a lot of people. But if Election Day were scheduled for a Saturday or a federal holiday, then the options change. In that case, you're facing the choice of voting or taking a day of leisure, and many people would just as soon go to the golf course or the mall as to stand in line at a polling location. Besides, the people who have the hardest time taking off work are low-skilled, low-income workers—the people who are most easily replaced if they upset their bosses. Those clerks, waiters, janitors, and the like are also the very people who are most likely to work on federal holidays—so again, it's not clear that the creation of an Election Day holiday would actually improve their ability to go to the polls.

For our purposes, the important thing is that the set of people who would choose to go to the polls on a Tuesday would be somewhat different from the set of people who would choose to go to the polls on a holiday. There are certainly people who feel trapped by their jobs; people who would like to vote but cannot take the time off work to do so. Others are voting on Election Day only because they'd rather vote than go to work—but most of those people would probably prefer to go to the beach than go to the polls, so an Election Day holiday would actually stop them from voting. There is no reason to believe that the "trapped at work" folks would vote for the same candidates that the "avoiding work" crowd would vote for. The choice to create an Election Day holiday would likely lead to different overall voting patterns, and potentially different electoral outcomes. So which set of voters more accurately represent the will of the people? Since both are an arbitrary subset of the population, the answer is probably neither.

The same logic applies to moving elections to the weekend, although in that case there are also religious effects. Saturday and Sunday are holy days to many Judeo-Christian denominations. Some of those denominations would surely see voting as a religious obligation perfectly in line with a day of rest and prayer, and voting among those parishioners might increase. Other denominations would see voting as a distraction from the Sabbath and would strongly discourage their parishioners from participating in elections. So if we change election days to be on weekends we will also likely change the electoral outcomes.

And what about the decision to hold elections in early November? Well, it turns out that November is a cold, rainy, and sometimes snowy month in many parts of the country. There is a reason that farmers try to have their crops harvested before November. And this inclement weather can also affect electoral outcomes.

In a widely cited study, political scientists Brad Gomez, Thomas Hansford, and George Kraus found that rain and snow have a significant impact in lowering Election Day turnout in U.S. presidential elections. More importantly, they found that bad weather can actually have substantial effects on the outcome of an election. According to their data, Republican candidates do significantly better on rainy and snowy days than Democratic candidates. For instance, in 1960 Election Day weather was extraordinarily good across the middle section of the country, helping John F. Kennedy eke out a victory against Richard Nixon. In 2000, a steady rainfall in the Florida panhandle might well have cost Al Gore enough votes to change the outcome of that extremely close election.

This study is not without its problems, and we shouldn't put too much stock into one result. In particular, we are skeptical about their finding that rain always benefits Republicans. But the larger point is a good one: If the weather is bad enough, because of excessive rain, snow, or cold, then some people who would have otherwise gone to the polls and voted will surely change their minds.

So with that in mind, think about what happened in the 2008 presidential primary season. That year many states moved up their primary dates, with the effect that the first primaries and caucuses were held in January (instead of the usual February). "Super Tuesday," the day when most people across the country voted in presidential primaries, was also moved up; many of the primaries that had previously been held in mid-March were instead held in early February.

Well, as you can probably guess, the weather across the Midwest, the Northeast, and the Rocky Mountain states is often a lot worse in January and February than it is in March. And sure enough, temperatures during the Iowa caucuses in 2008 hovered in the high teens, while a snowstorm swept across the Midwest on Super Tuesday. Of course, we cannot know exactly what the effect truly was because we have no way of knowing who would have voted had the weather been nicer or whom they would have voted for. But the inclement weather could have affected some people more than others; it seems likely that the elderly and infirm would be more influenced by blizzards than younger or healthier citizens. People who rely on public transportation might have been affected differently by the poor weather than people who own cars. In other words, this decision to move up elections could very well have had an effect on the primary races.

We would like to think election results are a reflection of the will of the people, but it's hard to see how that's possible when the outcomes depend so heavily on what day the elections are held. A snowstorm or a change in the day of the week should not change voter opinions. But it can change election outcomes.

Ballot Ordering
Think about the last time you bought an apple. If your market is anything like ours, there were a lot of choices. Obviously, you have to choose the

type of apple—Red Delicious, Granny Smith, and so on. Even after you've done that, you have a pile of perhaps fifty very similar apples to choose from. Some were probably obviously bruised, so you ruled those out. But then did you search through each apple looking for the perfect size, shape, and color? Probably not. Most likely you just grabbed the first apple that looked ripe and unblemished. This is what social scientists call *satisficing*: Instead of searching for the very best apple, you chose the first one that you came across that was minimally acceptable.

Satisficing is a good thing. Every day we are faced with countless choices that have very little importance to our happiness or prosperity. Which pair of socks to wear? Which pen to use? Which coffee shop to stop at? If we exhaustively researched and analyzed every choice we made, we'd waste all day, every day, focused on mundane decisions.

So, in many situations, satisficing makes a great deal of sense. But people satisfice a lot, and not just on the trivial things. In particular, there is good evidence to suggest that many voters satisfice on Election Day. In 1992, Stanford professor Jon Krosnick and his colleagues looked at the state of Ohio, where ballot order is randomized in each precinct. Krosnick looked at voting patterns in nearly 4,000 precincts for over 100 races. The results were striking; when a candidate's name happened to appear first, that candidate had, on average, a 2.5 percent advantage.

Eight years later, Krosnick followed up this study by looking at races in Ohio, North Dakota, and California. The results were very similar. Even in races where only two candidates were on the ballot, being first gave a 2.8 percent edge, on average. Most notably, ballot ordering didn't merely influence obscure local races. In all three states, George Bush received more votes in places where his name was first on the ballot than when it was last. The most extreme result was in California, where Bush got a whopping 9.4 percent larger vote share when he was listed first on the ballot (North Dakota and Ohio were less surprising at 1.7 percent and 0.8 percent, respectively). The same trend was found in races for senate seats. Candidates have an advantage when they are listed at the top of the ballot. It seems that voters don't always look for the best candidate, but often satisfice instead. They find the first candidate on the list that is good enough and vote for that person.

Different states have different ways of deciding how to order candidates on a ballot. Some states, like Ohio, randomize the order in which the names appear. This may be the fairest way to decide who gets the advantage of being at the top of the ballot, but randomization can have negative consequences. For instance, in the 2003 California gubernatorial recall election, there were 135 candidates running for governor, yet over 95 percent of voters ended up voting for one of four people. In that case, the randomized order made it difficult for most voters to find their candidate.

Other states, such as Virginia, list candidates from "major" parties first, thus making it easier for voters to find major-party candidates. But of course, this rule disadvantages third-party candidates, who are already facing an uphill battle. Massachusetts puts the incumbent first, Kentucky puts candidates from the party of the sitting U.S. president first, and Vermont lists candidates in alphabetical order. Each of these methods creates its own unique bias, favoring some candidates over others.

And yes, even a change of 1 percent can affect the outcome of an election. Democrat Al Gore lost Florida to Republican George Bush in the 2000 presidential election by fewer than 600 votes. Republican Dino Rossi lost to Democrat Christine Gregoire in Washington's 2004 gubernatorial election by fewer than 200 votes. Democrat Al Franken defeated Republican Norm Coleman by fewer than 500 votes in Minnesota's 2008 Senate race. In each one of those cases, the margin of victory was so small that the outcome could have been different had the names been ordered differently on the ballot.

Democrats for "John Ewards" and Pat Buchanan

In the 2004 presidential election, Democrat John Kerry and his running mate John Edwards (no relation to the author) won the state of Minnesota and all ten of its electoral votes. As a result, ten people were chosen by the Minnesota state legislature to vote in the Electoral College upon the promise that they would vote for John Kerry for president and for John Edwards for vice president. But when the time came to actually record those votes, one of the electors wrote on his or her ballot "John Ewards" for president instead of "John Kerry." (That's right, not only did this person write in the wrong name, he or she also misspelled it!) The Electoral College officials—the people appointed by Congress to actually count the votes—decided that the voter intent in that case was "John Edwards." All ten of the electors successful wrote "John Edwards" on the line for vice president. Officially, one of the Minnesota electors voted for Edwards for both president and vice president. Of course, none of the electors confessed to the error, but the result is that John Kerry received one fewer electoral vote for president than he "should" have.

We know that the voters in this case intended to vote for John Kerry; they all signed a piece of paper declaring their intent well before the election. These voters were educated and generally highly competent people, and it would be hard to think of a simpler way to design a ballot than simply having the voter write down his or her choice. Yet, even then, one of them voted for the wrong guy. Sadly, this wasn't an isolated incident.

In 2006, Rice University professor Mike Byrne and his colleagues had undergraduates vote in a simulated election. The students were given three identical ballots and were asked to fill them all out in the same way according to instructions they had been given before stepping into the voting booth. Some of them were even allowed to take their "voter guides" into the booth with them; they didn't have to remember who to vote for, it was written right in front of them. These voters were all well educated, smart, motivated, and familiar with the voting systems—the sort of population you would least expect to make errors in filling out a ballot. Nonetheless, more than 1 in 10 ballots had at least one error. Surprised by such a high error rate, Byrne ran the study again, this time sampling from a more representative subset of the American voter. That time, over 26 percent of ballots contained at least one error.

Of course, Byrne's study used simple elections with extremely common ballot designs. In real life, ballots are not always designed so clearly; you can imagine what that does to the error rate.

Palm Beach County is one of the largest and most reliably liberal counties in all of Florida. In 2000, Gore was counting on a big win in Palm Beach County if he had any hopes of winning the state. And sure enough, Gore did win big there, earning 63 percent of the county, or just under 270,000 votes. What surprised election observers was that Pat Buchanan, an extremely conservative Republican who was running as a Reform Party candidate, also did well in Palm Beach County. Buchanan's 3,000 votes in Palm Beach County gave him about ten times more votes than he was expecting from that county, and more than twice as many votes as he received in any other county in Florida.

What happened? The most likely explanation is voter error, stemming from a confusing ballot design. As you can see from figure 3.5, this so-called Butterfly Ballot lists candidates for president on both sides, with a

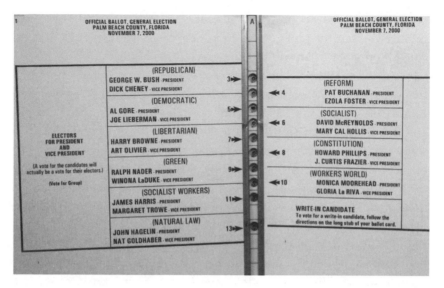

Figure 3.5

row of punch holes down the middle. A voter intending to vote for George Bush simply has to punch the top hole. A voter intending to vote for Al Gore should punch the third hole—despite the fact that Al Gore is listed second on the ballot. The second hole corresponds to Pat Buchanan, who is listed at the top of the opposite page. Of course, most voters navigated the ballot successfully; Gore did win that county by a large margin. But the 2000 election was so close that even a small number of mistakes could have affected the outcome. In a study by political scientist Jonathan Wand and colleagues, voter error due to the Butterfly Ballot design cost Al Gore at least 2,000 votes, easily enough to have changed the outcome of that election.

Voters often make mistakes on their ballots, even when they know who they want to vote for. Making the right decision on Election Day is meaningless if the voters can't accurately mark the ballot.

Vote Counting

Rise of the Machines

In ancient Athens, voting was commonly done one of two ways. Most of the time, the citizens at the assembly were asked to give a show of hands.

Officials would then judge which side received the greater number of votes and declare a winner. Other times, the citizens would place small stones or balls in an urn: either white or black depending on how they were voting. For a democracy in which there were fewer than 10,000 eligible voters, and in which voting required attendance at a lengthy debate, these procedures worked just fine.

Thanks to technology, we've moved beyond counting hands or stones, but the Butterfly Ballot demonstrates that there is still plenty of room for error. There is simply no perfect way of counting votes. More importantly, every imperfect way is different. The outcome of elections can depend not on the election itself, but instead on the choice of voting technology.

Old-fashioned lever voting machines and more modern electronic voting machines leave no paper trail; there is no way to verify after the fact that the machines counted the votes correctly or to do any sort of recount. In fact, the lack of verifiability is even more problematic with electronic voting machines than it is for the older technologies. The software for most of these machines is proprietary and only people who work for the companies know how it really works. As a result, there have been allegations that the manufacturers of the voting machines could implant instructions directly into the software to favor certain candidates.

Moreover, the technology is new, which makes the electronic machines more prone to breakdowns and technological glitches. For instance, in San Diego County's elections for the March 2004 presidential primary, the polls opened over an hour late in about half of the county's polling locations. Many voters were told to "come back later," although it is unclear how many actually did. In 2006, electronic machines in Sarasota County indicated that about 18,000 voters (one in seven) had otherwise completed their ballots but failed to vote in the race for Florida's Thirteenth Congressional District—a widely publicized election that was decided by fewer than 400 votes. In that case, there were widespread allegations that most of those people had voted in that election and a technical glitch had discarded the votes. But there was no way to verify what actually happened, and a winner was declared based on the machine tallies—even though those tallies were possibly flawed.

Even when elections are uncontroversial, lever and electronic voting machines are far from ideal. They are extremely heavy and bulky, which makes them difficult to set up and put away on Election Day and expensive to store for the rest of the year. As a result, richer districts (who can more easily afford to pay election workers and storage fees) have a distinct advantage in procuring more machines than poorer districts. Fewer machines in poorer areas means longer lines, which means that voting becomes more of a hassle, which can contribute to lower turnout. Moreover, these machines can be very complicated and difficult for some less technically savvy voters to use, which increases the odds of ballot errors.

Punch-card systems get around these issues by being much less expensive and leaving a paper trail. Unfortunately, that paper trail can be very difficult to follow. Sometimes a small bit of paper, called a *chad*, is left *hanging*. Sometimes the ballot is *dimpled*; there's a mark, but no hole has been punched in the ballot at all. In all of those cases, election workers, lawyers, and judges have to go back through and determine voter intent. Did the voter intend to vote for this candidate, or did he consciously stop himself before the paper was broken? It's a lot like determining whether or not a batter checked his swing in baseball—except that election outcomes can rest on the decisions. Mike Edwards can testify personally to how confusing these ballots can be; on at least two occasions, he was halfway through a ballot before realizing that he wasn't pushing down on the pin hard enough to break the paper. During the 2000 Florida recount there was so much confusion over hanging chads that Florida banned punch-card balloting for all future elections. Another problem with punch cards is that they allow voters to make the mistake of voting for two candidates for the same election. The problem is worse with punch cards than with other kinds of ballots because voters don't actually look at the punch card itself. Instead, they look at a fixed ballot, which gives the voter no visual indication whether he or she has already voted.

Optical scan ballots have worked better than their alternatives; they are cheap, relatively easy to use, and are familiar to any voter who has taken a standardized test in school. They also leave a paper trail and can be hand-counted if necessary. In fact, according to the Caltech/MIT Voting Technology Project, optical scan ballots are the most secure and reliable form of voting technology currently in use.

But no system is perfect. In the 2008 Minnesota Senate race, in which Al Franken defeated incumbent Norm Coleman by fewer than 500 votes, hand-counting the optical ballots revealed numerous voter mistakes. Some people had tried to change their votes by scribbling out one bubble and marking another. In other cases, voters had written notes in the margins in order to explain their mangled attempts to fill in one of the bubbles. These errors contributed quite a bit to the confusion, controversy, and ultimately the lawsuits that resulted from this extremely close election. The confusion effectively denied Minnesotans one of their senators for several months while the courts decided who actually won the election.

When voters step into the voting booth, they are supposed to leave a record of who they want to vote for. Unfortunately, voters often make mistakes. Some voter error is to be expected, but when that error results from confusing ballots or unfamiliar voting technologies, the results can have massive impacts on the outcome of elections. Similarly, candidates are supposed to win elections because they have the best ideas, and yet sometimes candidates win because their supporters were concentrated in counties that had clearer ballots or voter technology that was less prone to error.

State Election Officials

The 1876 presidential election took place just as the Jim Crow laws were sweeping the South, ending the brief period of enfranchisement for African Americans that had been allowed after the Civil War. That election was tightly contested, between Republican Rutherford B. Hayes and Democrat Samuel Tilden. Unsurprisingly, there was rampant voter intimidation across the South, mostly aimed at African Americans, who were most likely to vote Republican. So on Election Day, the states across the South each reported vote totals that strongly favored the Democrat Tilden (the preferred candidate of Southern whites). But three states, Florida, Louisiana, and South Carolina, were still governed by the pro-Republican officials and Union troops left over from the Civil War. The Republican election officials in those states decided that there was evidence of massive fraud. So to compensate for the large number of African Americans who were denied the vote, the Republican officials discarded large numbers of white Democratic votes. Then they certified that the Republican, Hayes, had won those states. Those states gave Hayes enough electoral votes to win the presidency—but of course, the Democrats around the country protested. To prevent a constitutional crisis, Congress created an independent commission to certify the electoral votes from each state. That commission ultimately gave the votes of Florida, South Carolina, and Louisiana to

Hayes, who was subsequently sworn in as the nineteenth president of the United States.

Those Republican officials might have done the right thing, at least in Louisiana and South Carolina. The black vote was heavily pro-Republican at the time, and Louisiana and South Carolina were majority black states; in a free and fair election, there is a very strong likelihood that those states would have gone for Hayes. But it would be extraordinarily naive to suggest that those officials weren't also acting with the best interests of their own party in mind.

We've come a long way since 1876. Jim Crow laws are a thing of the past and the Republican Party is no longer shunned by Southern whites. And yet our election officials are still as partisan as the Republican officials who threw the election in favor of Rutherford B. Hayes.

For instance, in most states there is an elected position called secretary of state. One of the main duties of most secretary of state offices is to act as the state's highest election official. They certify election results, oversee recount procedures, and sometimes can declare when recounts should or should not occur. They manage the voter registration rolls, the official lists of who can and cannot vote, and they inform voters about upcoming elections.

All of those decisions can affect the outcome of elections. Managing the voter registration lists effectively gives the secretaries of state the power to decide who can and cannot vote in an election. In some cases, people may be allowed to vote in the wrong places or without showing the proper documentation to verify address or citizenship. In other circumstances, people's names can be purged off of those registration rolls, effectively disenfranchising those voters. Aggressive information campaigns can result in higher voter turnout, while less aggressive campaigns can effectively dampen voter turnout. Most importantly, the role that secretaries of state play in recounts has been a factor in many recent high-profile elections.

For instance, in 2000, Florida Secretary of State Katherine Harris was that state's top election official. It was her job to certify that the votes had been counted properly, to declare an end to the election, and to formally declare the winner of the election. Most of the time, those are ceremonial duties, but in 2000 they had a profound effect on the election. In particular, it was Secretary Harris who could have ordered further recounts and defined the parameters of those recounts. When the Supreme Court ultimately ruled on *Bush v. Gore*, their ruling explicitly upheld her authority to terminate the recounts, thereby overturning the Florida State Supreme Court's ruling that Secretary Harris had violated Florida law by stopping them prematurely. According to the National Opinion Research Center at the University of Chicago, who gained access to the ballots after the election on behalf of a consortium of news organizations, the presidency hinged on which ballots were recounted. The limited recount requested by Harris favored Bush. A full recount of all counties, which Harris could have requested, would have favored Al Gore.

So who was Harris, and what made her qualified to make such important decisions?

Katherine Harris was first elected to public office as a Republican Florida state senator in 1994, and she was elected secretary of state in 1998. As a perceived up-and-coming conservative Florida politician, she had been chosen as a delegate to the Republican National Convention in 2000, and had served as a co-chair for George W. Bush's campaign in Florida. Katherine Harris was a professional politician and a loyal Republican.

That's right, a partisan Republican with clear loyalties to George W. Bush was asked to make decisions that helped to determine whether George W. Bush would win or lose a presidential election. That's a bit like a player moving from shortstop to home plate umpire in the middle of a World Series game. Even if the player were consciously trying to be neutral, he simply has too much invested in the outcome, too much emotional and financial stake, to ever be a completely fair arbiter. Making the player into the umpire would be unfair to the teams playing the game. It would also be unfair to the player, who would surely have his reputation and integrity called into question no matter how he ruled.

So we can sympathize with Katherine Harris. She was put in an impossible position—as are most secretaries of state around the country. It is simply absurd to expect that politically ambitious people can be neutral judges of election results. Yes, in theory the voters in each state should be picking secretaries of state who are unbiased individuals of impeccable character. Yet in 1998 when a couple million Florida voters went to the polls and selected Katherine Harris over Sandra Mortham as Florida secretary of state, they probably had no idea that their decision might help to determine the next president of the United States. After all, the voters in those elections are irrational human beings, choosing other irrational human beings, in elections that are often poorly publicized and poorly attended.

Unfortunately, that's not the only case where a small group of voters can unintentionally affect the outcome of a much larger election. Just ask the citizens of Ames, Iowa.

Strategic Voting

A Hot August Night

On August 11, 2007, 33,000 Republicans drove to the Iowa State campus in Ames to attend a GOP fundraiser and vote in an informal straw poll. Most of the people who voted that evening had been recruited to come to the event by the various presidential campaigns. The campaigns paid the transportation costs of many of the attendees, as well as their admission to the event itself. Mitt Romney, Mike Huckabee, Ron Paul, Sam Brownback, Tom Tancredo, and Tommy Thompson all took time out of their busy campaign schedules to come to the event and personally campaign in and around Ames. Election front-runners Rudy Giuliani and John McCain both chose not to participate—and both were widely criticized for "abandoning" Iowa. Mitt Romney, the favorite in Ames that evening, spent millions of dollars on the event, mostly on advertisements designed to encourage his supporters to attend.

The money paid off: Mitt Romney ended up winning the straw poll. The surprise candidate was Mike Huckabee, who came in second. Meanwhile, Tommy Thompson was so disheartened by his poor showing that he dropped out of the race.

Why on earth is the Iowa Straw Poll—an obviously biased election from a small number of voters in a small state—taken so seriously? Because those voters in Ames were not merely giving Mitt Romney and Mike Huckabee their votes in a meaningless election, they were also giving those candidates credibility in the eyes of the media and the rest of the voting public. That credibility ultimately led to millions of votes.

To see how this works, take a moment and think about all the people you know and respect, including family, friends, coworkers, political leaders, and celebrities. Think about who has the best ideas, who is the best motivator, who is the most intelligent, and who is the best administrator. Feel free to add to that list any other qualities you think Americans should look for in a great leader. Now, with that in mind, and without concern for electability or campaign financing, who do you think would make the best president of the United States?

Now here comes the million dollar question: Did you vote for that person in our most recent presidential election?

Chances are pretty good that you did not. Even if you like the president, you still may believe that your favorite uncle, or the local Congressional Representative, or your company's new brilliant vice president would do a better job at leading the country. Just look at the 2008 primary: Neither McCain nor Obama won a majority of votes in their own party's primaries. And yet the vast majority of people who voted against McCain in the GOP primary voted for him in the general election, just like the vast majority of people who voted against Obama in the primary voted for him in the general election. All of those Democrats who voted for Hillary Clinton in the primary could have written her name on the general election ballot; instead they overwhelmingly voted for Obama. They did so because their preferred candidate had no shot at winning. They didn't want to "throw away their vote," and so they voted for one of the favorites instead. This is what political scientists refer to as *strategic voting*.

To see how this works, imagine that Bob McVoter is voting in the 2008 New Hampshire Republican Party Primary. Here are the candidates that are on Bob's ballot, in order of his preference:

1. Mike Huckabee
2. Fred Thompson
3. Duncan Hunter
4. Rudy Giuliani
5. John McCain
6. Ron Paul
7. Mitt Romney

Bob really likes Mike Huckabee, the former governor of Arkansas, and has even considered donating money to Huckabee's campaign. At the same time, Bob has some pretty strong biases against a couple of the candidates. In particular, Bob is scared of Mitt Romney, a former governor of Massachusetts, becoming president because he believes that anyone who can win an election in Massachusetts must be a liberal elitist. He is also concerned about

Congressman and former Libertarian Party candidate Ron Paul, because he thinks that all Libertarians want to give marijuana to kindergarteners. (Hey, no one ever said that Bob was open-minded!) The rest of the candidates are acceptable, although Bob is unenthusiastic about any of them.

So Election Day arrives, and Bob sees the latest polling data on the morning news. Here are the results of the CNN/WMUR poll taken just before the 2008 New Hampshire Republican Primary:

John McCain	32%
Mitt Romney	28%
Mike Huckabee	14%
Rudy Giuliani	11%
Ron Paul	10%
Fred Thompson	1%
Duncan Hunter	1%
Undecided/Other	7%

So who should Bob vote for? On the one hand, he could just vote for his favorite candidate, Mike Huckabee. We all like going to the polls and supporting candidates whom we can really get behind, and this would make Bob feel pretty good about himself. But there's a problem: Huckabee isn't going to win the election, at least not based on the polling. So voting for Huckabee might be considered "throwing his vote away." It gets worse, because Mitt Romney is within striking distance of John McCain, whereas Huckabee is a long shot. Bob isn't a big McCain fan—he ranked McCain sixth out of the eight choices—but McCain does have the best chance of beating Romney. So, Bob decides that he will vote for McCain. He chooses the favorite (McCain) over his preference (Huckabee) in order to avoid a bad outcome (Romney).

But this begs an important question: How do candidates become "favorites" in an open race like a primary? Or, to put it another way, why did New Hampshire voters in 2008 choose to rally around John McCain and not one of the other candidates on the ballot?

High Noon at Grand Central Station

In the 1960s, Yale professor Thomas Schelling asked a version of the following question to people in New York and Connecticut:

> An old friend has asked you to meet with someone tomorrow. He was very clear about the date, but he neglected to mention either a time or a place. Where will you go and when will you be there?

It sounds like an impossible problem, right? How could two individuals possibly find each other in the middle of a city with millions of people when they don't even know what time to show up? Yet it turns out that the vast majority of New Yorkers when given this scenario would choose Grand Central Station, and almost all of them would choose to arrive at noon.

Does this happen because New Yorkers just love to eat lunch amid the bustling atmosphere of Grand Central Station? It's a beautiful building, admittedly, but no. Is it because Grand Central Station is such a convenient place to meet people? If you've ever been trampled by a herd of wild commuters dodging between groups of tourists taking pictures of the architecture, then you'd probably think otherwise. Instead, people believe that other New Yorkers are likely to think that Grand Central Station is a centrally located meeting place, and that noon is an obvious time to meet. So when they answer "I'd go to Grand Central Station at noon," really they are saying that they believe that most other people when asked that question would go to Grand Central Station at noon.

In this example "Grand Central Station" and "noon" are *focal points*. When people are trying to coordinate their behavior without the ability to communicate with each other, they tend to rally around natural focal points. Focal points usually are not "the best" answers. Often they aren't even particularly good answers. Instead, focal points tend to be "obvious" or "natural" answers.

For instance, let's imagine the same scenario—you're meeting someone that you don't know tomorrow in New York City—but neither of you are New Yorkers. So when and where do you show up? Noon is still the "obvious" time—but instead of meeting at Grand Central Station, people tend to choose to meet on the observation deck at the Empire State Building. We suppose you can thank *An Affair to Remember* (or *Love Affair*, or *Sleepless in Seattle*) for that. Of course, here's the problem: The observation deck of the Empire State Building is a horrible place to meet someone. It is extremely crowded: On most days it takes at least an hour to go through the metal detectors and up the elevator. It is also expensive, with adult tickets running over $18. If you had actually talked to the person you were meeting with, never in a million years would you think that meeting at the top of the Empire State Building was a good idea. There are a huge number of more easily accessible and less crowded New York City landmarks. But of course, the choice isn't up to you. After all, you're not going to the place that would be the best meeting spot. You're going to the place that your friend is most likely to be. As long as he or she thinks the same way, you'll both be right.

So when Bob McVoter reads the CNN poll before heading out to cast his ballot in New Hampshire, he is essentially checking on the focal points in this election. And in this case, the polling told him that the two focal points were John McCain and Mitt Romney. He could certainly vote for someone else, just like you could choose not to go to the Empire State Building. But by ignoring the focal points, he would fail to coordinate with the many other voters, and would end up "throwing his vote away."

The Importance of Meaningless Votes

Think about all of the people who ran for the GOP Republican Primary in 2008, and not merely the seven who were on the New Hampshire primary ballot. There were four former governors who threw their hats into the ring: Mitt Romney (MA), Mike Huckabee (AR), Tommy Thompson (WI), and Jim Gilmore (VA). There were two sitting U.S. senators: John McCain (AZ) and Sam Brownback (KS). There was one former senator, Fred Thompson (TN). There was one former mayor of New York City, Rudy Giuliani. And there were three members of the U.S. House of Representatives: Ron Paul (TX), Duncan Hunter (CA), and Tom Tancredo (CO). For most of 2007, the race was widely considered to be a three-person contest between John McCain, Rudy Giuliani, and Mitt Romney. Then, over the summer and fall, Fred Thompson briefly rose as a media darling, and fell apart just as fast. Why were McCain, Giuliani, Romney, and Thompson considered the front runners? Why did the media attention focus on the former governor of Massachusetts, and not the former governors of Wisconsin (who had once held a cabinet seat) or Virginia (who sat on a prominent Washington foreign policy advisory board)? Why was the senator from Arizona considered a stronger candidate for president than the senator from Kansas?

In short, how does a candidate become a "serious contender" instead of just an "also ran"? How does a candidate become a focal point?

One way is to come into the race with name recognition or notoriety. Rudy Giuliani wasn't just the mayor of New York City; he was perceived as the leader who helped get the country through the attacks of September 11. Fred Thompson wasn't just the former senator of Tennessee; he was also the admiral from *The Hunt for Red October* and the district attorney from *Law & Order*. John McCain wasn't just the senior senator from Arizona; he was the "maverick" who beat George W. Bush in New Hampshire back in 2000.

Another way to be taken seriously is through campaign financing. Mitt Romney wasn't just the former governor of Massachusetts; he was an incredibly rich businessperson who was willing to invest a large chunk of his personal wealth into building name recognition. As a more extreme example, independent Ross Perot briefly made the 1992 general election for president a three-way race by dumping a small fortune into his own candidacy; he even bought 30-minute slots during prime time on the major television networks to hawk his ideas.

Finally, you can be taken seriously by doing well in the polls and early voting. So let's say you have some great ideas about where the country should be headed, but don't have the media attention, name recognition, or financial backing to be taken seriously. How do you overcome that? First, you need to convince a small group of people in a key area to vote for you. Then you must use that support to convince other voters that you are a "serious" contender. Toward that end, it would really help if you could find a "meaningless" vote, where people might be willing to "throw their votes away" on a long shot, yet a vote that is high profile enough to garner significant media attention. In other words, you need the Ames Straw Poll.

So the candidates and pundits take that event very seriously. Yes, it was only a simple poll of 33,000 people who showed up on a college campus in a small city in Iowa. But it is also one of very few opportunities that candidates have to convince the media and the larger voting populations in the bigger states that they are "legitimate" or "viable" candidates. By finishing second, Huckabee publicly demonstrated to Republican voters around the country that he could compete with the more prominent candidates. Or to put it another way, the straw poll was a public declaration that Huckabee had the potential to be a focal point candidate.

How Good Strategy Is Bad for Democracy

The Road to the White House Goes through Hooksett

Morris Udall, an Arizona congressman who ran for President in 1976, used to tell a joke about the New Hampshire Primary: A guy in Manchester (NH) goes up to his friend and asks, "Are you going to vote for Mo for president?" His friend replies, "I don't know yet, I only met him twice." There is a lot of truth to that joke; presidential candidates spend months criss-crossing Iowa and New Hampshire, talking to voters in diners, cafes, and meeting halls in every small town in those states. Because of strategic voting concerns, candidates need to do well in these early primaries, and therefore the voters in those states get to know the candidates extraordinarily well. Meanwhile, voters in California and Texas, which are huge states with a large number of major media markets, have to pay hundreds of dollars apiece at fund-raising dinners for the same privilege. From the politicians' perspective, time that could be spent talking to hundreds or thousands of voters in Oakland, California, or Dallas, Texas, is instead spent talking to voters a dozen at a time in Bloomfield, Iowa, or Hooksett, New Hampshire.

More importantly, that attention cuts both ways. Candidates don't just spend their time on the campaign trail selling themselves to voters. They also spend that time, whether they know it or not, absorbing the problems and concerns of voters. Before anyone can become president, they have to spend months talking to corn farmers and dairy farmers, tractor manufacturers and bed-and-breakfast operators. They have to make promises to those voters and hear about their problems. They will certainly have their view of the country shaped by those experiences. But here's the problem: Not a single one of the nation's 100 largest cities is located in either Iowa or New Hampshire. Both of those states are over 95 percent white, and neither have significant immigrant populations. Additionally, there are numerous issues that have dramatic impacts on the politics and lives of millions of Americans, which have little or no impact on the Iowa and New Hampshire primaries: federal land usage, oil drilling, water rights, public transportation, and so on. A president may be from Illinois, or Texas, or Arkansas, and that surely has an impact on how he governs. But, essentially, all presidents are from New Hampshire and Iowa.

Pluralistically Ignorant

When you were in school, did you ever sit in class, wanting to ask a particular question, but not saying anything because you didn't want your fellow students to think that you were stupid? Of course, later you may have realized that most other people were just as confused as you were—but everyone in the class was too afraid to ask. That's *pluralistic ignorance*: A bunch of people all make incorrect assumptions about what other people believe, and act on that assumption to reinforce the group norm. Everyone in the class wanted to ask a question; everyone made the incorrect assumption about the norm (that most people found the material easy and therefore you shouldn't ask questions or you'd look stupid); and everyone acted on that assumption by staying quiet, thereby looking like they understood the material, and reinforcing the norm for everyone else.

In the early 1990s, psychologists Deborah Prentice and Dale Miller studied drinking on college campuses. They found that a large number of students felt pressured to drink heavily. For anyone who has been to college, that is not a shocking statement. What was surprising was the finding that the vast majority of students were uncomfortable with binge drinking, even most of those who were doing it. In other words, students were drinking a lot more than they wanted to because they looked around and saw everyone else drinking a lot. These individuals held private beliefs that they should curtail their drinking, but they also wanted to fit in, even though many of the people that they were trying to fit in with were also uncomfortable about drinking excessively. The tragedy of pluralistic ignorance is that if everyone drank less, everyone would be happier.

Pluralistic ignorance can cause the most popular candidate to lose an election. To see how, let's go back to the story of Bob McVoter. Remember that Bob is on his way to the vote in the New Hampshire Republican Party Primary when he sees the latest CNN poll. He notices then that his least favorite candidate, Romney, is a close second, while his favorite candidate, Huckabee, is a distant third. As a result, Bob chooses to vote for McCain, despite being fairly ambivalent about the senator from Arizona. But what if the 2008 New Hampshire Republican Primary was actually a case of pluralistic ignorance? Here was the poll that Bob saw before heading out to vote on that January morning in New Hampshire:

John McCain	32%
Mitt Romney	28%
Mike Huckabee	14%
Rudy Giuliani	11%
Ron Paul	10%
Fred Thompson	1%
Duncan Hunter	1%
Undecided/Other	7%

Presidential polls ask people "If the election were held today, who would you vote for?" The poll is not asking you to name your preferred candidate, because if you are planning on voting strategically, the pollsters want to know that. In particular, if Bob were asked "who would you vote for," he would probably respond "John McCain."

What if, instead, the poll had asked "who is your preferred candidate?" Bob would have responded "Mike Huckabee." He is only voting for McCain because he believes that McCain is more popular than Huckabee. But what if he's wrong? What if, in fact, most of McCain's supporters in New Hampshire were actually people like Bob—people who would honestly have preferred Huckabee? If that were the case, then Bob, and everyone like him, voted for the wrong guy. Just like the college kids who drank too much, they all could have been happier if all of them voted for their preferred candidate. Instead, they voted strategically, and the most popular candidate lost the election.

Of course, it is impossible for anyone to say for certain whether pluralistic ignorance is actually occurring in any given election. But the possibility certainly exists. Every election has candidates who are never taken seriously, either by the media or the average voter. Some of those candidates would surely gain widespread popularity if they were ever given a chance. Some of them may already be widely popular candidates, but be victims of pluralistic ignorance. The problem is that winning elections isn't always about being the best leader, the most popular candidate, or even the best politician.

The Problem with Primaries
During the 2002 California governor's election, Los Angeles Mayor Richard Riordan faced off against businessman Bill Simon in the Republican Party

Primary. Simon ran as a strong pro-life, pro-business conservative. Riordan, as the Republican mayor from the normally liberal city of Los Angeles, was widely seen as the moderate choice. Early polling showed that Riordan had a strong lead over Simon, and that he would give a strong challenge to the unpopular Democratic incumbent, Gray Davis. (In fact, Gray Davis was so unpopular that he would be recalled the following year and replaced by Arnold Schwarzenegger.) Riordan, meanwhile, was widely respected around the state, even among many Democrats.

But two things conspired to prevent Riordan from winning the election. First, California has a closed primary, which means that only registered Republicans could vote in the Republican Primary. Second, Gray Davis intervened in the GOP primary, producing television ads that claimed that Riordan was not conservative enough for California's Republican voters. Davis essentially advertised on behalf of Bill Simon. The result? Conservative Republicans picked Simon over Riordan in the GOP primary. Moderate and Independent California voters were never given the chance to vote for their preferred candidate. Simon then lost by a wide margin to Davis in the general election.

Political parties are a necessary component of modern democracies. They help to coordinate the behavior of large groups of politicians, which is especially useful for legislatures. Parties also provide information shortcuts to voters about where a candidate stands on a variety of issues (which we will discuss in detail in chapter 7). You don't need to memorize where each candidate stands on every issue; knowing that he's a Democrat gives you a strong indication about how the candidate will vote on a wide range of policies.

The problem is that political parties are not representative of the citizenry as a whole. The average Green Party member will, by definition, be more pro-environment than the average voter. In the same way, the average Republican will be more conservative than the average voter. So during a general election, voters don't see a list of the most skilled politicians on their ballots. Instead, they see one person chosen by the Democrats (who will tend to be more liberal), one person chosen by the Republicans (who will tend to be more conservative), one person chosen by the Greens (who will tend to be more pro-environment), and so on. This is how we ended up with the debacle of the 2002 California gubernatorial election. Conservative Republicans chose the conservative (Simon) over the moderate (Riordan), and thereby denied the rest of California from voting for their preferred candidate.

Although primaries are mostly an American invention, this problem exists in other countries as well. In most democracies across the world, candidates are chosen in closed-door meetings of the party elite. The public has no say whatsoever in whose name appears on the general election ballot. At least in a closed primary, candidates have to convince large numbers of other people from their own party to vote for them—even if those people are only representative of a small slice of the overall population.

At the other extreme, some American states use open primaries, in which any voter can vote in any primary. Open primaries allow moderate and independent voters to participate in primary races, and thereby assist moderate candidates. The problem with open primaries is that they allow groups of voters to participate in a party's primary in a harmful way. For example, before the 2008 presidential primaries in Ohio and Texas, Rush Limbaugh urged Republican voters in Texas and Ohio to vote in the Democratic Primary for Hillary Clinton over Barack Obama. He believed that the extended, and increasingly ugly, race between Clinton and Obama was hurting the Democratic Party:

> So yes, I'm asking [Republican voters] to cross over and, if they can stomach it—I know it's a difficult thing to do to vote for a Clinton—but it will sustain this soap opera, and it's something I think we need.

Limbaugh was not asking voters to support Clinton because he thought Clinton was the best candidate, or even because she was the best Democrat. He was asking voters to support Clinton because he thought doing so would harm the Democratic Party, and therefore make it more likely that the Republican would win the general election. It is unclear if Limbaugh's request had any effect, although Clinton did win the Ohio Primary.

However a party chooses a candidate, the selection process can undermine the public's ability to choose their preferred leaders. Closed primaries and intraparty elections can cause a political system to reject popular, moderate choices. Open primaries open the door to manipulation by the other side.

Summary

Campaigns are supposed to be about the best candidate winning, but in reality, politicians can lose elections in which they were the most popular choice. Candidates are supposed to focus their efforts on trying to please the most voters, but in reality, politicians pay more attention to the needs of New Hampshire voters (pop. 1.3 million) than California voters (pop. 37 million). Ballot design, voting machines, district maps—none of those things is supposed to determine the outcome of presidential elections. Our electoral system is supposed to guarantee that voters make the most important choices about our leaders. How can democracy possibly be successful when the small details of when, where, and how we vote can have such a huge impact on who wins our elections?

References

Lead Quote
Vaughan, B. N.d. BrainyQuote.com. Retrieved March 23, 2011, from http://www
.brainyquote.com/quotes/quotes/b/billvaugha103974.html.

Gerrymandering
Viser, M. 2008. Mass. GOP losing ground. *Boston Globe*, May 2. Retrieved from http://
www.boston.com/news/local/articles/2008/05/02/mass_gop_losing_ground/.

Incumbency Advantage
Cox, G. W., and J. Katz. 1992. Why did the incumbency advantage in US House elections grow? *American Political Science Review* 40 (2):478–497.

Friedman, J. N., and R. Holden. 2005. The rising incumbent advantage: What's gerrymandering got to do with it? November 14, 2005. Retrieved March 23, 2011 from http://ssrn.com/abstract=847656.

Zajonc, R. B. 1968. Attitudinal effects of mere exposure. *Journal of Personality and Social Psychology* 9 (2):1–27.

Election Day Timing
Farber, H. S. 2009. Increasing voter turnout: Is Democracy Day the answer? Working Paper, Princeton University. Retrieved March 23, 2011, from http://ideas.repec
.org/p/pri/cepsud/1135.html.

Gomez, B. T., T. G. Hansford, and G. A. Krause. 2007. The Republicans should pray for rain: Weather, turnout, and voting in U.S. presidential elections. *Journal of Politics* 69 (3):649–663.

Ballot Order
Krosnick, J. A., J. M. Miller, and M. P. Tichy. 2004. An unrecognized need for ballot reform: The effects of candidate name order on election outcomes. In *Rethinking the Vote: The Politics and Prospects of American Electoral Reform*, ed. A. N. Crigler, M. R. Just, and E. J. McCaffery. New York: Oxford University Press.

Miller, J. M., and J. A. Krosnick. 1998. The impact of candidate name order on election outcomes. *Public Opinion Quarterly* 62:291–330.

Voter Error
Byrne, M.D., Greene, K.K., Everett, S.P. 2007. Usability of voting systems: Baseline data for paper, punch card, and lever machines. In *CHI 2007 Proceedings*. New York: ACM Press.

Everett, S. P., M. D. Byrne, and K. K. Greene. 2006. Measuring the usability of paper ballots: Efficiency, effectiveness, and satisfaction. In *Proceedings for the Human Factors and Ergonomics Society 50th Annual Meeting*. Santa Monica, CA: Human Factors and Ergonomics Society.

Smith, D. 2004. Vote for Edwards an electoral shock. *Minneapolis Star Tribune*, December 14.

Wand, J., K. Shotts, W. R. Mebane, J. S. Sekhon, M. Herron, and H. E. Brady. 2001. The Butterfly did it: The aberrant vote for Buchanan in Palm Beach County, Florida. *American Political Science Review* 95 (4):793–810.

Voting Technologies
Caltech/MIT Voting Technology Project. 2001. Voting: What is and what could be. Retrieved March 23, 2011, from http://vote.caltech.edu/drupal/files/report/voting_what_is_what_could_be.pdf.

Fitrakis, B., and H. Wasserman. 2004. Diebold's political machine. *Mother Jones*, March 5. Retrieved March 23, 2011, from http://motherjones.com/politics/2004/03/diebolds-political-machine.

Kapochunas, R. 2006. Legal fight in Florida's 13th could stretch into 2007. *New York Times*, November 21. Reprinted from *Congressional Quarterly*. Retrieved March 23, 2011, from: http://www.nytimes.com/cq/2006/11/21/cq_1978.html.

Wasserman, J. 2004. Panel: Don't use Diebold touch-screen voting machines. *San Diego Union-Tribune*, April 22. Reprinted from The Associated Press. Retrieved March

23, 2011, from http://legacy.signonsandiego.com/news/politics/20040422-1251-ca
-electronicvoting.html.

Election Officials
Fessenden, F., and J. M. Broder. 2001. Study of disputed Florida ballots finds justices
did not cast the deciding vote. *New York Times*, November 12. Retrieved March 23,
2011, from http://www.nytimes.com/pages/politics/recount/.

Malbran, P. 2008. Red flag on purging voter rolls: CBS Evening News investigates
little-known, problem-ridden process that could endanger your vote. CBSNews.com,
September 30. Retrieved March 23, 2011, from http://www.cbsnews.com/stories/
2008/09/30/eveningnews/main4490682.shtml.

Office of the Clerk, United States Congress. Women in Congress: Katherine Harris.
Retrieved March 23, 2011, from http://womenincongress.house.gov/member
-profiles/profile.html?intID=101.

Perez, M. 2008. Voter purges. Brennan Center for Justice: Voting Rights and Election
Project, September 30. Retrieved March 23, 2011, from http://www.brennancenter
.org/content/resource/voter_purges.

Pre-NH polling for 2008 GOP primary
CNN/WMUR New Hampshire Primary Tracking Poll. N.d. Conducted by the University of New Hampshire Survey Center. Retrieved from http://www.unh.edu/
survey-center/news/pdf/primary2008_gopprim10708.pdf.

Criticism of Giuliani and McCain for Missing Iowa Straw Poll
Beuamont, T. 2007. McCain, Giuliani skip Iowa Straw Poll. *USA Today*, June 6.
Reprinted from The Associated Press. Retrieved March 24, 2011, from http://www
.usatoday.com/news/politics/2007-06-06-iowa-straw-poll_N.htm.

Focal Points
Schelling, T. C. 1960. *The Strategy of Conflict*, 55–56. Cambridge, MA: Harvard
University Press.

Perceived Electability
Cillizza, C. 2007. Romney, Rudy, and the electability question. The Fix blog at
WashingtonPost.com, November 5. Retrieved March 24, 2011, from http://voices
.washingtonpost.com/thefix/eye-on-2008/romney-rudy-and-the-electabili.html.

Obama: Electability concerns? 2008. First Read blog at MSNBC.com, April 16.
Retrieved from http://firstread.msnbc.msn.com/_news/2008/04/16/4433678-obama
-electability-concerns.

Rudin, K. 2007. Is Hillary Clinton electable? Political Junkie at NPR.org, November 1. Retrieved March 24, 2011, from http://www.npr.org/templates/story/story.php?storyId=15843708.

Wilson, R. 2007. McCain's electability argument. Real Clear Politics, November 28. Retrieved March 24, 2011, from http://www.realclearpolitics.com/articles/2007/11/mccains_electability_argument.html.

Pluralistic Ignorance

Prentice, D. A., and D. T. Miller. 1993. Pluralistic ignorance and alcohol use on campus: Some consequences of misperceiving the social norm. *Journal of Personality and Social Psychology* 64:243–256.

Primary Elections

Gledhill, L. 2001. Riordan has edge on Davis in polls. *San Francisco Chronicle*, December 13. Retrieved June 24, 2011, from http://www.sfgate.com/cgi-bin/article.cgi?f=/c/a/2001/12/13/MN236557.DTL.

Ingraham, L. 2008. Interview: Rush Limbaugh Explains why he's urging Republicans in Texas and Ohio to vote for Hillary Clinton on Super Tuesday 2. *The O'Reilly Factor*, March 3. Retrieved June 24, 2011, from http://www.foxnews.com/story/0,2933,334669,00.html.

Woodruff, J., B. Schneider, C. Crowley, and K. Snow. 2002. "Fight" seen in California's governor's race. CNN, March 6. Retrieved June 24, 2011, from http://archives.cnn.com/2002/ALLPOLITICS/03/06/california.primary/index.html.

Pictures

Massachusetts District 9 map by www.GovTrack.us. N.d. Street data from OpenStreetMap.org. Retrieved March 23, 2011, from http://www.govtrack.us/congress/printablemaps.xpd.

Amoeba picture by Pearson Scott Foresman. Retrieved March 23, 2011, from http://commons.wikimedia.org/wiki/File:Amoeba_(PSF).png.

4   Too Many Voices

Polling is merely an instrument for gauging public opinion. When a president or any other leader pays attention to poll results, he is, in effect, paying attention to the views of the people. Any other interpretation is nonsense.
—George Horace Gallup

Listening to the Crowd

If you've ever watched *The Price Is Right*, you know that the game show largely involves contestants trying to guess the prices of common household items while the audience shouts at them. Most contestants use one of two strategies. The first type of contestant completely ignores what the audience has to say. They confidently state their answers, with little regard to the surrounding cacophony. The second type tries to listen to the crowd. Every once in a while listening to the audience actually works: The majority of the audience knows that the answer is $200, they will all shout "two hundred dollars," and the contestant will guess $200. But most of the time the different members of the audience all shout different answers. One audience member will shout "two hundred dollars," another will shout "one hundred fifty dollars," a third will shout "five hundred dollars," and some prankster in the first row will shout "thirty thousand dollars." Of course what the contestant actually hears is "two fifty hundred five thirty dollars." In those cases this second type of contestant will look out at the audience with a puzzled expression and eventually shrug or pantomime that she has no idea what's being said. And in the end, the second contestant does exactly what the first did: make up an answer and hope that it was right.

Democracy is a lot like *The Price Is Right*. It is a system of government premised on the idea that most politicians at least make an effort to listen to The People most of the time. When we describe politicians as "representatives" and "servants of the people" we are underscoring the idea that the people who govern us are supposed to pay attention to what we want. Just like on *The Price Is Right*, every once in a while the people will come to a consensus about an issue and they will clearly express their will—we'll discuss these rare circumstances in chapter 8.

Unfortunately, most voters don't fully understand what they want or how to get it. Moreover, different voters have conflicting preferences and contradictory demands. As a result, the politician who tries to listen to the will of the people will not hear a clearly articulated set of preferences. Instead, that politician will hear a cacophony of voices all telling him to go in different directions. Just like the contestant on *The Price Is Right*, the politician is faced with the choice of either doing his own thing or standing there looking confused.

Hearing Voices

Think for a moment about who you voted for—or if you didn't vote, who you were rooting for—during the most recent presidential campaign.

Now, why did you vote for him or her? Ignore for a moment all the stuff about irrationality, biases, and first impressions that we discussed in the first few chapters: Why did you think you voted for that person? What message were you trying to send, and to whom were you trying to send it?

Below are just some of the reasons that people voted for Barack Obama in 2008. (For the sake of simplicity we'll just use Obama, but we could easily craft a similar list for any candidate in any election.)

• Some voters were trying to punish the GOP for their job performance.

• Some voters wanted specific policy changes: withdrawal from Iraq, new health care policy, etc.

• Some voters just liked Barack Obama and thought that he would make a good president.

• Some voters wanted to punish McCain for something that he, or his surrogates, had done during the campaign.

• Some voters thought that McCain was out of touch or would have made a bad president.

So put yourself in Obama's shoes. You've just been elected president, and you want to be a faithful representative of the American people. Which message, or messages, do you respond to? After all, each message implies a different way of governing.

Some people would have voted for you despite your policies, because they liked you personally or thought that you were a good leader. Those voters might very well want a continuation of the conservative policies of your predecessor. Other voters are going to want dramatic and meaningful reversals of policy in a large number of different areas. A third group voted for you because you appeared to be a thoughtful and nuanced thinker on the campaign trail. Those voters will want you to go slowly and find compromise positions on the most important issues. If you, as a newly elected president, want to represent the will of your constituency, then what should you do: fast change, methodical change, or no change?

Meanwhile, many people voted for you because they disliked your opponent, or were offended by your opponent's campaign tactics, but fundamentally thought that the previous president was doing a good job. These voters will probably want you to be civil and respectful toward your predecessor. On the other hand, many other voters want to see dramatic, clear denunciations of your predecessor; they may even demand a criminal investigation into the actions of the previous administration. So what should you do: Be respectful toward the previous president or treat him as a pariah?

Similarly, many voters will expect that you will treat the losers of the election with respect and listen to their counsel on important matters. But, of course, other people voted for you because they thought that your opponents had bad ideas for the country. So should you listen to your rivals or shun them?

And let's not forget that as president you are supposed to represent all the people, not just the people who voted for you. Many American citizens voted for the other guy and think that your policies are wrong. But listening to those voters will obviously anger many of the people who voted for you. Which voters do you represent?

Then there is the problem that the voters' bad information may cause them to send flat-out contradictory messages. Remember in chapter 1 we discussed how voters believe both that the foreign aid budget ought to be cut in half, and that a realistic figure for that budget should be about 10 percent of the total U.S. budget. But in fact, the foreign aid budget is less than 1 percent of the total U.S. budget. So as president, how do you faithfully represent the wishes of the people on that issue: Should you lower the foreign aid budget even further, or raise the foreign aid budget to 10 percent?

To get around this confusion, politicians are forced to rely on polling. In theory, polling should allow politicians to at least determine what the majority of people believe about a particular topic. In practice, however, polls are not nearly as informative as we would like to believe. Even the best polls often ask the wrong questions of the wrong people and in the wrong way. As a result, politicians who rely too heavily on polling data may find themselves no better off than the befuddled *Price Is Right* contestant.

Sampling the People

On July 28, 2008, a *USA Today* headline proclaimed that John McCain was gaining on Barack Obama in the latest presidential election polling. The article noted that in a poll of registered voters conducted by *USA Today*/ Gallup, McCain had cut Obama's lead from six points to three points. The article also noted that among likely voters, McCain had actually pulled ahead of Obama, going up by five points when a month earlier Obama had led by four. If you read to the bottom of the article, however, you would have found that the Daily Tracking Poll run by Gallup showed that Obama was holding an eight-point lead among registered voters. How is it possible that the same polling organization, on the same day, could accurately report that McCain had cut Obama's lead, while also reporting that McCain had passed Obama and that Obama's lead over McCain was holding steady?

Before we answer that question, we encourage you to forget politics for a moment and start thinking about jellybeans.

Imagine that you are handed a big bag of 10,000 red and blue jellybeans, and you want to know what percentage of the bag is red and what percentage is blue. One way to find out would be to dump the whole bag out on the floor and count every last bean. But that would take much too long: You just want to satisfy your curiosity before you get down to the serious business of eating, not make a career as a bean-counter. Instead, you can make a pretty good estimate based on just a small selection, or a sample.

So you grab a handful of random beans, count that sample, and then use that count to estimate how many beans are red and how many are blue. Odds are that if you grab enough beans for your sample, your estimate will be pretty close to accurate.

In theory, a poll is very similar. The pollster calls up some number of randomly selected people and asks them who they will vote for. Unfortunately, people are a lot more complicated than jellybeans. Jellybeans never misunderstand your questions or give you misleading answers. And jellybeans never refuse to be counted.

Apparently the Average American Didn't Read Literary Digest

In 1936, *Literary Digest* conducted a poll of over 2 million people (a huge number of people—consider that the Gallup poll of Presidential Job Approval usually surveys fewer than 2,000 people). *Literary Digest* was a reasonably popular magazine at the time, and their poll had proven accurate in several previous elections. Based on their 1936 poll, *Literary Digest* announced that Republican Alf Landon would easily defeat incumbent president Franklin Roosevelt to become the next president of the United States. In reality, Landon was crushed by Roosevelt; he even failed to win his native Kansas (where he was governor at the time). This was one of the greatest landslides in U.S. history, in the opposite direction that the *Literary Digest* poll predicted. How could a sample of so many people be so wrong?

The answer lies in *which* people were surveyed. Let's think back to those jellybeans for a moment. We assumed that the sample of jellybeans from which you made your estimate was chosen "randomly." But how did you get your supposedly random sample? Maybe you grabbed whatever jellybeans were at the top of the bag. That works great if the jellybeans are all mixed together. But let's say that whoever bought the jellybeans first scooped some red jellybeans into the bag, and then scooped the blue ones in. In this case, the beans at the top of the bag will be disproportionately blue, and your sample won't be random at all.

What if you vigorously shook the bag for a while to ensure an even distribution of jellybeans within the bag, closed your eyes, and then pulled your beans out of the bag? That would be a pretty good methodology for randomizing a bag of jellybeans. Unfortunately for pollsters, the electorate doesn't respond well to vigorous shaking. In fact, for the electorate there is no practical way to ensure a random and unbiased sampling.

In the case of *Literary Digest*, the sample was chosen from three sources: people who were subscribers to the *Digest*, car registration lists, and telephone listings. In 1936, while the country was struggling with the Great Depression, most Americans could not afford to buy cars, they could not afford to own telephones, and they could not afford to subscribe to literary magazines. This meant that the *Digest* surveyed mostly wealthy people. The poll got the election result wrong because it failed to ask the opinions of the poor and the middle class—groups that overwhelmingly favored Roosevelt. For a poll to get an accurate picture of the American people, it needs to sample from a group that is representative of the American people. If the poll samples from an unrepresentative group (like car owners in 1936), then the sample is *biased*, and there is a very good chance that the poll will be inaccurate.

Thankfully, sampling has gotten a lot more sophisticated since the Great Depression. Polling organizations generally use computers to randomly call phone numbers, and then poll workers can ask their questions. The computers randomly select phone numbers without any difficulty—that part works fine. But these surveys can still produce a biased sample. Some voters still don't own telephones (or only use cell phones, which are often left out of phone surveys), while other voters screen their calls. Some voters don't speak English well enough to answer the questions of the pollsters. And some voters will simply refuse to answer a pollster's questions.

Of course, none of those things would be a problem if the voting patterns of those groups were the same as the voting patterns of the population as a whole. But when the voting patterns of the people who are surveyed are different than the voting patterns of the people who are not surveyed, then you get the same problem that *Literary Digest* had in 1936. And that's ultimately the problem: non-English speakers, people with caller ID, people who cannot afford telephones, and people who use only cell phones do not necessarily have the same political attitudes as people who respond to phone surveys.

As bad as phone polling can be, it is usually better than the alternatives. Internet polling is particularly problematic. Some Internet polls, like the Harris Poll, maintain a database of willing poll participants from which to sample respondents. Of course, the people who are willing to sign up for the database and spend the time to fill out the surveys are not necessarily representative of the entire population. Even with this problem, Harris is still one of the best when it comes to Internet polling. At the other end of the spectrum, casual Web polls are worthless. For instance, before the 2008 presidential election Ron Paul supporters decided that it would be good publicity for their candidate if Ron Paul won every publicly available Web poll out there. By voting early and often, they succeeded. Although their efforts did gain some publicity, they also underscored how awful those polls were to begin with.

Other methods of sampling aren't any better. Door-to-door polling is extremely expensive and inefficient. Polls by mail require the respondent to fill out the form and put it back in the mailbox. They also require a higher degree of English literacy and a stable mailing address. While in some cases it is possible to "correct" for a biased sample, doing so requires a number of statistical guesses about the nature of the biases—guesses that even the best pollsters can get wrong. So when it comes to political surveys, even the best polls are biased.

So now put yourself into the shoes of the governor of a state, and imagine that the big issue of the day is immigration. Your advisors hand you a poll that tells you that your state is divided on immigration, but that a small majority is in favor of harsher punishments on undocumented immigrants. Then you find out that the poll failed to account for non-English speakers. Likely non-English speakers have a much different view of immigration, on average, than English speakers—but you don't really know how different. The poll isn't useless; it still gives an accurate picture of what a large portion of the electorate believes. Unfortunately, because the sample was biased, the poll doesn't actually tell you the true will of all the people. Just like our poor *The Price Is Right* contestant, you're left shrugging and taking your best guess.

The Likely and the Unlikely

Imagine that you're having a dinner party and invite ten of your friends. Three of your friends are vegetarians, while two eat almost nothing except for meat. Two others are on a low-carb diet, another has a peanut allergy, and yet another dislikes shellfish. So what do you serve for dinner? Before you answer, you might want to make sure that all of the people that you invited will actually attend. After all, you only really care about the dietary habits of your friends who will actually be there. So if the vegetarians are not coming, then you can just throw a couple of steaks on the grill and get down to planning the entertainment.

In the same way, many politicians and pollsters who are interested in election results really only care about the people who are going to vote. After all, politicians want to win elections and pollsters want to know who will win elections. In that sense, politicians and pollsters are primarily interested in the opinions of those people who will vote in the next election. But predicting who will bother to vote is a huge problem. We all know, roughly, how many adults there are in the United States. We can know at any given moment how many of those adults are registered to vote. What we don't know is who will actually show up on Election Day.

So how do you determine who will actually vote? Well, one possibility is that you ask people if they are planning on voting in the upcoming election. Simple and straightforward, right? Well, unfortunately, there are quite a few people who will tell you that they are planning on voting, but who won't actually show up to the polls on election day. People say that they will do a lot of things; that doesn't mean that they will actually do them.

So instead of relying on what people say they'll do, you could only count people who voted the last time around. These are people who have demonstrated an ability to show up to the polls on time, and this method will give you a much more conservative estimate of who will likely vote. It turns out, however, that this estimate is often too conservative. It ignores first-time eligible voters: new citizens and people who have turned 18 since the last election. And younger voters often have different views from older voters—ignoring them will skew your sample. It also ignores the fact that each election is different, and there will often be groups of voters who were uninspired by any candidate four years ago, but who find themselves enthusiastic about the possibility of voting for one candidate or another this time around (or vice versa).

Every polling organization has a different way of estimating the likely voter turnout, and many of them can get pretty sophisticated. Suffice it to say, however, that no matter how sophisticated the estimate, at the end of the day it's somewhat of a guess—and it's a guess that can have a profound impact on the results of a poll.

So remember that *USA Today*/Gallup poll that we mentioned earlier, where Obama held a three-point lead among registered voters, while

McCain held a five-point lead among "likely" voters? Gallup, in that poll, used a conservative estimate of who is "likely" to vote. It turned out that Obama was the popular choice among people who were planning to vote but who were not considered "likely" voters by Gallup's model. And sure enough, Obama's margin of victory was in part driven by his success among "unlikely" voters.

Whereas figuring out how to sample jellybeans is easy, figuring out how to sample the electorate is an impossible challenge. There's no way to know who to sample, and there's no dependable way to go about getting an unbiased sample of those people anyway. Of course, the problems don't stop there. Even if you know who to talk to, you still have to figure out what to ask them. If you want to know the color of a jellybean, you can just look at it. Assuming the lighting isn't particularly strange, you can get what you want to know without much trouble. But when you're dealing with people, there's a lot more you have to take into account than lighting.

Questioning the Questions

Context, Context, Context

Back in the late 1960s, psychologist Allen Parducci asked people about the immorality of various illegal behaviors on a fixed scale. The people were randomly divided into two groups. For one group the first few questions on the survey asked about serious felonies: murder, arson, rape, and so on. The other group was instead asked questions about minor misdemeanors: traffic violations, jaywalking, graffiti, and so on. Both groups then answered a question about shoplifting. The people taking the felonies survey thought that shoplifting was only a minor offense, whereas the people taking the misdemeanors survey thought that shoplifting was a really big deal—even though they were asked the exact same question and the groups were otherwise indistinguishable from each other.

Even though the question didn't ask them to do so, the respondents were implicitly comparing shoplifting to the other listed crimes. Compared to jaywalking, shoplifting is a big deal—but compared to murder, shoplifting is a trivial offense. The answers that people give to polling questions depend critically on what other questions were also asked. In short: Context matters.

In another classic study that was done during the cold war, researchers asked identical groups of people the following two questions:

1. Should American reporters be allowed into Communist nations?

2. Should reporters from Communist countries be allowed into the United States?

One group was asked about American reporters first, the other group was asked about Communist reporters first. What happened? Most people in both surveys thought that American reporters should be allowed to report from Communist nations. But people's responses to whether Communist reporters should be given access to America depended on whether it was the first or second question. When the question about Communists was asked first, only a little over half of the respondents thought that the Communists should be allowed to report from America. But when asked about American reporters first, three-quarters of the respondents thought that Communist reporters should also be given access to America. After having just agreed that U.S. reporters should be let into Communist countries, it would be unfair to not allow the Communists to report from the United States in reciprocity. The context that the first question provided changed people's responses to the second question.

In some cases, the particular wording of a question can provide the crucial bit of context that can affect results. For instance, we already discussed in chapter 2 how Americans feel differently about "the estate tax" and "the death tax," even though the two phrases refer to the exact same lines in the tax code. Of course, there is no "right" wording to this question, just like there is no "right" way to order the questions about Communist reporters. All poll questions occur within a particular context, which will make it difficult for any politician to use polling to gauge the will of the people.[1]

---

1. At the extreme, context and wording effects can even be used to actually change our opinions. Imagine that you're sitting at your kitchen table one day when your phone rings. The person on the other end of the line identifies himself as working for some polling agency that you've never heard of, and politely asks if you have a few minutes of time to answer some questions. He starts off with a couple basic questions that sound pretty standard:

"If the election were held today, who would you vote for?"

"How much do you know about each of the candidates?"

I Don't Think That Word Means What You Think It Means

Are you conservative? Before you answer that question, please consider
all of the possible meanings of the word *conservative*. *Conservative* could
be used in reference to people who call themselves conservative. "Rush
Limbaugh is conservative." *Conservative* could refer to simply being old-
fashioned. "Bob wore a conservative tie." *Conservative* could refer to being
resistant to change. "Susan opted for the more conservative approach
and did nothing." *Conservative* could refer to a particular political ideology. "Barry Goldwater, Irving Kristol, and William Buckley are the fathers
of modern conservative thought." So, are you conservative? Obviously,
your answer will depend on the context. Bill Clinton might say "yes"
to that question when talking about his ties, whereas Rush Limbaugh
might say "no" when he is advocating for massive changes to Social
Security.

Polls run into this problem frequently. Unless the pollster is very careful
about the context, a simple question like "are you conservative" could be
very misleading. A politician looking at the poll results might make infer-
ences about people's political attitudes, even though many of the respondents were actually referring to their wardrobes. And it's not just *conservative*
that has this problem. Many words that are commonly used in American

---

Eventually, however, the questions take a subtle turn. The questions will start focus-
ing on one of the candidates, asking about details of their lives or policies that
you've never heard about before:

"Would you be more or less likely to vote for Joan d'Candidate if you found out
that she was having an extramarital affair?"

"A recent report by the *Washington Post* indicated that Joan d'Candidate has close
ties to a convicted felon. Does that information make you more or less likely to
support her?"

Congratulations, you've just taken a *push poll*. A push poll isn't actually designed
to gather any useful information. These polls are actually funded by the campaigns
(or groups working on behalf of the campaigns) and can be thought of as negative
advertising. Because the pollster sounded like an authoritative, unbiased source—at
least at first—these kinds of questions are actually quite effective at introducing
misinformation to the electorate. Moreover, because the information given to the
electorate was phrased as a question, it allows the candidate to maintain the moral
high ground. After all, the push poll didn't actually say that Joan d'Candidate was
having an affair or was good buddies with a convicted felon; it merely asked a
hypothetical question.

politics can have multiple or ambiguous meanings: *liberal, nation, freedom, democrat, state, conflict,* to name just a few.

The problem gets worse: Not only do words have multiple definitions, sometimes the meaning of a sentence has nothing to do with the meanings of the words that comprise that sentence. Linguist H. P. Grice famously noted that there is a difference between the logical meaning of words and how people actually use and interpret them. For instance, even a simple word like *always* can mean different things in different contexts. *Always* is supposed to mean "each and every time." The baseball team that scores the most runs always wins the game. However, sometimes *always* actually means "most of the time," as when a baseball fan complains that the Yankees always win.

Grice's insight wasn't just about the meaning of individual words. It's about how we interpret language more generally. When your friend tells you that his lawyer is a shark, he doesn't mean that the lawyer is a cold-blooded ocean predator. Similarly, think about what a mother is actually promising when she tells her son "if you don't clean your room, you won't get any ice cream." She's saying that not cleaning his room will prevent him from getting ice cream. She never actually says that cleaning his room will lead to ice cream—and yet what the kid actually hears is "I'll give you ice cream, if you clean your room."

These kinds of subtleties can create confusion in polls when different responders interpret a question in different ways. For instance, the Internet Movie Database (IMDB) compiles user reviews of an incredibly large number of films. As of December 16, 2010, their Top 50 list contained both *Citizen Kane* and *Toy Story 3*. While they are both excellent movies, the fact is that the IMDB users who ranked those movies were answering a fundamentally different question when they gave *Citizen Kane* 8.6 out of 10 stars than when they gave *Toy Story 3* 8.7 out of 10 stars. *Toy Story 3* is great because it is fun, although we suspect that it won't be remembered as an incredibly influential piece of filmmaking; *Citizen Kane* is great because it revolutionized the art form of modern cinema, although as a piece of entertainment it can be a bit slow-moving at times. These movies are not really comparable, and yet they were given virtually identical ratings.

Politicians are probably not bothered by inconsistencies on lists of the greatest films of all time. But the same problems can crop up in political polling. For instance, what does it mean to ask "should teachers be paid more"? This question could be interpreted as "do you think that we should raise teacher salaries to attract better people to the profession," "do you think that current teachers are being exploited based on their low wages," or even "do you think that the city can afford to pay teachers more?" In reality, different people are going to look at the same question, and interpret it in completely different ways. The result for the politician is *The Price Is Right* all over again; lots of messages, but very little clarity.

Tripping on the Concrete

Throughout the 2008 election, polls consistently showed that health care reform was one of the most important issues and that a solid majority of Americans wanted reform. Yet in September 2009, the AP reported poll results showing that 49 percent of Americans were opposed to health care reform, with only 34 percent in favor. What's the difference? Americans hadn't changed; the question had. In 2008, the question was hypothetical. Did most Americans want easier access to health care and lower health care costs? Absolutely. In 2009, however, there was a particular health care reform bill being debated. When people opposed health care reform in 2009, they were really opposing a particular bill. The costs were more real and the compromises that were made to get that piece of legislation through Congress upset people.

Sometimes people feel differently about an abstract concept than they do about a concrete event, policy, or idea. In this case, the abstract concept (health care reform) was quite popular, but the concrete policy (the 2010 health care reform bill) was not. In other cases, people may prefer the concrete to the abstract. Consider how people think about Congress. In an NBC News/*Wall Street Journal* poll conducted in March 2010, only 17 percent of people approved of the way that Congress, as a whole, was doing its job. In that same poll, 45 percent approved of the job that their particular representative was doing. And of course, in the elections later that year, the vast majority of incumbent representatives were returned to office. We may hate Congress and hate politicians, even as we love our particular congressional representative. Similarly, back in chapter 1 we discussed a poll that showed that parents generally liked their own schools, even as they were skeptical about schools in other parts of the country. The abstract concept of "the quality of American schools" brought up very different feelings than the concrete question of "the quality of your child's school."

The difference between abstract principles and concrete examples can be extremely problematic in both law and politics. A person might believe that shoplifters ought to be prosecuted to the full extent of the law, and yet believe that Jean Valjean deserves no punishment for stealing a loaf of bread to save his starving niece. Or a man who believes that environmentalists are ruining American business might take exception to a local factory dumping toxic waste into the stream where his grandfather taught him to fish. These kinds of examples create very treacherous ground for politicians, even ones who believe that they are faithfully representing the public's wishes.

For instance, in 1998 then Texas Governor George W. Bush enjoyed broad political support, especially among the conservative and Christian elements of the Texas Republican Party. In particular, those Bush supporters firmly supported the frequently used death penalty in Texas, and strongly approved of Bush's hands-off approach when it came to grants of clemency for death row inmates. But when Karla Faye Tucker was scheduled for execution—a confessed murderer who had made a profound conversion to Christianity while in prison—Governor Bush was blindsided when many of his most prominent conservative supporters criticized him for failing to act on her behalf. Bush held steady to the general rule, but faced a political backlash when he failed to adapt to a specific situation.

Governor Bush probably thought that the polls that showed strong support in Texas for the death penalty would have applied to Karla Faye Tucker—just like they applied to the dozens of other people executed in Texas that year. In the same way, President Obama likely thought that the 2008 polls showing strong support for Health Care Reform would have applied to the 2009 health care reform bill. In both cases, however, they were wrong. Even a politician who consults accurate polling data that demonstrates strong public support for an abstract concept can trip up when it comes to applying that will to concrete issues.

Tipping the Scales

During the Iraq War, Alex Todorov and Crystal Hall asked a randomly selected group of people the following question:

> Please indicate the average amount of time that you have spent watching, reading and listening to the media coverage of the situation in Iraq (TV, newspapers, magazines, online), per week, since the first week of the war.

a) up to ½ hour

b) ½ to 1 hour

c) 1 to 1½ hours

d) 1½ to 2 hours

e) 2 to 2½ hours

f) more than 2½ hours.

Only 38 percent of respondents reported that they spent more than 2 1/2 hours each week reading or watching war-related news coverage. The researchers also asked a second, basically identical group of people the exact same question, only this time the multiple choice answers had changed:

a) up to 2½ hours,

b) 2½ to 3 hours

c) 3 to 3½ hours

d) 3½ to 4 hours

e) 4 to 4½ hours

f) more than 4½ hours.

This time 68 percent of respondents answered that they spent more than 2 1/2 hours reading or watching war-related coverage.

In theory, the responders should have recalled their media consumption habits before answering the question, and then simply circled the answer that matched their memory. This study demonstrates that reality is not so simple. In practice, people look at the answers first, and then use that as one factor in answering the question. So in the first group, 2 1/2 hours seemed like a lot, at least compared with the other answers; in the second group, 2 1/2 hours didn't seem like very much at all. In both cases, the responders adjusted their answers accordingly. This is just one example of a phenomenon that has been repeatedly demonstrated in the survey research literature: People will tend to avoid "extreme" answers, and prefer to place themselves in the middle, no matter what scale was used. Of course, this can cause serious problems for anyone trying to interpret that poll. How can a politician know what the electorate wants when the polls yield different answers depending on how they're worded?

Of course, there are plenty of other ways that the framing of a set of answers can alter a poll's results. In 1991, psychologists Norbert Schwarz and Hans-J. Hippler asked different groups of people to rate a series of politicians on a scale from 0 to 10. Then they asked other groups of people to rate the same politicians on a scale from –5 to 5. A 5 on the first scale should have been identical to a 0 on the second scale; in both cases, those were the middle values that were supposed to indicate that the politician was doing an average job. And intuitively we would have expected that politicians who were below average on one scale would also have been below average on the other scale. But that's not what happened. It turned out that people were reluctant to give negative scores, and thus were much more willing to give subpar scores to politicians on the 0 to 10 scale than on the –5 to 5 scale. A –1 just feels worse to most people than a 4, even though the two numbers might mean exactly the same thing. So if you are a politician who scored a 0 on the –5 to 5 scale (which is average), but a 4 on the 0 to 10 scale (which is below average), it isn't clear how to interpret these results.

Other kinds of multiple-choice answers in polls and surveys lead to misconceptions in different ways. One common type of survey question asks people to pick an item out of a long list. For instance, after the 2004 presidential election, some commentators made a big deal about postelection polls that indicated that "moral values" was the most important issue in the election. Here are the results of a National Election Pool poll taken of actual voters to find out the most important issue of the 2004 presidential election:

Moral Values	22%
Terrorism	19%
War in Iraq	15%
Health Care	5%
Taxes	4%
Education	4%

People who thought that "Moral Values" were the most important issue were extremely likely to favor President Bush. This led many in the media to proclaim that these "values voters" were the key element in President Bush's reelection. However, as prominent pollster Jan van Lohuizen commented, that "moral values" number is misleading. In 2004, most Bush voters were relatively content with the economy and the tax code, they were happy with the direction of the War in Iraq and the War on Terror, and they were not especially concerned about either health care or education. For many of those voters "moral values" was a catch-phrase encompassing not only abortion and gay marriage (both of which were hot-button social conservative issues) but also the general moral character of the candidate. Kerry voters, on the other hand, were generally unhappy with all of the specific policy issues mentioned in the poll. Bush supporters who were generally content with the state of the country rallied to the "moral values" answer; Kerry voters split themselves up among those who were most unhappy with Iraq, or with the economy, or with health care or with education. The single broad category of "moral values" papered over the interesting differences between Bush voters—and in this case, misled most of the nation's leading pundits to inaccurate conclusions about the election.

Polls can ask the right questions of the right people and still cause confusion because of how the answers are worded, and unfortunately for pollsters and politicians, there is no such thing as neutral wording.

One Person's Gain Is Another Person's Loss

Of course, even when the sample is reasonable, the questions are well crafted, and the answers are framed appropriately, it can still be very difficult to draw conclusions from polling data.

Let's go back to those Gallup poll results regarding the 2008 presidential race between McCain and Obama. The full poll results are given in figure 4.1. Those *USA Today*/Gallup poll results were reported under the headline "McCain Gains on Obama." That is an accurate assessment: Obama's lead among registered voters narrowed considerably during the month between the two polls. But there are other valid interpretations of those results. "Obama Maintains Lead" would have been perfectly reasonable, given that the movement in the Registered Voters poll was well within the margin of error. "Race Still Too Close to Call" would also have been reasonable, given that a tie was within the margin of error in all of those poll results. Or, they could have focused on the "likely voters" poll and headlined their article "McCain Passes Obama."

How is a politician supposed to interpret that data? It is hard to know which poll results one should pay attention to. So should Obama have been worried about McCain, or not?

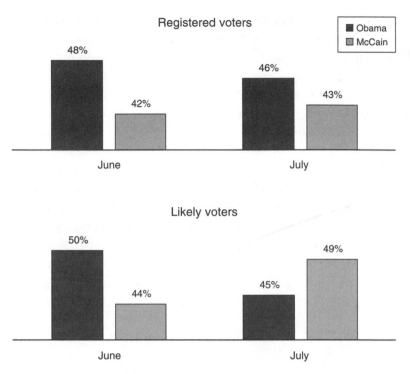

Figure 4.1

July 28, 2008, *USA Today*/Gallup presidential poll. Margin of error for all of the above polls: 4 percent. (A margin of error of 4 percent means that the pollsters are 95 percent confident that the reported poll numbers are within 4 percent of the true value.)

Even when looking at exactly the same poll results, reasonable people could draw very different conclusions. For instance, on March 8, 2011, *USA Today* reported on their website about a recent change in Obama's performance in Gallup's Daily Tracking Poll under the headline "Obama Weekly Approval Rating Lowest of the Year." Meanwhile, The Fix blog at WashingtonPost.com analyzed the exact same Gallup polling data under the headline "President Obama and the Leveling Effect." The authors at The Fix noted that Obama's Daily Tracking Poll numbers had remained within a very narrow range for the previous nine months. Both interpretations of the (identical) poll were technically correct, the data were gathered by one of the world's most respected polling organizations in one of their most reliable surveys, and neither the *USA Today* nor the political analysts for the *Washington Post* seemed to be giving a partisan interpretation of the data. And yet they came to very different conclusions. Sometimes good polls can have multiple correct interpretations.

And sometimes good polls are just wrong. There is an old joke that if someone tells you that you are "one in a million," they are really just saying that there are 1,000 people in China exactly like you. That same logic applies to polling. Polls are built around 95 percent confidence intervals, which means that we can be 95 percent sure that any given poll is correct. On the other hand, one out of twenty polls will be inaccurate, even if those polls were conducted without any bias of any kind. Before the 2008 election, there were at least half a dozen polling organizations, each running a weekly poll for two months (or more) leading up to the presidential election. Six polls a week for the nine weeks means fifty-four polls between the Republican Convention and Election Day. Fifty-four polls, and each poll has a one in twenty chance of being wrong, which means that we can expect that two or three of those polls, all of which were conducted by legitimate polling organizations, were simply inaccurate. It would be reasonable for even as many as six or seven of those fifty-four polls to be wrong; and it is possible that every last one of them was correct. Sadly, we just have no way of knowing which polls were accurate and which polls were flawed.

Of course, it is not exactly shocking to say that news organizations and political pundits cherry-pick polling data out of contradictory results to prove their respective points. But keep in mind that polls are not simply there to give pundits something to talk about. Polls are supposed to play an important role in modern democracies: to allow "We the People" to communicate our will to our leaders. Contradictory results and unidentifiable errors on even the best polls can interfere with the ability of political leaders to do the jobs that we hired them to do.

Summary

Leaders of democracies are supposed to listen to their constituents and to obey the will of the people. But how do they know what that will really is? Elections provide only minimal guidance when it comes to actual governing; there are simply too many voters sending too many contradictory messages. So politicians must rely on polls to understand what the people really want. But even the best polling is very difficult to interpret accurately. It is simply impossible to ask the right people the right questions with the answers framed in just the right way. That's on top of the basic problems that we discussed in chapters 1 and 2: People have poor memories and may not always answer questions accurately and honestly. How can democracy possibly be successful when the people cannot reliably communicate with their leaders?

References

Lead Quote
Gallup, G. H. N.d. BrainyQuote.com. Retrieved March 24, 2011, from http://www.brainyquote.com/quotes/quotes/g/georgegall113366.html.

Poll Sampling Problems
American Association of Public Opinion Research. 2011. Polls and survey FAQs. Retrieved March 24, 2011,from http://www.aapor.org/Poll_andamp_Survey_FAQs/1927.htm.

Gallup. October 4, 2010. Understanding Gallup's likely voter model. Retrieved March 24, 2011, from http://www.gallup.com/poll/143372/understanding-gallup-likely-voter-models.aspx.

Krosnick, J. A. 1999. Survey research. *Annual Review of Psychology* 50:537–567.

Lawrence, J. 2008. McCain gains on Obama in poll. *USA Today*, July 28. Retrieved March 24, 2011, from http://www.usatoday.com/news/politics/election2008/2008-07-28-poll_N.htm.

Squire, P. 1988. Why the 1936 *Literary Digest* poll failed. *Public Opinion Quarterly* 52:125–133.

Wastler, A. 2007. An open letter to the Ron Paul faithful. CNBC.com, October 11. Retrieved March 24, 2011, from http://www.cnbc.com/id/21257762/An_Open_Letter_to_the_Ron_Paul_Faithful.

Problems with Questions: Context and Language
Grice, H. P. 1957. Meaning. *Philosophical Review* 66 (3):377–388.

Hyman, H. H., and P. B. Sheatsley. 1950. The current status of American public Opinion. In *The Teaching of Contemporary Affairs: Twenty-first Yearbook of the National Council of Social Studies*, ed. J. C. Payne. Silver Springs, MD: National Council for the Social Studies.

Internet Movie Database. 2010. IMDB Top 250. Retrieved December 16, 2010, from http://www.imdb.com/chart/top.

Langer, G. 2009. Advancing Obama's Address: A summary of health care data. The Numbers at ABCNews.com, September 9. Retrieved March 24, 2011, from http://blogs.abcnews.com/thenumbers/2009/09/advancing-obamas-address-a-summary-of-health-care-data.html.

NBC News and Wall Street Journal Survey. 2010. Poll conducted by Peter Hart and Bill McInturff, March 11, 13–14. Retrieved March 24, 2011, from http://online.wsj.com/public/resources/documents/wsjnbcpoll03162010.pdf.

Parducci, A. 1968. The relativism of absolute judgment. *Scientific American* 219 (6):84–90.

Schuman, H., G. Kalton, and J. Ludwig. 1983. Context and contiguity in survey questionnaires. *Public Opinion Quarterly* 47 (1):112–115.

The Henry J. Kaiser Family Foundation. October 2008. Kaiser Health Tracking Poll: Election 2008. Retrieved March 24, 2011, from http://www.kff.org/kaiserpolls/h08_7832.cfm.

Verhovek, S. H. 1998. Execution in Texas: The overview; Divisive case of a killer of two ends as Texas executes Tucker. *New York Times*, February 4. Retrieved March 24, 2011, from http://www.nytimes.com/1998/02/04/us/execution-texas-overview-divisive-case-killer-two-ends-texas-executes-tucker.html?ref=karlafayetucker.

Problems with Questions: Framing the Answers

Hall, C. May 3, 2004. How much do you know about the war with Iraq? Lecture conducted at Princeton University, Princeton, NJ.

Menand, L. 2004. Permanent fatal errors: Did the voters send a message? *New Yorker*, December 6. Retrieved March 24, 2011, from http://www.hoching.com/menand/articles/NewYorkerIRiSS.pdf.

Schwarz, N., and H. J. Hippler. 1995. The numeric values of rating scales: A comparison of their impact in mail surveys and telephone interviews. *International Journal of Public Opinion Research* 7 (1):72–74.

Different Interpretations

Cillizza, C., and A. Blake. 2011. President Obama and the leveling effect. The Fix blog at WashingtonPost.com, March 9. Retrieved March 25, 2011, from http://voices.washingtonpost.com/thefix/morning-fix/president-obama-and-the-leveli.html.

Jackson, D. 2011. Obama weekly approval rating lowest of the year. The Oval blog at USAToday.com, March 8. Retrieved March 25, 2011, from http://content.usatoday.com/communities/theoval/post/2011/03/obama-weekly-approval-rating-lowest-of-the-year/1.

II Restoring Some Sanity

It has been said that democracy is the worst form of government except all the others that have been tried.

—Winston Churchill

Vote for the Crook

When Jacques Chirac ran for reelection as the president of France in 2002, he wasn't just fighting to stay in office. He was fighting to stay out of jail. His problems stemmed from a series of corruption charges against people who had been close to Chirac while he was mayor of Paris. By the time Chirac was connected to the crimes, he had already been elected president of France—and the French courts ruled that as president, he was immune from prosecution for acts that he committed before his election. In other words, if Chirac lost in 2002 he would be formally investigated and likely indicted. If he won, he would be free for another six years.

Who was Chirac's main competition in that election? Jean-Marie Le Pen. Le Pen has made many statements over the years expressing sympathy for the Nazis and questioning the historical accuracy of many Holocaust accounts. In 2002, he based his campaign around a series of draconian measures aimed at expelling immigrants, especially Muslim immigrants, from France. He has also publicly questioned whether blacks or Jews could ever be true Frenchmen. Unsurprisingly, the public rallied around Chirac's reelection, and "Vote for the Crook, Not the Fascist" signs began appearing around Paris. Sure enough, the crook won in a landslide. Chirac has since retired from politics and has finally been indicted.

That story should sound eerily familiar to anyone who lived in Louisiana in the early 1990s. In that case, the crook was Edwin Edwards (no relation to the author). Edwards had already served three different terms as governor of Louisiana, the last one ending in 1987. During his third term he was indicted on corruption charges, tried, and acquitted—although there remained a widespread belief that Edwards was guilty. So in 1991, when he announced that he was running for a fourth term as governor, he was considered a long shot. Fortunately for Edwards, name recognition, charisma, and an ability to manipulate the system can get you a long way, and he emerged as the front-runner.

His biggest competition was David Duke. David Duke was formerly a Grand Wizard of the Knights of the Ku Klux Klan, the founder of the National Association for the Advancement of White People, and the author of a book that argues for "racial separation." Edwards's supporters began carrying signs asking voters to "Vote for the Crook. It's Important." And people did: Edwards won easily. After his term was over Edwards was arrested and tried again on corruption charges. He was found guilty in 2002 and spent the next eight years in prison.

Democratic systems are supposed to produce multiple good options so that voters can pick qualified leaders. But in fact, every once in a while the system fails so miserably that not only do crooks win elections, but the world actually roots for the crook because the alternative is so much worse. Of course, Edwards and Chirac are not the most unsavory politicians ever elected. In democracies around the world voters have elected adulterers, bigots, criminals, and even on occasion the dead.

As depressing as that thought might be, by this point you probably are not surprised. After all, so far we have discussed how voters cannot possibly have enough information to make good choices; how we are inherently irrational and biased; how some candidates have unfair advantages in elections; and how even well-meaning politicians cannot possibly represent the true will of the people. It's no wonder that people like Chirac and Edwards get elected.

But of course, democracy isn't the only possible system of government. There are plenty of other forms of government out there that do not rely on the flawed votes of an irrational electorate. So let's take a look at the alternatives, and see if we can find one that's an improvement over our flawed system.

The Contenders

Historically, the most common form of government has been to give absolute authority to a monarch. You become the monarch by being the favored or eldest child of the previous ruler. The idea isn't absurd, in principle: Just find a decent man or woman to be king or queen, and then have his or her descendants rule. This system of government places a lot of faith both in genetics and in the parenting skills of the ruler. On the other hand, if the alternative is to place that faith in an uninformed and irrational public, then some might argue that a monarch might do a better job of governing.

Another very common form of government is oligarchy: rule by a small group of people, usually the upper class or aristocracy. The Roman Republic worked that way, as did many European governments during the Middle Ages. These groups of rulers are supposedly made up of the richest, smartest, most powerful, and/or most capable people in the country. Unlike democracy, this form of government ought to guarantee that the rulers won't be ignorant or utterly incompetent. Besides, the oligarchs are people with a lot of money and power invested in their country's success; in theory that ought to be a pretty good incentive for them to act in the best interests of the country as a whole.

In some modern nations, the oligarchy is composed of members of a single political party. For instance, in the People's Republic of China, the most powerful people in the country are not necessarily those who hold the titles of "President" or "Prime Minister." The most powerful people in the country are the leaders of the Communist Party. Membership in the Communist Party allows you to choose who those leaders are, and therefore membership in and advancement through the party are tightly controlled. This form of government at least guarantees that all of the people who rule will have a strong understanding of politics and policy.

Another possibility would be to take people who have dedicated their lives to God and put them in charge, as in Iran or in the Papal States of medieval Italy. Virtually every major religion in the world stresses the need to take care of our fellow man and to act with compassion, charity, and justice. These sound like wonderful virtues around which to build a government, even if you don't believe that God is taking an active role in the running of the country.

Finally, we could let the military run the country. After all, many countries have been ruled by military leaders: Sometimes these are called "military dictatorships," while other times we refer to them as *juntas*, which are simply councils of military rulers. Soldiers are people who have dedicated their lives to serving their country and are willing to make the ultimate sacrifice to do so. Perhaps they would make better decisions than politicians who are chosen because your neighbor thinks that they would be fun people to have over for a beer and a football game.

All of these forms of government might sound like reasonable possibilities, and there have certainly been plenty of political philosophers over the years who have argued in favor of each of them. But there is a problem: Despite the theories, none of these systems of government work nearly as well as democracy. Which countries ensure their citizens the most rights and civil liberties? Democracies. Which countries are better at fostering international peace and stability? Democracies. Which countries provide the most tangible benefits to their citizens? Democracies. When it comes to improving people's lives, democracies do it better.

Democratic Citizens Have More Liberty

Imagine that you wanted to have a small group of friends and neighbors over on a regular basis to read and discuss the Bible. In the United States these kinds of meetings are commonplace. If you lived in the People's Republic of China, you would first need to get a permit from the government, which is only given out if you are members of "approved" churches— approved because they have agreed not to speak out against the Chinese government or Chinese Communist Party in any way. If your weekly Bible study or house church did not have a permit, then you would risk being arrested, fined, or imprisoned.

In 2008, a group of Egyptian students held a peaceful demonstration to demonstrate solidarity with a nearby group of factory workers. They were arrested for holding an illegal protest. In the United States, if you did not have the proper permits to hold your vigil then you might risk having to spend the night in a county jail. In Egypt, there were no permits to get, and the leaders of this nonviolent protest were imprisoned for four months.

In the United States, we may grumble at the poor implementation of our Constitutional right to a "speedy" trial. After all, it can take months or years for difficult cases to work their way through our judicial system. Despite that lethargic pace, less than 1 percent of people in jail or prison are awaiting trial or have otherwise been detained without having been convicted in a court of law. Compare that to Nigeria in 2010, where 60 percent of the people in jail had yet to be tried or convicted—likely because most of them were innocent of any crime at all.

In the United States, we take for granted the many community newspapers, Internet blogs, and independent television stations, which all have the freedom to criticize the government as much as they want. In Belarus, all media distribution outlets are tightly controlled by the central government, and the government reserves the right to close any newspaper, television station, or website of which the government disapproves.

In the United States, cell phones are sold at convenience stores, and Internet access is widely available to anyone who can afford it. In Cuba, the general public has only been allowed to purchase cell phones and computers since 2008, and as of 2011 the central government still mandated preapproval of any individual who wished to access the Internet.

Of course, democracies aren't perfect. We can find plenty of anecdotal evidence that democracies are freer than nondemocracies, but we can also find plenty of cases where democracies have stripped citizens of their rights and liberties. In Germany, the public's ability to engage in a free exchange of ideas does not include statements that support Nazis. In France, the freedom of religion does not extend to allowing women to wear religious headdress in public schools. And the United States has regularly violated the rights of minorities to live freely without harassment or imprisonment, from Native Americans to Japanese Americans to Muslim Americans. So let's test whether or not democracies are actually better at providing rights and liberties to their citizens than nondemocracies.

For this test, we will focus on two freedoms that seem particularly vulnerable: freedom of the press and freedom of religion. The press at times is critical of governments, and at times they print unpopular things. Therefore, one might expect that democratic governments would be just as prone to crack down on journalists as other forms of government. As for religion, in many democracies political leaders advertise their religiosity, and often attempt to demonize the members of minority religions in order to get elected. Therefore, we might expect that democracies would not be any better at guaranteeing the freedoms of religious minorities than nondemocracies.

Before we carry out our test, we need to provide some measure of what makes a country a democracy. Thankfully, the Economist Intelligence Unit (EIU) maintains a ranking of countries, based on a wide variety of statistics, which evaluates exactly how democratic different countries are.[1] For this simple test we will not go into detail regarding their numbers. Instead, we will focus on the four categories into which the EIU places countries: "Full Democracies," "Flawed Democracies," "Hybrid Regimes," and "Authoritarian Regimes." Generally speaking, Full and Flawed Democracies are considered democratic, whereas Hybrid Regimes and Autocratic Regimes are not—although there is certainly debate about various borderline cases. In 2010, there were 26 Full Democracies, 53 Flawed Democracies, 32 Hybrid Regimes, and 55 Authoritarian Regimes. Notice that about half of the countries in the world are at least somewhat democratic.

One of the most basic rights that countries can give to their citizens is to guarantee freedom of the press. And one of the most harmful things a government can do to the freedom of the press is to imprison reporters who print unfavorable stories. According to the Committee to Protect Journalists,[2] in 2010 there were 145 journalists in 28 countries[3] worldwide who were in prison because of a story that they reported on or published. None of them was imprisoned in an EIU Full Democracy, and only two were imprisoned in Flawed Democracies (Indonesia and Moldova). In other words, the vast majority of imprisoned journalists in the world are held by the half of countries that are not democratic.

---

1. The Economist Intelligence Unit is a division of the *Economist* magazine that maintains a dataset on the political structures and freedoms of almost all countries in the world. We also ran the same tests with data from Freedom House, another organization with similar goals although different methods, and the results were basically identical.

2. The Committee to Protect Journalists is an international organization dedicated to protecting journalists and exposing restrictions on the press.

3. China, Iran, Eritrea, Burma, Uzbekistan, Vietnam, Cuba, Ethiopia, Turkey, Sudan, Bahrain, Kyrgyzstan, Syria, Afghanistan, Azerbaijan, Bangladesh, Burundi, Egypt, The Gambia, Indonesia, Iraq, Kazakhstan, Kuwait, Moldova, Russia, Saudi Arabia, Tunisia, Yemen.

Another one of the most important liberties is religious freedom: the ability to worship whatever god or gods you choose (or to not worship any if that is your preference). The Pew Research Center categorizes countries based on government restrictions of religious freedom. According to their 2009 rankings, ten countries have Very High Restrictions.[4] Not a single one of them is a Full Democracy according to the EIU, and only one of them (Malaysia) is even a Flawed Democracy.[5] Of the 33 countries with High Restrictions,[6] none of them is a Full Democracy, and only six are listed as Flawed Democracies (Bulgaria, Greece, India, Indonesia, Israel, and Moldova).[7] That's a total of only seven democracies among the 43 countries that have high or very high restrictions on the freedom of religion. If democracy were no different from nondemocracy, then we would have expected more than 20.

The citizens of democracies take for granted basic freedoms that are actually exceedingly rare in the history of the world. Democratic governments are much less likely to restrict access to the holy books of "unapproved" religions. They are less likely to tell us what can or cannot be printed in newspapers. And they are less likely to prevent us from meeting with friends, neighbors, and strangers to discuss politics or religion. In almost every democracy in the world we can purchase books and newspapers that express a wide variety of viewpoints, many of which are extremely critical of current orthodoxy. If we do get arrested, then we can expect a hearing in open court, with an attorney present—and if the court rules in our favor we can expect to be immediately set free. Democracy seems to give rise to an environment where these kinds of basic human rights can take hold and prosper.

---

4. Saudi Arabia, Iran, Uzbekistan, China, Egypt, Burma, Maldives, Eritrea, Malaysia, Brunei.

5. The EIU does not rank either Brunei or Maldives, two of the top ten, because of their small populations.

6. Indonesia, Mauritania, Pakistan, Turkey, Vietnam, Algeria, Belarus, Russia, Turkmenistan, Libya, Sudan, Tajikistan, Jordan, Afghanistan, Morocco, Laos, Syria, India, Tunisia, Azerbaijan, Kuwait, Kazakhstan, Yemen, Iraq, Western Sahara, Bulgaria, Singapore, Moldova, Greece, Israel, Cuba, Oman, Somalia.

7. The EIU does not rank either Western Sahara or Somalia, two of these 33 nations; Western Sahara because it is so small and Somalia because of an ongoing civil war that makes data collection almost impossible.

"We the People" are willing to elect anyone with a chiseled jaw and a famous last name, we believe in contradictory policies driven by fear and instinct, and we let our leaders manipulate us into keeping their jobs despite their often poor performance in office. Despite all of that, democracies protect the rights of their citizens better than nondemocracies.

Democracies Are Better at Fostering Peace

World War II, World War I, the Franco-Prussian War, the Franco-Austrian War, the Crimean War, the Austro-Prussian War, the First Schleswig War, the Second Schleswig War, the French Revolutionary and Napoleonic Wars. Those ten wars were all fought on European soil between 1800 and 1950, and all involved either France or Germany (and in most cases, both). During that time period there was a war involving at least one of these European powers in almost one out of every three years.

How many wars have Germany or France fought on continental Europe since 1950? Zero. Instead, these countries share some of the closest diplomatic and trade ties that the world has ever seen. Their citizens can travel freely between the two nations, without even showing a passport, and they even share the same currency. The thought of a Franco-German War right now is almost laughable.

So what happened? There were a lot of factors involved in the cessation of hostilities between these ancient rivals. But one of the most important was democracy. In his 1795 essay "Perpetual Peace," Immanuel Kant predicted that democracies would be able to coexist peacefully in a way that other states could not. It turns out that Kant was at least partly correct. Political scientists have coined the term *democratic peace* to describe the fact that democracies are relatively unlikely to fight with other democracies.[8]

The democratic peace is probably the most important, and most misunderstood, finding in modern political science. In particular, it is impor-

---

8. Some have been so bold as to state that no two democracies have ever fought a war with each other. The truth of that statement depends on exactly what they mean by "war" and "democracy." We won't go into the details, but suffice it to say that it would probably be an overstatement to claim that democracies never fight each other. Democracies do fight each other, just not as often as other states fight each other, or even as often as democracies fight other states.

tant not to overstate the democratic peace. The theory does not claim that democracies will act peacefully toward nondemocracies. The United States alone has started wars with Great Britain (1812), Mexico (1846), Spain (1898), and Iraq (2003), and initiated numerous smaller conflicts with many other countries around the world. Democracies are more peaceful with regard to each other, but they can be pretty violent in their relationships with nondemocracies.

So given this caveat, why is the democratic peace such an important finding?

First, the democratic peace indicates strongly that there is something peculiar about democracy. Monarchies fight with other monarchies; military dictatorships fight with other military dictatorships; Communist one-party states fight with other Communist one-party states; theocracies fight with other theocracies. Democracy is different.

Second, democracy gives hope that the spread of democracy around the world will reduce conflict. Western Europe has had sixty years of continual peace for perhaps the first time ever. Even if that peace isn't permanent, any reduction in the number of wars is a tremendous benefit to the citizens of those countries.

The particular leaders that democracies elect may not always be smarter or more capable or friendlier than the leaders of other countries. Yet at the end of the day, the spread of democracy offers the hope of peace to the citizens of democracies in a way that is unavailable to the citizens of countries with other forms of government.

Democracies Take Better Care of Their People

Newspapers are commonly filled with reports of the "special relationships" and "sweetheart deals" that some politician is giving to some "special interest group," and no one ever seems to do anything about it. Politicians always seem to be rewarding their friends and leaving the people to foot the bill. The wealthy and powerful seem to receive enormous benefits from government, while the poor and underprivileged seem to be perpetually ignored. These are common criticisms of democratic governments. So it would seem that democracies would be pretty bad at providing tangible benefits to the poorest members of society, because the rich, powerful, and connected seem to get it all.

But if you think democracies are bad, consider the case of Mobutu Sese Seko, the dictator of Zaire (now called the Democratic Republic of the Congo or DRC) from 1965 to 1997. The DRC is one of the poorest countries in the world; the World Bank estimates that the average per capita income in the Congo in 2008 was less than $1 per day. Mobutu himself was not exactly from a wealthy family; his mother was a hotel maid when the country was ruled by the Belgians, and Mobutu enlisted in the army as a very young man.

Yet after rising to the rank of general and taking power from the democratically elected political leadership, Mobutu died as one of the wealthiest men in the world, having enriched himself from the state coffers to the tune of $5 billion, according to the nonprofit international watchdog organization Transparency International. Mobutu traveled in a fleet of Mercedes Benz limousines between his palaces along roads that his government was reportedly too poor to fix. He maintained a pristine airfield in the small village where he grew up, so that he could charter Concorde air jet flights to and from Paris for his family's shopping trips. He spread this wealth to a small group of generals, high government officials, and his personal bodyguards, even while government workers often went unpaid in the rest of the country.

Of course, Mobutu is an excessive example, but the general trend outside of democracies is for leaders to reward themselves and their friends and to skimp whenever possible on benefiting the common man. Although no democracy is perfect in this regard, it turns out that the rulers in democracies are much more likely to govern for the benefit of their people than to hoard wealth for their own personal use.

For instance, South Africa under apartheid was an oligarchy run by and for the small white minority. Not only were blacks forbidden from participating in the political process, they were also given few civil rights and had access to almost no public services of any kind. When apartheid fell apart, the new democratic government took steps to implement a series of reforms to improve the lives of average citizens. Among their principal concerns was access to clean water and reliable sanitation. The new democratic government even wrote into their new constitution that the government would work to ensure access to clean water for every South African. The result was an immediate and dramatic increase in the number of black South Africans with access to those basic public services.

This story is not uncommon. David Lake and Matthew Baum ran a series of analyses in 2001 to try to determine if democracies were better at providing basic public services than nondemocracies. In particular, they looked at secondary school enrollment, access to safe drinking water, immunization against disease, and infant mortality rates (an indicator of access to reasonable health care). It turns out that democracies do a much better job of providing these public services than nondemocracies. In particular, countries that transitioned to democracy from other forms of government noticed an immediate improvement in those categories relative to countries that transitioned from one undemocratic government to another or from a democratic government to a nondemocratic government. Other researchers have found similar correlations with democracy and literacy rates, life expectancy, public sanitation, and the like. Lake and Baum also noticed that when countries moved away from democracy, they tended to regress on their provision of basic services. For instance, when a military coup toppled an unstable democratic regime in Nigeria in 1983, the percentage of Nigerian children who were given immunizations against basic diseases halved within three years.

In other words, democracies are much more likely than other governments to use a country's resources to benefit the people who live in that country. We may be electing people because of their looks, their money, or sheer randomness, and yet once those people get into office they do a better job of governing than do the military leaders, religious leaders, and children of previous monarchs that rule in other countries.

The Paradox

So there you have the basic paradox of democracy. Voters are irrational and elections are inherently flawed, but democracy is successful. Or to put it another way, Winston Churchill was exactly right: Democracy is the worst form of government, except for everything else.

Keep in mind that we do not intend to argue at any point that democracy is perfect, that democracies never fail, or that democracies never have their problems. There are plenty of examples of civil wars that tore apart democratic states or of elected politicians declaring themselves "president for life." Moreover, we do not mean to suggest that democracies never violate the rights of their citizens, or go to war, or fail to provide basic public services. Democracy has its flaws, but it is substantially better than the alternatives.

In the following chapters we'll give a number of reasons why democracy works so well despite its flaws. We'll discuss how mental shortcuts can make us effective voters despite our ignorance, and how the statistical properties of elections can make the group smarter than any individual within it; how widespread participation in democracy improves society; how our regular elections provide stability and limit internal conflicts; and how the ability for voters to rally around particular issues and vote out politicians can improve the performance of all of a democracy's leaders. In short, there are plenty of reasons why regularly asking millions of crazy people to vote in biased elections for flawed leaders is actually a really smart thing to do.[9]

References

Lead Quote
Churchill, W. November 1947. Speech in front of the British House of Commons.

Crooks vs. Fascists
Broughton, Philip Delves. 2002. French get choice of "crook or fascist." *Telegraph* (United Kingdom), April 26. Retrieved March 25, 2011, from http://www.telegraph.co.uk/news/worldnews/europe/france/1392313/French-get-choice-of-crook-or-fascist.html.

CNN.com. 2002. Chirac landslide against Le Pen. CNN.com, May 6. Retrieved March 25, 2011, from http://edition.cnn.com/2002/WORLD/europe/05/05/france.win/index.html.

Riley, M., D. Winbush, and R. Woodbury. 1991. Louisiana: The no-win election. *Time*, November 25. Retrieved March 25, 2011, from http://www.time.com/time/magazine/article/0,9171,974345,00.html.

Sack, K. 1998. Former Louisiana governor is indicted in extortion case. *New York Times*, November 7. Retrieved March 25, 2011, from http://www.nytimes.com/1998/11/07/us/former-louisiana-governor-is-indicted-in-extortion-case.html?src=pm.

---

9. To paraphrase Billy Joel, democracy may be crazy. But it just may be the lunatic we're looking for.

Democracy and Liberty

Amnesty International. 2010. Nigeria: 2010 annual report. Retrieved March 25, 2011, from http://www.amnesty.org/en/library/asset/AFR44/018/2010/en/bda62d59 -ec36-48fb-8215-0b4f3b987e5b/afr440182010en.html#37.2010%20Annual%20 Report|outline.

Committee to Protect Journalists. 2010. 2010 prison census. Retrieved March 25, 2011, from http://www.cpj.org/imprisoned/2010.php.

Economist Intelligence Unit. 2010. Democracy index 2010: Democracy in retreat. Retrieved March 25, 2011, from http://graphics.eiu.com/PDF/Democracy_Index _2010_web.pdf.

Freedom House. 2010. Freedom the World 2010: Erosion of freedom intensifies. Retrieved March 25, 2011, from http://www.freedomhouse.org/uploads/fiw10/ FIW_2010_Tables_and_Graphs.pdf.

Pew Forum on Religion and Public Life. 2009. Global restrictions on religion. Pew Research Center. Retrieved March 25, 2011, from http://pewforum.org/ uploadedFiles/Topics/Issues/Government/restrictions-fullreport.pdf.

Reuters. July 27, 2008. Egypt arrests 16 from anti-protest government group. Retrieved March 25, 2011, from http://www.reuters.com/article/2008/07/27/ idUSL7398588.

Silitski, V. 2010. Nations in transit 2010: Belarus. Freedom House. Retrieved March 25, 2011, from http://www.freedomhouse.eu/images/Reports/NIT-2010-Belarus-final .pdf.

Weissert, W. 2008. Cubans buzzing over first legal cell phones. National Geographic News, April 15, from The Associated Press. Retrieved March 25, 2011, from http:// news.nationalgeographic.com/news/2008/04/080415-AP-cuba-cell.html.

Democracy and Peace

Kant, I. 1795. *Perpetual Peace: A Philosophical Sketch.* Trans. M. Campbell Smith. London: Swan Sonnenschein.

Ray, J. L. 2009. *Democracy and International Conflict: An Evaluation of the Democratic Peace Proposition.* Columbia, SC: University of South Carolina Press.

Democracy and Tangible Benefits

CNN. 1997. Mobutu dies in exile in Morocco. CNN.com, September 7. Retrieved March 25, 2011, from http://articles.cnn.com/1997-09-07/world/9709_07_mobutu .wrap_1_joseph-desire-mobutu-zaires-mobutu-sese-seko-after?_s=PM:WORLD.

Deacon, R. 2009. Public good provision under dictatorship and democracy. *Public Choice* 139 (1–2):241–262.

Lake, D., and M. Baum. 2001. The invisible hand of democracy. *Comparative Political Studies* 34 (6):587–621.

Mutume, G. 2004. South Africa sets pace on rural water. *Africa Renewal* 18 (2):21. Retrieved March 25, 2011, from http://www.un.org/ecosocdev/geninfo/afrec/vol18no2/182water.htm.

Vollmer, S., and M. Ziegler. 2009. Political institutions and human development—Does democracy fulfil its "constructive" and "instrumental" role? World Bank Policy Research Working Paper Series, No. 4818, January 1. Retrieved June 27, 2011, from http://growth-institutions.ec.unipi.it/pages/Democracy/political.pdf.

5 Procedure, Process, and Prophecy

Though force can protect in emergency, only justice, fairness, consideration and cooperation can finally lead men to the dawn of eternal peace.
—Dwight D. Eisenhower

On Tea and Taxes

Did you know that our founding fathers fought, and died, so that they could pay higher taxes?

Okay, that's a gross oversimplification, but not a completely false one. For several decades before the American Revolutionary War, the British had largely left the American colonists alone. But the costs of running a global empire are pretty steep, and eventually the British needed to raise some more revenue. So they decided to tax trade into and out of the American colonies and to institute new trade restrictions that would prevent the Americans from trading with Britain's competitors. The American colonists responded with civil disobedience and vandalism, which eventually escalated into a full-blown war of independence. Once those colonists had their independence, they discovered that running a stable and effective government is also pretty expensive—not to mention the fact that they had incurred quite a bit of debt during the war that needed to be paid off. So what did our founding fathers do? They raised taxes to significantly higher rates than the British had ever proposed, and they did so willingly.

Of course, the war wasn't really about taxes. It was about fairness and having a say in our own destiny (among other things). The colonists didn't mind paying higher taxes; they simply objected to "taxation without representation."

This behavior represents a puzzle. A "rational" human ought to be more concerned with the costs and benefits of an action than with the fairness of the process. War is an extremely costly behavior: Lives are lost, trade is disrupted, and there are no guarantees that your side will be victorious. In fact, the American colonists were rebelling against one of the most powerful nations in the history of the world—success was by no means predetermined. And at the end of the war, most Americans weren't economically better off. So why would the American colonists risk so much, to gain so little?

It turns out that people are less interested in "getting a good deal" than they are in ensuring a fair process. The colonists cared more about having a say than they cared about paying higher taxes.

As we've seen, voters are irrational and they make some pretty awful decisions sometimes. But it turns out that having the opportunity to make those decisions is tremendously motivational, and leads to all sorts of positive benefits for society.

Procedural Justice

All You Have to Do Is Ask
In the workplace, rules exist for a reason. Some rules, such as dress codes and sexual harassment policies, are designed to help create an atmosphere conducive to work and free from unnecessary distractions. Other rules, such as restrictions on personal calls and taking office supplies home, are an attempt to avoid misuse of company resources. Rules serve to improve communication across different divisions of a company, protect customer privacy, increase efficiency, comply with government regulations, and decrease fraud. Not all policies are successful, but on the whole companies are more effective when employees follow the rules.

So, we shouldn't be surprised to learn that companies have spent a lot of effort trying to figure out ways to get employees to follow the rules. The most common way is the *carrot-and-stick method*. When employees follow the rules, they are rewarded in the form of bonuses, public recognition, and promotions. When they break the rules, they are punished by getting scolded, being docked pay, and possibly being fired. It's pretty straightforward.

There is, however, a significant problem: The carrot-and-stick approach requires that the boss knows who is following the rules, which requires monitoring. To know who is getting reimbursed for inappropriate expenses you need to run occasional audits and have employees fill out expense reports. To make sure employees aren't making personal calls or watching YouTube videos on company time, you need to monitor calls and computer use. And this sort of monitoring is expensive. Monitoring software isn't free, auditors don't just volunteer their time, and even filling out expense reports takes time away from other, more productive things that employees could be doing.

To make matters worse, although employees want to earn the rewards and avoid the punishments, they may decide to corrupt or circumvent the incentive system rather than follow the rules. Many online video games have "boss buttons" that people can click when the boss walks in to make it look like they were working instead of goofing off. People can fudge numbers on reimbursement forms or take sick days when they aren't sick. Moreover, all too often the incentive structures encourage poor behavior. One Australian organization that wanted to ensure that its employees answered phones promptly started rewarding employees for the number of phone calls answered in fewer than two rings. Employees took to answering quickly and immediately hanging up, forcing the caller to call back multiple times. The result was more calls and larger bonuses! In that case the incentive structure was not only costly, but actively undermined the organization's ability to be successful.

Clearly, it's much better if employees follow the rules because they want to rather than because they have to. So when do people voluntarily follow rules? When those rules are perceived to be legitimate. In 2005, New York University psychologists Tom Tyler and Stephen Blader surveyed over 500 workers at a large financial services company. They considered low-level clerical workers, high-level administrators, customer service specialists, and all levels in between. The researchers measured the extent to which the employees felt that the organization's policies were fairly designed, and how often the employees followed the rules. They also measured the effectiveness of the carrot-and-stick approach, asking employees to guess their likelihood of being caught if they were to break the rules, and just how bad they thought the punishment would be.

It turns out that the workers' decisions about whether to follow the rules were influenced more by whether they believed that the rules were fair than by whether they thought they would get caught and punished. Of course, it's reasonable to maintain a healthy dose of skepticism about these findings. After all, the accuracy of these results relies on people admitting that they've broken the rules. While the surveys were all anonymous and confidential, it's easy to imagine that rule-breaking might not be something people would feel comfortable admitting.

So Tyler and Blader followed up by looking at over 2,000 workers from a variety of industries and company types, ranging from small businesses to multinational conglomerates. Importantly, in addition to having workers self-report their own behavior, the researchers also had the *supervisors* of the workers report on how often the workers broke the rules. In this way, they could make sure the findings from the earlier studies weren't just the result of rule-breaking employees lying to the researchers. Two interesting findings emerged. First, the workers' self-reports of how often they broke the rules didn't differ from what their supervisors reported. It turns out that people were honest when filling out the surveys. More importantly, when the researchers looked at the supervisors' reports they found that the carrot-and-stick approach didn't predict rule-following nearly as well as whether the rules were perceived as fair.

In other words, when people believe that the rules are legitimate, they are more likely to follow them. Subsequent research has shown that when people think that the corporate procedures are just, people have higher job satisfaction, are more loyal to their employer, and like their boss more. This *procedural justice* also leads people to engage in so-called extra-role activities, going above and beyond the call of duty, volunteering for tasks outside of their formal job description, and otherwise working harder. Fairer processes lead to more motivated workers, which in turn makes for more effective organizations.

Just like the workplace, society works best when people follow the rules. Just like the workplace, those rules are expensive to enforce. The police can't be everywhere at once, and so for societies to function properly people need to be willing to obey the law by choice rather than by threat of sanctions. And just like the workplace, people follow the rules most often when they believe that those rules are legitimate and procedurally just.

Over the past five decades, there have been dozens of studies on the relationship between how fair and legitimate people think the law is, and how likely they are to follow it voluntarily. These studies have been run on teenagers, college students, and adults. They've been run all around the

United States and Europe. They've been run on former law breakers and law-abiding citizens. The results have come out strikingly similar: The more that people view the law as legitimate, the more they're willing to follow it.

Similarly, the more that people believe that procedures for distribution of resources are fair, the more they engage in behaviors that are constructive to society. For example, Tom Tyler teamed up with University of California, Berkeley scholar Peter Degoey to look at how people behaved during the 1991 California drought. The drought led to a severe water shortage, and California needed people to conserve water before the situation deteriorated further and led to a crisis. Tyler and Degoey surveyed over 400 San Franciscans about their willingness to voluntarily reduce water usage. The researchers recorded the extent to which participants believed that methods for setting water prices and for rationing water were fair. They also asked people to report how severe the water shortage was, and how severe they expected it to be in the future. Remarkably, a person's belief about the severity of the crisis did not affect how much water he or she used. Instead, people used less water when they were convinced that the procedures for pricing and allocating water were fair.

Procedural justice does more than just encourage people to conserve scarce resources. It is extremely important for maintaining stability in society as well. For example, Tom Tyler has demonstrated that criminal behavior among an ethnic group will decrease if that group feels that it is treated more fairly, and increase if the group feels that it is treated unfairly. He has shown that we can lower crime rates among young urban black males by convincing them that society (e.g., courts, police, schools, employers) is fair. As a result, the use of racial profiling and other crime-reduction strategies that feel unjust can backfire and lead to more problems than they solve.

We can apply procedural justice more broadly to the stability of an entire society. In order for any society to function well, people need to go to work and school, they need to earn and spend money, they need to follow the law and respect the authority of the police and the courts. If people believe that the government and the economy are basically fair and just, then they are more likely to participate in society in productive ways: They will listen to the police, actively engage in the economy, trust in the legal system, and so on. If people believe that these same systems are unfair and unjust, then they are more likely to resist authority: They will riot in the streets, save their money under their mattresses, and resolve their disputes with their own fists and weapons.

It turns out that democracy has all of the characteristics that drive intuitions about fairness. First and foremost among these is the notion of participation. From legal mediation, to interactions with the police, to suggestion boxes at work: When people have the ability to state their case or express their opinions, they tend to find the process fairer—even when those opinions can't affect the final outcome.

In 1990, E. Allen Lind and his colleagues gave people fifteen minutes to fill out ten scheduling forms—a very challenging task. Some people were simply told how many forms they needed to fill out and had no opportunity to provide input. A second group was asked for their opinion before the number of forms was revealed—ostensibly their input was taken into account when deciding on the difficulty of the task. Crucially, a third group of people was told the number of forms they would need to fill out and then asked for their feedback on that number, even though there was no way to change it. Unsurprisingly, being able to influence the final decision led people to evaluate the task as more fair. But even when one's input didn't influence the final outcome, people gave over 20 percent higher fairness ratings than when they didn't get to give input at all.

This study also confirmed that people are more productive when they believe in the fairness of a situation. When people believed the process was fair, they were more motivated and were more successful at the task. When people had no input they only completed 4.6 of the 10 forms on average. When they were able to express their opinion, but their opinion didn't affect the outcome, they successfully completed 5.9 forms. And when they believed that their participation had influenced the nature of the task, they completed 6.7 forms. In other words, when participants' opinions were heard, it improved their efficiency by upward of 25 percent; when their input was perceived to make a difference, it improved their efficiency by almost 50 percent.

Democratic societies benefit from the fact that the process allows everybody to participate. Even when our favored candidate loses, we still had the opportunity to express our desires. Lab studies have shown that people both cooperate more and pay more "taxes" to a group pool of money when they are allowed to vote on what will happen to that money. This is true whether they are on the winning side of that vote or not. When our opinions are expressed, we work harder, are more engaged, and follow the rules.

On the other hand, when we don't get to participate, it can actually incite destructive behavior. For example, on June 10, 1968, U.S. President Lyndon Johnson formed the National Commission on the Causes and Prevention of Violence in an attempt to reduce the rising chaos and violence sweeping through the nation, especially on college campuses. The commission was chaired by Milton Eisenhower, brother of former president Dwight D. Eisenhower, and a widely respected former president of Kansas State, Penn State, and Johns Hopkins Universities. After studying the causes of unrest, the commission concluded that 18-year-olds were "almost entirely disenfranchised" and called for the voting age to be lowered to 18. The goal was to provide youth with "a direct constructive and democratic channel for making their views felt."

As epitomized by the famous slogan "old enough to go to war, old enough to vote," 18-year-olds wanted their voices to be heard in the decision making. When the principle of participation wasn't held up, then they engaged in civil disobedience (and sometimes not-so-civil disobedience). Not only were they no longer productive members of society, they actually siphoned off resources by requiring police attention, and causing damage to university property that needed to be repaired. Milton Eisenhower saw what the British Empire in 1776 did not. By making people feel involved in the decisions that affect their lives, you make them less likely to rebel against society. In 1971, the voting age was lowered to extend voting rights to 18-year-olds.

Participation isn't the only thing that leads to perceptions of fairness. For instance, even fair laws can be enforced unfairly, and so people need to believe that their leaders are respectful and trustworthy. In a democracy, people have the ability to remove officials from office who they think are untrustworthy. In fact, in this case the voters' tendency to rely on first impressions of candidates actually works in our favor. After all, perceived trustworthiness is one of those factors that can drive our first impressions of candidates. We tend to trust the people for whom we vote, which improves our belief that our government is fair.

Another major component of perceived fairness is what Tyler calls *neutrality*: "people seek a 'level playing field' in which nobody is unfairly disadvantaged." The democratic process sets rules that we are all supposed to follow no matter how rich, powerful, or famous we may be. The U.S. Constitution and Bill of Rights explicitly guarantee equality. In other words, everybody gets a vote, and everybody's vote counts as much as his or her neighbor's vote.

When this isn't the case, the result is instability, unrest, and chaos. Consider the women's suffrage movement of the early 1900s. In late December, 1910, the British Parliament had failed to pass a bill giving women the right to vote. This led to immediate protests, some of which led to violence. A *Pittsburgh Post-Gazette* headline summed up the riots: "Suffragettes Again on the Rampage." One advocate for women's suffrage was quoted as saying "we are gentlewomen and the thought of violence is abhorrent to us . . . but we are strong enough to master our natural qualms. The vote is our right and we will stop at nothing to get it." This disturbance was not small; the article reported that the movement had over 300,000 members and the Women's Social and Political Union was well known for acts of arson and vandalism in their protests against being denied the vote. In the United States, the movements to abolish slavery, to give women the right to vote, and to eliminate Jim Crow laws were some of the most widespread and disruptive political movements in American history. In each of those cases, the movement strove to "level the playing field"—to make sure that different groups were given equal treatment under the law.

When people think the system is fair, they tend to work hard, cooperate, and generally strengthen the country. When people think the system isn't fair, they tend to do the bare minimum, and sometimes might actually work to undermine the system. Democracies appear fair and just, and we are all better off for it.

Are You the Kind of Person Who Lets People Rummage through Your Drawers?

How many of your friends would let half a dozen strangers come over to their house and rummage through their closets and drawers? In the mid-1960s, Stanford psychologists Jonathan Freedman and Scott Fraser called up housewives in California, and asked them if they would participate in a short survey about what household products people were using. They then conducted an eight-question survey about soaps (e.g., "what brand of soap do you use in your kitchen sink?"). Three days later, the experimenters called a second time, and asked the women if they would agree to a follow-up survey. The second survey would "involve five or six men from our staff coming into your home some morning for about two hours to enumerate and classify all the household products that you have. They will have to have full freedom in your house to go through the cupboards and storage places."

Amazingly, over half of the women agreed to this second request. Why would they be so helpful? Well, consider this—when a different group of housewives was given the same request, only without having taken the eight-question survey a few days earlier, less than 25 percent were willing to help out. The difference between these groups was a clever application of the psychological principle of *consistency*: People have a strong motivating drive to be consistent in their thoughts, attitudes, and behaviors.

The first request was quite innocuous—eight quick questions hardly take any time—so people were willing to help out. But by agreeing to take the survey, the women set a precedent. They had marked themselves as the sort of people who help out in consumer surveys. Then, when the second request was made, the psychological pressure toward acting consistently came into play. Women who normally wouldn't have agreed to that second request couldn't say no without feeling like they were contradicting the identity they had established.

There are countless demonstrations of these sorts of phenomena. Undergraduates compelled to write an essay in favor of tuition increases later show more positive attitudes toward tuition increases—something that undergraduates are typically opposed to. University development offices often ask young alumni for small gifts, $5 to $10, knowing that once the students get into the habit of giving, they'll be more likely to give larger gifts later. Salesmen use tactics such as "foot in the door," "low-balling," and "bait and switch," which all prey on our unwillingness to contradict what we've done before.

When citizens cast a vote, they establish that they care about the candidates, the system, and the country. They become invested in democracy. Casting a vote, like answering a brief series of questions about soap, is quick and easy. It also feels good; everybody likes it when people care about your opinions. Most importantly, voting psychologically commits you to further behaviors. Because of consistency pressures, people who vote are more likely to engage in other behaviors that support democracy.

For example, voters are more likely to donate to the Federal Election Committee for public financing of political campaigns on their tax forms. When people become more civically engaged, it strengthens communities, builds trust, and generally helps society. The fact that voting creates a sense of commitment to our community helps democracies function more effectively.

Self-Fulfilling Prophecies

Manipulating Markets and IQs

The Chicago Board Options Exchange (CBOE) opened in 1973 and almost immediately became an important market for derivatives trading. That same year a couple of prominent economists named Fischer Black and Myron Scholes published a set of formulas that could be used to predict options prices. Unfortunately, these formulas didn't do a very good job of predicting CBOE prices—missing by as much as 40 percent in the first few months that the CBOE was open.

But eventually the traders got hold of the formulas and started using them to determine how much to bid for various options. Bids that were directly determined by the equations were obviously well predicted by the equations. This use by traders improved the accuracy of the formulas, and as the equations became more accurate more traders started using them. This cycle continued until, by the late 1970s, the formulas were off by less than 3 percent. Black and Scholes went on to win the Nobel Prize for their theory, in part owing to its tremendous accuracy in predicting derivatives markets.

This story is a classic case of a self-fulfilling prophecy: a prediction that comes true because you believe that the prediction will come true. The Black–Scholes formula wasn't initially able to predict prices. It was only because people believed in it, and started making bids based on it, that it became accurate. The Black–Scholes formula didn't so much predict derivatives pricing as it established derivatives pricing. This formula is hardly the only self-fulfilling prophecy that occurs in economic systems. When prominent economists publicly predict declines in the stock market, then many people will rush to pull their money out of the market to avoid taking a loss. This, in turn, will cause the market to fall, validating the predictions of the economists.

Importantly, self-fulfilling prophecies don't just happen in financial markets. Beliefs can exert strong and subtle pressures on human behaviors, which in turn influence how others behave and often validate those initial beliefs. For example, in 1965, Harvard professor Robert Rosenthal and elementary school principal Lenore Jacobson told teachers at a public elementary school that certain students in their classes had been identified as "growth spurters" by the "Harvard Test of Inflected Acquisition." The teachers were told that these spurters were at the cusp of major intellectual growth, and should be expected to advance rapidly during the year, even if they hadn't previously shown any signs of being exceptional students.

In reality, there was no "Harvard Test of Inflected Acquisition"; the so-called spurters were chosen at random from the class. The reason that the students hadn't shown any signs of being exceptional was because they were no different from any other students in the class. The only difference between the children identified as spurters and the rest of the class was that the teachers were told that the spurters were special.

Except that by the end of the school year, the difference wasn't just in the teachers' heads anymore. Rosenthal and Jacobsen measured the student's IQs and found that students who had been arbitrarily labeled as spurters had actually spurted. For example, first-grade spurters had IQ gains of over 27 points, compared to only a 12-point gain for the nonspurters. The teachers' beliefs that the students were intellectually gifted led them to give more attention and encouragement to those students and actually created the outcome that they expected to happen.

These sorts of self-fulfilling prophecies occur all the time. People who believe they will be successful at dating exude confidence when on dates. Since confidence is usually considered sexy, someone's belief that he or she will have a good date makes it more likely that the date will be successful. If you expect an interaction with somebody to go poorly then you are likely to act awkwardly around that person. The other person will be put off by your awkward behavior, thus validating your belief. In one study, men had a "get to know you" conversation with women over the phone. The men were shown photos, ostensibly of the person that they were talking to. In reality, the photos had no resemblance to the conversation partner—but were instead chosen to be of highly attractive or else unattractive women. The conversations were recorded, and third parties who were unaware of the pictures listened to what the women had said. Women who had been (randomly) assigned to the attractive photo condition were rated as more attractive—by the third parties who hadn't even seen the pictures! The men who believed that they were talking to beautiful women acted differently, the women responded accordingly, and the people who were listening in on the conversations came to believe it too.

In other cases, the social or environmental cues that create these expectations can be very subtle. Consider a study done by Stanford psychologist Lee Ross and his colleagues. Ross asked a number of people to play a "prisoner's dilemma" game. In this game, each player has the option of acting in a self-interested manner or else cooperating. If both players cooperate then everyone wins a small amount, whereas if both players act self-interestedly, they both go home with little or nothing. The problem is that if only one player cooperates, then the "sucker" loses big while the selfish person wins big at his opponent's expense.

Although everybody played exactly the same game, half of the players were told that the game was called "the Wall Street Game" while the other half were told it was "the Community Game." Players of the Community Game cooperated at a significantly higher rate than players of the Wall Street Game. Players of the Community Game expected cooperation, while players of the Wall Street Game expected selfishness—even though the rules of both games were identical. Simply changing the name of the game changed the prophecy.

It's not just names that can serve as subtle cues about the nature of the prophecy. Even when the name of the game was the same, the psychologists discovered that they could change people's behavior simply by priming them with basic images: People shown Wall Street related images such as a briefcase were more likely to choose the self-interested option. In democracies we are constantly primed with notions of community, justice, fairness, and equality; this priming leads us to behave in ways consistent with these democratic notions.

All stable societies and governments rely on self-fulfilling prophecies. If people believe that the economy is fundamentally sound and fair, then they will participate in that economy, thus creating economic growth. If people believe that the government is stable and legitimate, then they are more likely to obey the law, which in turn helps create stability. On the other hand, when these beliefs are shattered, an economy or a government can fall apart very quickly, which is one reason why revolutions or economic chaos can seem to spread from one country to another. When one country's economy or government falls apart, the citizens of other countries start getting nervous—and that nervousness can cause collapse. This spreading uncertainty helps explain, for instance, why virtually every Eastern European Communist regime fell apart within a couple years of each other, while the Communist countries in other parts of the world seemed largely unaffected.

Yet although all stable governments rely on self-fulfilling prophecies to maintain control, democracies have certain advantages. All governments, including democratic ones, rely on basic beliefs about the stability of our government and economy. But democracy also relies on more general beliefs, or cultural norms, about equality, freedom, and prosperity. Those beliefs are constantly reinforced through education, through political advertising, and even through everyday social interactions. Those beliefs, in turn, create self-fulfilling prophecies.

For instance, in most democracies, there is a widely held belief that everyone is equal. These cultural beliefs about equality are regularly reinforced by campaign ads, statements by pundits and politicians, and even casual comments made on prime-time television shows. In psychological terms, we are constantly being primed by notions of equality. So not only is the belief in equality self-fulfilling (we believe that people are equal, therefore we treat them as equals), in fact the cultural belief in equality creates an environment in which we are frequently encouraged to think about the importance of treating people equally. Simply put, democracy works well because we believe that it works well.

Reciprocity

I'll Scratch Your Back if You Scratch Mine

In the late 1970s, Arizona State psychologist Bob Cialdini and his colleagues stopped random visitors on campus and asked them if they would be willing to volunteer two hours one afternoon to chaperone a group of children from a nearby juvenile detention center on a trip to the zoo. Unsurprisingly, very few people were willing to do this—less than 17 percent. Other random visitors were first asked if they'd be willing to spend two hours a week for two full years being a mentor to children from the detention center, and then were asked if they might consider taking a group of kids to the zoo. Not a single person was willing to sign up for the extended mentoring—but after having said no to that onerous request, a full 50 percent were willing to help out with the zoo trip.

So why was the second group of people willing to help out? Because of what psychologists call the *principle of reciprocity*. It's the notion captured by the old adage "I'll scratch your back if you scratch mine." When somebody else helps you out or makes a concession, then it's only fair to help them out or make a concession in return. It's the principle behind many bargaining sessions where each party gives a little until they meet in the middle of their initial offers. In the case of taking juvenile delinquents to the zoo, the experimenter compromised quite a bit—lowering the request from a weekly commitment for two years to a single day's commitment. The least one can do is meet him halfway and help out that one time. This principle doesn't just apply to recruiting volunteers for working with juvenile delinquents. The Disabled American Veterans organization uses the same idea when soliciting donations. Nearly twice as many people donate to the cause when the request includes a set of free personalized address labels. The veterans group offers something that makes people feel obligated to help out in return. Similarly, Hare Krishna used to hand out flowers in airports when asking for donations (at least, until they were prohibited from doing so in deference to airport security).

In order to be elected, a democratic politician has to make promises and beg for votes. For instance, presidential candidates spend months, or sometimes years, traveling around the country asking for people's support. On Election Day, the winner will receive the votes of tens of millions of citizens, and as a result will be given the job that he or she has been coveting for years.

That process creates a strong sense of reciprocity. Even though the voters may have been motivated by silly things, the fact is they gave their votes to the politician. The politician quite literally owes his or her job to the voters. When it comes to policymaking, democratic politicians will feel some obligation to help the people who helped put them in power. Democracies may not express the will of the people, but they do exert the right psychological pressures on their leaders to create policies that benefit the voters.

Summary

Next time you watch a game of football, take note of the offensive line. As noted by ESPN.com columnist and Brookings Scholar Gregg Easterbrook, when the quarterback gets sacked you will almost certainly see at least one of the linemen—the players who are supposed to be protecting the quarterback—standing around and doing nothing. No matter how brilliant the coach, and how clever the play calling, when the linemen slack off and the quarterback gets hit, the play isn't going to work. On the other hand, next time you see a really big play—somebody breaking free for an eighty-yard run—you'll almost always see a lineman going beyond the call of duty, hustling across the field to make a key block. This hustle turns what might have been a small gain into a huge success.

Politicians can make policies, just as coaches can call plays. But in the end, the success of the team or the country depends on the people in the trenches doing their jobs. Democracies don't necessarily lead to stronger policies, but they do lead to a more motivated citizenry. Democracies are perceived as fair, so people are more willing to play by the rules. Democracies get people invested in society through voting, so people act in a self-consistent manner and become civically engaged. Democracies prime us with concepts associated with equality and stability, which encourage us to treat each other as equals and to invest in the future, thereby contributing to a more equal and stable society. And democracies keep the leaders beholden to the people through norms of reciprocity, creating strong incentives for leaders to work for the people's interest above and beyond their own self-interest. As flawed as our votes and our elections might be, the simple fact that we are asked to vote and that those votes matter make democracies effective.

References

Lead Quote
Eisenhower, D. D. N.d. Retrieved April 17, 2011, from http://www.brainyquote.com/quotes/quotes/d/dwightdei165216.html.

Procedural Justice
Baack, B. 2001. The economics of the American Revolutionary War. EH.Net Encyclopedia, November 13, edited by Robert Whaples. Updated August 5,

2010. Retrieved April 17, 2011, from http://eh.net/encyclopedia/article/baack.war.revolutionary.us.

Cooper, J. 2007. *Cognitive Dissonance: 50 Years of a Classic Theory*. London: Sage.

Copeland, C., and D. Laband. 2002. Expressiveness and voting. *Public Choice* 110:351–363.

Freedman, J. L., and S. C. Fraser. 1996. Compliance without pressure: The foot-in-the-door technique. *Journal of Personality and Social Psychology* 4:196–202.

Lind, E. A., R. Kanfer, and P. C. Earley. 1990. Voice, control, and procedural justice: Instrumental and noninstrumental concerns in fairness judgments. *Journal of Personality and Social Psychology* 59:952–959.

Saldin, R. P. 2011. Strange bedfellows: War and minority rights. *World Affairs*, March/April. Retrieved April 17, 2011, from http://www.worldaffairsjournal.org/articles/2011-MarApr/full-Saldin-MA-2011.html.

Stewart, C. 1910. Suffragettes are again on the rampage: Militant women in England have another spell of strenuous activity—ministry and police alarmed. *Pittsburgh Press*, December 18, Theatrical Section, page 5.

Tyler, T. R. 1990. *Why People Obey the Law*. New Haven: Yale University Press. Reissued with a new afterword: Princeton University Press, 2006.

Tyler, T. R. 2000. Social justice: Outcome and procedure. *International Journal of Psychology* 35 (2):117–125.

Tyler, T. R., and S. L. Blader. 2005. Can businesses effectively regulate employee conduct? The antecedents of rule following in work settings. *Academy of Management Journal* 45 (6):1143–1158.

Tyler, T. R., and P. Degoey. 1995. Collective restraint in social dilemmas: Procedural justice and social identification effects on support for authorities. *Journal of Personality and Social Psychology* 69:482–497.

Tyler, T. R., and C. Wakslak. 2004. Profiling and the legitimacy of the police: Procedural justice, attributions of motive, and the acceptance of social authority. *Criminology* 42:13–42.

Wahl, I., S. Muehlbacher, and E. Krichler. 2010. Impact of voting on tax payments. *Kyklos* 64 (1):144–158.

Self-Fulfilling Prophecies
Ferraro, F., J. Pfeffer, and R. I. Sutton. 2005. Economic language and assumptions: How theories can become self-fulfilling. *Academy of Management Review* 30 (1):8–24.

Kay, A. C., and L. Ross. 2003. The perceptual push: The interplay of implicit cues and explicit situational construals on behavioral intentions in the prisoner's dilemma. *Journal of Experimental Social Psychology* 39 (6):634–643.

Liberman, V., S. M. Samuels, and L. Ross. 2004. The name of the game: Predictive power of reputations versus situational labels in determining prisoner's dilemma game moves. *Personality and Social Psychology Bulletin* 30 (9):1175–1185.

Rosenthal, R., and L. Jacobson. 1968. Pygmalion in the classroom. *Urban Review* 3 (1):16–20.

Snyder, M., E. D. Tanke, and E. Berscheid. 1977. Social perception and interpersonal behavior: On the self-fulfilling nature of social stereotypes. *Journal of Experimental Social Psychology* 35:656–666.

Reciprocity

Cialdini, R. B. 2001. *Influence! Science and Practice*. Needham Heights, MA: Allyn & Bacon.

Cialdini, R. B., J. E. Vincent, S. K. Lewis, J. Catalan, D. Wheeler, and B. L. Darby. 1975. Reciprocal concessions procedure for inducing compliance: The door in the face technique. *Journal of Personality and Social Psychology* 31 (2):206–215.

Conclusion

Easterbrook, G. 2006. Stop the INT insanity! ESPN.com. Retrieved April 17, 2011, from http://sports.espn.go.com/espn/page2/story?page=easterbrook/061121.

6 Letting Off Steam

All democracies are based on the proposition that power is very dangerous and that it is extremely important not to let any one person or small group have too much power for too long a time.

—Aldous Huxley

A Remarkable Event

On Tuesday, January 20, 2009, Barack Obama was sworn into office as president of the United States in front of an estimated crowd of over 1 million people gathered on the National Mall in Washington, D.C. After the inauguration was completed, George W. Bush, the former president, quietly boarded an airplane headed for Dallas, Texas. No one in the United States was particularly surprised; Obama did win the election, after all. But in the history of humankind this was a remarkable event. These two men disagreed on virtually every important policy issue facing the country, to the extent that each of them had accused the other of doing substantial harm to the security and reputation of the nation. The Democrats celebrated their victory, the Republicans tried to figure out how to win the next round of elections, and the country stayed at peace.

Leading up to that election, many Americans were extremely unhappy with their government. But there was no rioting that crippled commerce in America's big cities, nor any organized nationwide strikes that brought the economy to the brink of disaster. The Republican Party did not stockpile weapons in preparation for civil war. The government never declared martial law. The military was never called in to deal with chaos in the streets. Instead, we had a hotly contested presidential election that resulted in a new president from a different political party who promised hope and change. Tough times led to a change in leadership, but without any massive social or political chaos that would have done further harm to the economy and without any government crackdowns that would have led to the loss of civil liberties. Widespread discontent in the United States had led to a dramatic change in leadership, and our sitting president responded by buying a house in Dallas and handing over the White House keys to a political rival.

Compare this with what happened in Poland under Communist rule. In the late 1970s, widespread unrest over perceived government misman-agement of a faltering economy led to a series of strikes organized by Soli-darity, a national labor union led by Lech Walesa. In Communist Poland, there was no mechanism for replacing unpopular leaders. So what did the government do? They declared martial law and ordered the military to arrest the leaders of the protest movement and to break up further protests and strikes. Walesa himself spent most of the next year in jail. The coun-try's downward spiral continued throughout the 1980s. Martial law became a way of life, international sanctions restricted the influx of goods, infla-tion became so rampant that the Communist government established stores that accepted Western currency, and the government began ration-ing basic foodstuffs. Eight years later, after the Soviet Union withdrew some support from the Polish Communists, the government collapsed under the weight of its own unpopularity.

In nondemocracies, economic and political instability is often accom-panied by civil unrest, violence, and even war. In 1905, a depression in Russia and a war with Japan was crippling the Russian economy, and so a priest led thousands of protesters to march on the tsar's palace. The tsar, Nicholas II, panicked and ordered his army to fire on the crowd; hundreds of Russians were killed or wounded. In 1989, when tens of thousands of students gathered in Tiananmen Square in protest, the government responded by using military force to clear the square, killing hundreds. In 2009, when widespread protests about an unfair election in Iran threatened the government, the Iranian leadership imprisoned hundreds of protest leaders and shut down virtually all mass media for weeks.

You get the idea.

In a democracy, the most powerful people in the country regularly trade power back and forth between them. This alternation of power helps to build a culture of cooperation and reduces incentives for anyone to get too greedy. In nondemocracies, power is only transferred with the death or retirement of the previous ruler(s), and every succession is a potential civil war. Moreover, when economic crisis or social turmoil creates a popular demand for change, democracies can easily respond by "voting the bums out." In nondemocracies, there may be plenty of bums, but no elections to get rid of them. Elections act like a release valve. Without them, pressure will build and societies are more likely to explode.

What's a Dictator to Do?

Releasing the Pressure

In the late 1780s, France was faced with a crippling national debt and was having trouble managing the country's numerous crises. In particular, veterans from France's many wars weren't receiving their pensions, and the government also found itself unable to deal with a wave of crop failures that caused a spike in the price of bread. Meanwhile, the nobility was widely resented because they were exempt from all taxation, and King Louis XVI and his wife, Marie Antoinette, were widely perceived as out of touch with the French people. What happened? Widespread food riots resulted in the destruction of many noble estates; veterans rioted in the streets of Paris; and peasants began to hoard food and weapons—in short, widespread civil unrest. The king tried to get the nobility to pay more taxes but they refused, and the French middle class responded by forming their own government and encouraging open rebellion against the throne. The result was revolution.

Louis XVI probably tried his best, but ultimately, the people of France demanded change of a rigid, inflexible government. The monarch and the nobility were so entrenched in their positions that they could not properly respond to the economic crisis. The French people were so desperate for "change" that they turned their government over to the murderous Robespierre and the power-hungry Napoleon.

Surely the French royalty and nobility could have handled the situation better. But before we pin too much blame on poor Louis, put yourself in the shoes of the absolute dictator of a country in crisis. (We'll call you an absolute dictator instead of a monarch, just so that you don't have any pesky nobility to get in your way.) Maybe the crisis is of your own making, maybe it's not. It doesn't really matter; all countries sometimes go through periods of crisis. What really matters is that you rule over increasingly unhappy people. Strikes and protests are popping up across the country as your citizens struggle to make their voices heard. This chaos and instability is causing increased criticism of the government, both internationally and also among some groups who used to be friendly to your regime. As a result of the crisis and the criticism, your regime is collapsing. What do you do? Your options look something like those given in figure 6.1.

Let's go through these options, starting with the top. Your first decision is whether or not to even try to hold onto power. After all, you could simply use the crisis as an excuse to flee the country. Sadly, retirement does have its downsides. First, there is the obvious problem that you would no longer be in charge, and presumably you liked being in charge. Second, there is no political mechanism by which you can step down and still guarantee the physical and economic security of yourself, your family, and the many people who worked for you. If you lose power, then you and

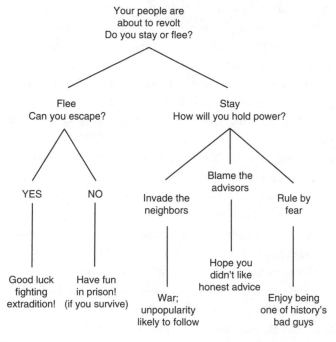

Figure 6.1
A dictator's dilemma.

your followers will be completely at the whim of whoever steps up next. Maybe they will promise to hold democratic elections and guarantee that the members of the old regime will not fall victim to a political witch hunt. Unfortunately for you, most drastic regime changes lead to the harassment, imprisonment, exile, and sometimes even execution of those who used to be in power.

Just look at the Communist leaders who were toppled when the Iron Curtain fell in the late 1980s: Poland's Wojciech Jaruzelski has been charged with multiple war crimes and has only avoided imprisonment owing to his poor health; East Germany's Erich Honecker was convicted of treason, released when diagnosed with terminal lung cancer, and died in exile in Chile; Bulgaria's Todor Zhivkov was arrested and imprisoned; Romania's Nicolae Ceauşescu was executed within days of the coup that took down his government; Albania's Ramiz Alia went to prison for five years . . . you get the point. Most fallen dictators face exile, imprisonment, or death.

Even people who were loyal to the previous regime, but not actually in charge, can face persecution after a regime change. For instance, Nova Scotia experienced a dramatic influx of immigrants from the United States during the 1780s and 1790s. Why? Because in the United States those who had been prominently allied with the British during the Revolutionary War found themselves subject to harassment. They faced the threat of petty violence and vandalism, their neighbors boycotted their shops, and they were mocked and ostracized in their own communities. Eventually many of them fled to Canada.

So let's say that you do manage to flee the country and that you aren't bothered too much by leaving your former supporters to feel the wrath of the new regime. You still need to be wary of extradition. Just ask Alberto Fujimori of Peru what can go wrong. Fujimori was elected president of a newly created Peruvian democracy in 1990, only to declare himself "President for Life." A decade later, he was forced out of power and fled to Japan. The Peruvian regime demanded that he be returned to Peru to face trial for human rights abuses and embezzlement. Japan refused to extradite him, but in 2005 Fujimori traveled to Chile where he was arrested, extradited to Peru, and convicted.

If that doesn't sound like the retirement you had hoped for, perhaps we should consider your alternatives. You're the dictator: There must be some way that you can try to hold onto power! And as you can see from figure

6.1, there are a few possibilities, although we should warn you that all of these methods benefit your regime at the expense of your people.

Option 1: Rally around the Flag

You could start a war to try to take advantage of the "rally around the flag" effect to stay in power. The rally around the flag effect is simply the observation that political leaders often get a substantial bump in popularity any time that their countries go to war or are the victims of external aggression. For example, George W. Bush had a job approval rating of 51 percent the week before September 11, 2001, according to Gallup. The week after the 9/11 attacks, his approval rating jumped 35 points to 86 percent. When the United States invaded Iraq in March 2003, Bush's approval rating jumped 13 points, from 58 percent to 71 percent, within a one-week period. Or we can look at Jimmy Carter in 1979. His Gallup poll approval rating hovered around 30 percent most of that year; in the weeks after Iranian students captured hostages at the American Embassy there, his approval rating jumped to over 50 percent. Please note that we are not proposing that the popularity boost was the purpose of the Iraq invasion or that Bush or Carter had anything to do with those acts of terrorism. Yet it is undeniable that President Bush received popularity boosts from both the 9/11 attacks and the invasion of Iraq, and that Carter received a boost from the Iranian Hostage Crisis.

These popularity bursts make a lot of sense: International wars and foreign policy crises are often accompanied by an upsurge in patriotic feelings, while opponents of a regime tend to back off a bit, to avoid being labeled as somehow sympathetic to the enemy. But if you are trying to use this effect to maintain power by starting a war, you should be wary. First, political scientists have noted that being attacked generally leads to larger boosts than initiating attacks against other countries; notice that Bush got a much larger spike after 9/11 than after launching the Iraq War. Second, these effects on popularity are very temporary. Carter received his boost in late 1979, but Reagan still beat him in 1980. The boost that Bush received from 9/11 was notable both in terms of its strength and longevity, and yet two years later his popularity had dipped to pre-9/11 levels. And it only took four months for Bush's popularity to drop to its prewar levels after the start of the Iraq War. Finally, war is a very risky thing to gamble on. Take the Iraq War: Although the war led to a short-term boost in Bush's popularity, it also contributed to his extremely low popularity numbers during his second term.

Of course, despite these problems, there have been political leaders who have tried to start wars in order to benefit from this effect—to distract people from economic, social, or political turmoil at home. For instance, in 1982 an unpopular Argentinian military regime invaded the nearby British-controlled Falkland Islands. The resulting war ended disastrously for the Argentinians. The British successfully retook the islands, defeated the Argentinian fleet, and the Argentinian military regime fell apart.

The rally around the flag effect failed the Argentinians for two basic reasons. First, people may feel a surge in patriotism at the beginning of wars, but in general peace is cheaper and leaves more of their children alive. Second, all wars are risky, many wars are unpopular no matter how successful they are, and people especially hate losing them. Starting a war may cause your people to forget their problems for a day, but in the long run they will most likely hate you all the more.

Option 2: Shifting the Blame

So maybe it's not such a great idea to blame a foreign country for your nation's problems. You could always blame your advisors instead. Trump up some charges of incompetence or treason against the other people who are running the government, probably those who have disagreed with you or questioned your wisdom. Publicly express your shock and betrayal at their insidious deeds, and have those people imprisoned or executed. You should also make sure to change a few of the country's key economic policies; between that and the change in leadership, that might be enough to placate the crowds.

Unfortunately, there are problems with this course of action as well. Drastic changes in government policies often cause as many problems as they fix. Moreover, you are unlikely to get honest opinions from any of your advisors ever again.

For instance, during Stalin's rule of the USSR, he repeatedly purged his top political and military advisors. Eventually, the only people left around him were terrified of any independent thought or action. Nikolai Bukharin, for example, was one of Stalin's most loyal followers during the party skirmishes that followed Lenin's death in 1924. Bukharin was also one of the most powerful supporters of the Soviet Union's New Economic Policy

(NEP), a broad-based plan for economic development in the 1920s that allowed farmers to sell grain in local markets. Then a grain shortage in 1928 led Stalin to abandon the NEP in favor of widespread collectivization of farms. When Bukharin protested, Stalin had him removed from the Communist Party, and eventually Bukharin was executed on trumped-up charges. Meanwhile, many of the most successful farmers under the NEP rules were arrested and blamed for the grain shortage. The lesson to Russians everywhere was clear: Don't oppose Stalin and don't trust him. Collectivization led to a dramatic drop in grain production, but no one stepped up to oppose it; in fact, official publications became unanimous in their praise of the program.

Stalin isn't the only leader to have tried this tactic. In 1958, Mao Zedong was concerned with China's economic development. So he instituted the Great Leap Forward, a disastrous economic policy that resulted in widespread famine. When a national war hero, Peng Dehuai, expressed concern about the starvation, he was purged from the party along with anyone else who even mentioned that there was a famine. This purge quieted dissent temporarily, although it caused several prominent members of the Chinese government to begin to question Mao's leadership (most notably Deng Xiaoping, who would rule China after Mao's death). During the early 1960s, this group managed to convince the Chinese Communist Party to quietly reverse many of the Great Leap Forward's programs. Mao responded by beginning a series of public campaigns for "education" and "cultural development" that effectively increased his own public status at the expense of his political enemies. That movement evolved into the "Cultural Revolution," in which angry rioters were encouraged to attack various high-ranking officials who had fallen out of Mao's favor. These leaders would then be arrested and either imprisoned or executed. This policy helped to placate the crowds and simultaneously strengthened Mao's power, but it also caused quite a bit of chaos and instability. Moreover, it quashed any remaining dissent from within the party that could have checked the excesses of Mao's rule. Just like in the USSR, blaming the advisors helped the dictator to stay in power, but his country was the worse off for his actions.

Option 3: The Iron Fist
If scapegoating your advisors doesn't sound like a good idea, there is a third possibility: Create a police state and rule by fear. For instance, the

government could declare martial law; imprison, exile, or kill any prominent dissenters; encourage neighbors to report each other to the police;
and so on. In one form or another, terrorizing your own people is one of
the most common strategies used by autocrats throughout history to keep
power: Ivan the Terrible, Vlad the Impaler, Hitler, and Pol Pot, just to name
a few. Mass terror can keep dictators in power, but once again the cost for
your people is very high. Living in constant fear stifles innovation, can
decrease productivity, and even has negative long-term health effects. Also,
you will demand that your people lose their lives, their liberties, and their
happiness just so that you can keep your job.

No matter what course a dictator takes to stay in power, it will massively
disrupt the country's economy. Every single one of those strategies diverts
resources from improving the lives of citizens toward ensuring the political
stability of an unpopular regime. And every single one of those ideas inherently limits the freedoms and liberties of the citizenry. When times are
bad, people want changes in their leadership, and nondemocracies are
unable to respond without hurting their own citizens.

What's a Protestor to Do?

Raging Against the Machine
To this point we've focused on the actions of the guy in charge, but let's
not forget that there are plenty of people who are out of power but who
would like to be in charge. In nondemocracies the opposition can do
almost as much damage to a people's happiness and well-being as the
country's rulers.

So remember back to the chapter on procedural justice. When people
have a say in the process they are more likely to be productive, law-abiding
citizens. And when they don't have a say in the process? Well, like those
English suffragettes that we mentioned earlier, they can cause trouble.

So this time think of yourself as the leader of a group of particularly
oppressed people—an opposition leader in an autocratic country. (A similar
logic applies to oppressed minorities in democratic countries, a point
that we will discuss later.) You know that you cannot hope to influence
the system through "normal" channels. Most autocrats and dictators
don't take criticism too well—see the previous section about the imprisonment or execution of political rivals. There are no elections available
for you to run in, no political polling to express your opinions, and no

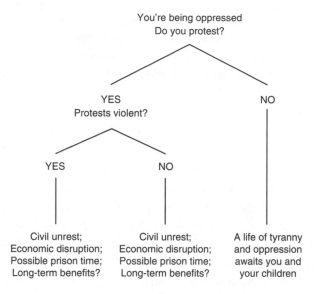

Figure 6.2
Fighting oppression.

representatives that you can effectively lobby. So how do you influence the political process?

As you can see from figure 6.2, one possibility is to encourage your followers toward peaceful civil disobedience. You can organize protests, marches, strikes, and other public demonstrations, demanding political change. It is easy for us to think of those things as fairly benign. But after days and weeks of disrupting traffic, shutting down factories and farms, preventing goods from being delivered to stores, such activities can become more than a minor annoyance. Think about it: How many truckloads of food are delivered every day to keep a city fed? How many truckloads of garbage are carted away every week? What would happen then if all the truck drivers in a country went on strike for three weeks? Or if groups of people blocked the major highways in and out of town, causing those trucks consistently to be delayed? As you can imagine, even the most peaceful demonstrations can quickly escalate into a huge problem.

A number of the great leaders of the twentieth century directed peaceful protest movements on behalf of oppressed groups, including Lech Walesa in Poland (protesting Communist rule), Mahatma Gandhi in India (protesting British rule), and Martin Luther King, Jr., in the American South (protesting Jim Crow laws). But although these men are rightfully lauded for their long-term contributions to peace and freedom, in each case the short-term result was a lot of turmoil for their societies. For instance, the Montgomery, Alabama, bus boycott was a hardship on the citizens of Montgomery. Black citizens were forced to find alternate means of transportation and often faced harassment for doing so. Meanwhile, whites had to contend with massive cutbacks in bus service (which was hit financially by the decrease in ridership) and an economic slump caused by a drop in the number of black shoppers. The boycott also touched off a wave of extremist violence from white racist organizations, including multiple bombings of the homes and churches of black leaders. The boycott was a great moment in American history, but also a very hard time to live in Montgomery.

Of course, not all protests are peaceful. Instead of coordinating letter writing campaigns, marches, and public speeches, you could coordinate bombings, assassinations, and terrorist strikes. The violent option was chosen by the Irish Republican Army (protesting British rule), the African National Congress (protesting apartheid in South Africa), and the National Liberation Front (protesting French rule in Algeria), among others. These protests are just as disruptive to a nation's economy as their peaceful counterparts, and have the additional consequence of causing civilian deaths.

In the long run, fighting oppression and tyranny may make the world a better place if your protest movement is successful. But peaceful or not, your actions will cause a lot of short-term pain and hardship for the very people you are trying to help. If you lived in a democracy, you would have the option of changing society through significantly less disruptive means. Nondemocracies deny you that opportunity.

There have certainly been many instances of violent and disruptive protests in democratic countries. The difference is in degree. Strikes, protests, and terrorist acts in democratic nations tend to be isolated events aimed at particular goals. Workers strike for higher wages, greater benefits, and fewer hours; protestors march against particular government policies or court actions; fanatics commit violent acts to further their particular aims; and of course, criminals of all types will use instability of any kind to cover up or justify their antisocial behavior. And democratic governments do sometimes respond with excessive force, even occasionally leading to the deaths of protestors. But those events do not tend to cause the dramatic disruption that can occur when a section of the population rises up against an autocratic ruler, who responds with a wave of arrests or violence.

In fact, the worst protests in democracies tend to come as a direct result of a group's oppression. The United States in 1960 was a democracy, but the Jim Crow laws guaranteed that the African American population in the South was denied access to the political system. Similarly, Britain and France were democratic throughout the twentieth century, but their colonial policies disenfranchised many people and led to open rebellion in their colonies. In each of those cases, a democratic state exercised autocratic control over an oppressed group.

In democracies, elections allow people to express their discontent through their ballots. In nondemocracies, the only way to change the system is to disrupt the economy. Especially in the short term, the opposition is forced to weaken the country.

Succession Failures

Not all crises stem from economic or social turmoil. Sometimes the problems are purely political. In fact, in a nondemocracy, every regime change is a potentially debilitating crisis.

In a democracy, new governments come along every few years. In nondemocracies, power transitions are much less common—usually only when the heads of the previous regime die or retire (either by choice or by force). In a democracy, regular elections and the establishment of pro-democratic beliefs and traditions ensure smooth transitions. Nondemocracies have to do things a little differently. Historically, guaranteeing the smooth transition of power from one regime to another is one of the most difficult things that a regime has to do. If the transition goes poorly, the results are bad: economic chaos, riots, civil war, or foreign invasion. To avoid that, nondemocracies have usually transferred power in one of four ways:

Heir apparent Power is transferred automatically to the nearest living (usually male) relative. This works fine if everything goes right: The king has a son, dies about twenty years later, and his eldest son takes charge. But things can get problematic if the king has only daughters, if the king doesn't have any children at all, if the king lives too long and his children become impatient, if the king dies while the son is still a young child, if the king has illegitimate children, or if the eldest son is especially cruel, incompetent, or insane.

Oligarchic elections   In the pre-Roman German tradition, every time a king died a group of the most powerful men in the kingdom would gather together and elect the next monarch. This tradition was carried forward in the Holy Roman Empire. Of course, the problem is that small groups of men (even powerful men) can easily be bullied or bribed. Repeated allegations of bullying or bribery can undercut any sense of widespread legitimacy. As we will discuss later, the loss of legitimacy can make it more likely that the losers of those elections will resort to violence to take power.

Contest   The Ottoman Empire actually embraced chaotic successions. The Sultan would appoint all of his sons to be governors of different provinces when they came of age. The sons would then attempt to subvert and/or assassinate each other during their father's lifetime. When the old Sultan died, the remaining sons would struggle against each other to succeed the father. The next Sultan would be the last man standing. It worked better than you might think, but we doubt that anyone would seriously argue that encouraging violence among potential heirs to the throne is a healthy way to run a modern nation-state.

Selection   In some countries, the heir to the throne is chosen by the previous monarch. During the height of the Roman Empire, emperors were chosen in this manner. Before their death, an emperor would "adopt" an heir, presumably picking the most capable man for the job. It worked well five times, from Nerva to Marcus Aurelius. But disaster struck when Marcus Aurelius chose his natural born son, Commodus, to succeed him. Although the Russell Crowe *Gladiator* version of these events is historical nonsense, there has been a lot of historical consternation about how a great man like Marcus Aurelius could choose to name his own son, the obviously incompetent Commodus, as heir. The obvious answer, of course, is that even great men can be bad judges of the character of their own children. And that's a huge problem: An entire society can be thrown into turmoil because a man is overly fond of his son. The other issue with this type of system is that sometimes emperors die unexpectedly. If the emperor dies without selecting an heir, chaos will ensue.

What's a President to Do?

The Thin Line between a Straitjacket and a Crown

Of course, no system of government is perfect, and democracies do fail. New democracies in particular seem prone to failure. We've already mentioned Alberto Fujimori of Peru, who was democratically elected only to declare himself President for Life. Unfortunately, there have been a number of self-declared presidents for life over the last two centuries of democratic experiments. So why don't all democracies collapse in that way? Once invested with power, why don't all leaders refuse to give it up? Why do we continue to hold elections and abide by their results?

To answer this question, we need to first delve a little deeper into the concept of legitimacy. So with that in mind, here is a fun experiment that you can try at home: When you wake up tomorrow, declare yourself king or queen. Start referring to yourself with the royal "we." ("We would like our breakfast now.") Insist that your family and friends wait on you hand and foot and refer to you as "your royal highness." Quit your job and levy taxes on your neighbors to pay for your lavish lifestyle. On second thought, don't try this experiment unless you're willing to find yourself under psychiatric evaluation.

So what's the difference between you and Louis-Dieudonné? More commonly known as Louis XIV of France, he was one of Europe's most powerful monarchs and one of history's most notorious gluttons. He relied on the people around him to do everything for him, often even demanding that high nobles serve as his personal valets (not exactly a glamorous job in an age before indoor plumbing). Anyone who refused his whims was subject to some very harsh punishment.

So why was Louis XIV able to get away with it, whereas you can't? Legitimacy. People believed that Louis XIV was the rightful and legitimate king of France. His soldiers believed it. His bureaucrats believed it. If anyone challenged that rule . . . well, there were plenty of soldiers and bureaucrats to deal with the disloyal. Legitimacy is really just a type of self-fulfilling prophecy: If we all believe that Louis is king, then we all act like he's king, which effectively makes Louis king. If we all act like Louis is just some crazy Frenchman, then we all treat him like some crazy Frenchman, and then Louis is just a strange guy wearing a crown.

Democracies are not ruled by monarchs, but their leaders still must maintain legitimacy in order to govern. Imagine that a president who had just lost an election wanted to take drastic, unconstitutional action in order to hold onto his office. Well, even the president of the United States cannot act alone. He relies on thousands of aides, staff, security, and civil servants to carry out his wishes, not to mention the courts, the police, and the military. For the president to carry out a coup like that, he would need the support of all of those groups. As long as the vast majority of that larger group of people believes in the fundamental legitimacy of the democratic institutions, then the president's coup would fail.

Of course, the particular institutions may vary. In the United States, we believe in the primacy of the Constitution and in the power of courts to interpret and enforce the Constitution. In Great Britain, there is no written constitution. When the British refer to their constitution, they are referring to two things: (1) the primacy of the English Parliament to make decisions for the good of the country and (2) the unwritten understanding that there are certain actions that even Parliament should not take without dire need. Americans sometimes shake their heads at the British system because they don't have a written constitution—but the U.S. Constitution is just a two hundred-year-old piece of paper. The paper is important only because we all believe in what it says and in what it represents. The Articles of Confederation were ratified in 1781 and served as the precursor to the Constitution. And yet, the Articles no longer have the authority of the Constitution, despite being an older piece of paper signed by an equally prestigious group of Founding Fathers. It isn't the age or nature of the Constitution that provides its power, but rather its legitimacy.[1]

In other words, democracies transfer power smoothly between different rulers because everyone believes that power is supposed to be transferred smoothly. Democratic traditions and beliefs simply set expectations about the future. Those expectations lead the people within a democracy to believe that the winner of an election will become the next president. As

---

1. We should note that there are many different elements that go into making a democracy "legitimate" or otherwise providing stability to a democratic regime, including many cultural norms such as tolerance of different opinions, obedience to the rule of law, civic engagement, and the rights of minority interests.

a result of that belief, those people take the steps necessary to ensure a smooth transition—and will oppose any individual who tries to interfere with that transition.

Al Gore as Revolutionary?

So let's revisit the controversial *Bush v. Gore* decision that effectively handed the 2000 presidential election to George W. Bush. Al Gore certainly wanted to be president. He strongly disagreed with both the logic and the result of the Supreme Court decision that forced a stop to the Florida recounts and handed Bush the victory. There were many Constitutional lawyers who agreed that it was a poor decision, and basically all Democrats agreed that it was a bad result. So why did Al Gore give up?

What else could he do? A strong norm in our society is to adhere to the rulings of the courts. A *norm* is simply a sociological term for a cultural rule. In this case, the norm is that the courts are the final arbiters of the most important controversies in our lives and that court rulings must be followed. That is not a Constitutional doctrine, by the way. Nowhere in the U.S. Constitution does it give the Supreme Court the power to overrule Congress or to decide the outcome of disputed presidential elections. Yet many social scientists would argue that the norm of obeying judges is so ingrained in our society that functionally we have no choice in the matter. Al Gore lost when he argued his case in front of the highest court in the land; to fight against that decision would be to ask a huge group of people to push back against a deeply ingrained norm. The prophecy demanded self-fulfillment.

Besides, what's so bad about losing an election? The Democrats were certainly disappointed that they lost the 2000 election, Al Gore in particular. But the losers of that election did pretty well for themselves in the long run. Al Gore went on to be a college professor, star in an Oscar-winning documentary about global warming, and win a Nobel Peace Prize. The Democrats got beat up pretty badly by the Bush team for a couple years, but by 2006 they controlled Congress and by 2008 they were back in control of the White House. Losses in democracies are temporary: Political parties live to fight again, and the individual candidates can often earn more money (and sometimes prestige) in the private sector anyway. In other words, not only are there strong cultural norms that push candidates to play by the rules, but there are also strong practical incentives that

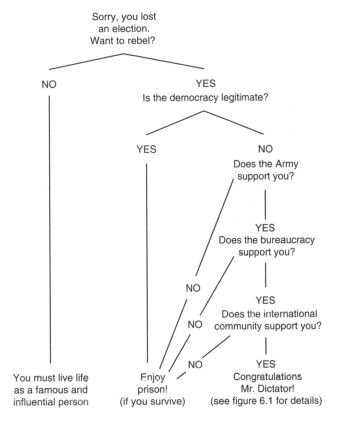

Figure 6.3
Democratic stability.

reward good behavior. Figure 6.3 shows the different options for the recent loser of a presidential election.

So think back to the 2008 presidential election, in which Barack Obama defeated John McCain in the race to succeed George W. Bush. The Republican Party could have refused to hand over power, but that action would have been very risky. First, although there are more generals, soldiers, police, and judges who vote Republican than vote Democratic, it is not at all clear that those people would support a conservative coup d'état. If the political leadership were to attempt a coup and not get enough support, they would find themselves imprisoned and on trial for treason. If it were to become public knowledge that the leaders of the GOP were even considering such an action, it could effectively end their political careers. Or to put it another way, attempting a coup would have stripped the GOP of their legitimacy as rulers.

On the other hand, there are much lower costs involved in respecting the election outcomes. Republicans spent the next few years trying to slow down the progress of any legislative program they disagreed with, and forced some pretty major compromises on most of Obama's key legislative programs. They won control of the House of Representatives in the 2010 elections, and there is a decent chance that they will be back in the White House once Obama's term is up anyway. As for John McCain? He's still a widely respected senator.

The Greatest Man in the World

But what if the democracy is not well established? What is to keep the leaders of a new democracy from just refusing to hand power over to their political rivals?

This is a question that all new democracies must face. King George III of England was once asked if he thought that George Washington would actually step down and turn the army back over to a powerless American Congress. King George replied, "If he does that, he will be the greatest man in the world." The new American democratic institutions did not have a lot of legitimacy: King George knew it, George Washington knew it, and surely the heads of the Continental Congress knew it. But Washington stepped down anyway, which gave Congress time to demonstrate its ability to govern, and preserved American democracy.

Most democracies have a number of false starts before finding their George Washington. France had democratic experiments fail twice, with two different Napoleons declaring themselves emperor. England's Parliament thought that they were taking charge after executing Charles I, only to see power fall to the tyrannical Oliver Cromwell. Germany's Weimar Constitution was considered a model for the rest of the world to emulate, until the Nazis got themselves elected and Hitler took over. Until a democracy has established some legitimacy independent of the individuals who run the country, it is extremely vulnerable to the rise of populist dictators.

This problem has led one group to establish a reward for the heads of new democracies who retire in accordance with their respective constitutions. The Mo Ibrahim Foundation awards the Ibrahim Prize of $5 million to "a democratically elected former African Executive Head of State or Government who has served their term in office within the limits set by the country's constitution and has left office in the last three years." If the leader does manage to play a positive role in his country's political scene after he retires, he can receive another $200,000 each year for the next decade. The idea is to make the retirement option more appealing than the dictator option for young democracies, until a pro-democratic norm can be established. Then the norm can reinforce itself.[2]

Finally, we should note that even if you overthrow an illegitimate regime, there is no guarantee that your coup will be successful. New regimes can be brought down by many different factors. For instance, it is important for new regimes to maintain the support of their country's army and gain at least some support from the international community; after all, it's hard to maintain power when some unfriendly group has rolled tanks into your capital, whether those tanks belong to your country or to someone else's. It's also hard to maintain power if you can't convince the people who manage the daily operations of the government to work on behalf of your regime. Taking power is risky, even if you are replacing an unpopular regime. And if you're trying to wrest control in an established, legitimate democracy, retirement starts to look pretty appealing.

The Importance of Smooth Transitions

Government by Lottery

Being able to transition power smoothly, in good times or bad, is a huge advantage for democracies. In fact, some have even argued that it is the only important difference between democracies and nondemocracies. These theorists point to many of the same problems that we discussed in Part I to try to argue that we can get rid of this whole "will of the people" myth altogether and find a way to maintain regular power transitions without the bother of a popular election.

There are two common proposals for what this postdemocratic government might look like. One possibility is to adapt an idea first used in

---

2. Some new democracies have also attempted to develop these norms of democratic legitimacy and power sharing by consciously establishing power-sharing arrangements between dominant political factions, although these arrangements have met with mixed success.

ancient Athens called *sortition*. To fill some of their offices, the Athenians would hold a lottery to choose random citizens. The chosen citizens would then be forced into public service until their term expired, at which time someone else would be chosen. So imagine that you were asked to serve in Congress the same way that you are called to jury duty. Political scientist Robert Dahl has proposed that modern democracies could use this method to choose their legislatures and thereby eliminate many of the corrupting influences of popular elections. Under a sortition system, no one "runs" for president or Congress. Special interests could no longer purchase influence through "campaign contributions," and we would all save a lot of time, money, and energy not having to worry about campaigning.

The other possibility, which has been proposed by political philosopher Bruce Ackerman among others, is called *lottery voting*. Under this proposal, all voters would indicate their preferred candidate on their ballot, just like in normal democratic elections. But no ballots would be counted. Instead, a single random ballot would be selected, and whomever was chosen on that ballot would be elected. In this case, you would still get campaigns by people who wanted to be in power; after all, if you want to be president then you can maximize your chances by having your name appear on as many ballots as possible. The advantage is that, in the long run, this system does a better job than standard representative democracy at advancing the concerns of large minorities. In our system, majorities rule, and they can consistently ignore the wishes of even large minorities. Under lottery voting, large minorities would have a decent chance of having their candidates picked, and their policies enacted.

Both of these systems allow for the regular and smooth transition of power, even in times of social or economic turbulence. They just try to do away with the craziness of elections and voter bias. But ultimately, both of them are bad ideas because transitioning power smoothly is not the only advantage of a democracy. By ignoring those other advantages, we can easily create more problems than we would solve.

The Importance of Process

Just as one example, both the sortition and lottery voting methods fall short on most measures of procedural justice. Procedural justice, if you remember, is the idea that people are more likely to cooperate and behave if they believe that the rules are fair. Part of this fairness is the ability to have input and to influence the outcomes. In other words, one of the great benefits of democracy is that people get to participate in the process and they can feel like their votes really matter. Both of these proposals fail to make average citizens feel like an important part of the political process.

In the sortition system, individuals are chosen randomly to serve in Congress; in the lottery, a small group of individuals are selected at random to choose the members of Congress. In our current system, when Congress acts, every citizen bears some responsibility for choosing the people who made that decision. If you hate your representative or senator, then you have the option to work for the opposition's campaign in the next election. But win or lose, you had an impact on the race and your voice was heard. Now compare that to the connection you feel to juries, which are composed of randomly selected groups of people. Do you feel responsible for the actions of juries in your area? We surely like to second guess those jurors who freed O.J. Simpson or who gave a $2.65 million verdict to a woman who spilled coffee on herself (*Leibeck v. McDonald's*). But we don't feel that we had any say in the selection of those juries or any ability to influence the decisions that they came to.

Moreover, the selection processes themselves, no matter how perfectly designed, will surely be called into question. Both systems allow for people to be selected as leaders who are either grossly unqualified or indifferent to the "honor" of being chosen. These factors are bound to seem unfair to many people. Besides which, all truly random selection mechanisms go through periods where they seem anything but random. If you flip a coin enough times, you will get streaks of 6 or 7 heads in a row. (As of the writing of this book the NFC has won fourteen consecutive opening coin tosses in the Super Bowl!) Play enough hands of poker, and you will go through periods where it feels like every other hand contains a straight or full house, while at other times you will go a dozen hands in a row and see nothing better than a low pair. In the same way, a randomly selected Congress will at times contain shockingly small percentages of some particular ethnic group, gender, or political party. At other times, the randomly selected Congress will contain people under indictment for severe criminal behavior or people who believe that the right way to solve all of America's problems is through the use of nuclear weapons. Those events, even though they are "expected," will surely cause many people to question the inherent fairness of the system.

Democracies have a huge advantage because they ensure smooth transitions of power, but it would be a mistake to assume that any system of government which solves the power transition problem will do just as well.

Summary

In democratic countries, elections allow for regular, orderly, and peaceful successions, in good times or bad. Nondemocracies simply do not have that luxury. Successions are times of instability and chaos. Economic crises can cause widespread government crackdowns and inhibit both economic growth and individual liberty. And opposition groups are forced to create further instability in order to protest government policies. Democracies may be flawed, but they are uniquely capable of responding to turmoil and crisis, and even of dramatically changing themselves, without widespread chaos or violence.

References

Lead Quote
Wallace, M. 1958. Interview with Aldous Huxley, May 18. Retrieved March 25, 2011 from   http://www.hrc.utexas.edu/multimedia/video/2008/wallace/huxley_aldous _t.html.

Transitions to Democracy
Haggard, S., and R. P. Kaufman. 1995. *The Political Economy of Democratic Transitions*. Princeton, NJ: Princeton University Press.

Olson, M. 2000. *Power and Prosperity: Outgrowing Communist and Capitalist Dictatorships*. New York: Basic Books.

Roeder, P. G. 1993. *Red Sunset: The Failure of Soviet Politics*. Princeton, NJ: Princeton University Press.

Wood, E. J. 2000. *Forging Democracy from Below: Insurgent Transitions in South Africa and El Salvador*. Cambridge: Cambridge University Press.

Rebellion against Autocratic Regimes
Bendix, R. 1978. *Kings of People: Power and the Mandate to Rule*. Berkeley, CA: University of California Press.

Gurr, T. R. 2000. *Peoples versus States: Minorities at Risk in the New Century*. Washington, D.C.: United States Institute of Peace Press.

Magangna, V. 1991. *Communities of Grain: Rural Rebellion in Comparative Perspective.* Cornell, NY: Cornell University Press.

Mann, M. 1993. *The Sources of Social Power,* vol. 2: *The Rise of Classes and Nation-States, 1760–1914.* Cambridge: Cambridge University Press.

Moore, B. 1966. *Social Origins of Dictatorship and Democracy: Lord and Peasant in the Making of the Modern World.* Boston: Beacon Press.

Popkin, S. 1972. *The Rational Peasant: The Political Economy of Rural Society in Vietnam.* Berkeley, CA: University of California Press.

Scott, J. C. 1987. *Weapons of the Weak: Everyday Forms of Peasant Resistance.* New Haven, CT: Yale University Press.

Rally around the Flag Effect

Baker, W. D., and J. R. Oneal. 2001. Patriotism or opinion leadership: The nature and origins of the "rally 'round the flag" effect. *Journal of Conflict Resolution* 45 (5):661–687.

Chiozza, G., and H. E. Goemans. 2003. Peace through insecurity: Tenure and international conflict. *Journal of Conflict Resolution* 47 (4):443–467.

Mueller, J. E. 1973. *War, Presidents, and Public Opinion.* New York: Wiley.

Richards, D., T. C. Morgan, R. Wilson, V. Schwebach, and G. Young. 1993. Good times, bad times, and the diversionary use of force: A tale of some not-so-free agents. *Journal of Conflict Resolution* 37 (3):504–535.

Roper Center Public Opinion Archives. 2011. Presidential approval. University of Connecticut. Retrieved March 25, 2011 from http://webapps.ropercenter.uconn .edu/CFIDE/roper/presidential/webroot/presidential_rating.cfm.

American Revolution

Boaz, D. 2006. The man who would not be king. CATO Institute. Retrieved March 25, 2011, from http://www.cato.org/pub_display.php?pub_id=5593.

USHistory.org. 2011. When does the revolution end: The Loyalists. US History Online Textbook. Retrieved March 25, 2011, from http://www.ushistory.org/us/13c .asp.

Peru

New York Times. 2009. Times Topic: Alberto K. Fujimori. Retrieved March 25, 2011, from http://topics.nytimes.com/topics/reference/timestopics/people/f/alberto_k _fujimori/index.html.

Falklands War
Hickman, K. N.d. The Falklands War: An overview. Retrieved March 25, 2011, from http://militaryhistory.about.com/od/battleswars1900s/p/falklands.htm.

French Revolution
Furey, F. 1995. *Revolutionary France, 1770–1880*. Translated by Antonia Nevill. Oxford: Blackwell.

Jordan, D. P. 1979. *The King's Trial: Louis XVI vs. The French Revolution*. Berkeley, CA: University of California Press.

Peaceful Protests
Ash, T. G. 2002. *The Polish Revolution: Solidarity*, 3rd ed. New Haven: Yale University Press.

Randall, K. 1989. Martin Luther King's Constitution: A legal history of the Montgomery Bus Boycott. *Yale Law Journal* 98 (April): 999–1067. Retrieved March 25, 2011, from http://academic.udayton.edu/race/02rights/Civilrights03b.htm.

Soviet Russia and Stalin
Kershaw, I., and M. Lewin, eds. 1997. *Stalinism and Nazism: Dictatorships in Comparison*. Cambridge: Cambridge University Press.

Riasanovsky, N. V. 2000. *A History of Russia*, 6th ed. Oxford: Oxford University Press.

Mao, the Great Leap Forward, and the Cultural Revolution
Chang, J., and J. Halliday. 2005. *Mao: The Unknown Story*. New York: Anchor Books.

Fairbank, J. K., and M. Goldman. 1992. *China: A New History*. Cambridge: Harvard University Press.

History's Bad Guys
Flexner, S., and D. Flexner. 1992. *The Pessimist's Guide to History*. New York: Avon Books.

Marcus Aurelius and Commodus
Dio, C. 2001 [ca. 229]. *Roman History*, vol. IX, Books 72–73. Trans. Earnest Cary. Loeb Classical Library. Cambridge, MA: Harvard University Press.

Gibbon, E. 1776. *The History of the Decline and Fall of the Roman Empire*, vol. 1, ch. 4. London: Strahan & Cadell.

Ottoman Succession

Quataert, D. 2005. *The Ottoman Empire, 1700–1922*, 2nd ed. Cambridge: Cambridge University Press.

Sortition and Lottery Voting

Ackerman, B. 1991. *Social Justice in the Liberal State*. New Haven, CT: Yale University Press.

Callenbach, E., and M. Phillips. 1985. *A Citizen Legislature*. Berkeley, CA: Banyan Tree Books.

Dahl, R. 1991. *Democracy and Its Critics*. New Haven, CT: Yale University Press.

7 Overcoming Our Weaknesses

So, two cheers for Democracy: one because it admits variety and two because it permits criticism.

—E. M. Forster

Ignorance Is Bliss

Which has more people: San Diego or San Antonio? It's a tough question, isn't it? San Antonio is a large Texas city with an NBA team (the Spurs), a famous historical landmark (the Alamo), and is renowned for its River Walk and its close ties to Mexican culture. San Diego is a large California city with both an NFL team (the Chargers) and a MLB team (the Padres), the Legoland amusement park, and is renowned for its zoo and its beaches. There are good reasons to pick either one. In 2002, psychologist Daniel Goldstein and his colleagues asked this question to both Americans and Germans. The researchers found that only about two-thirds of Americans correctly answered San Diego. But every single one of the Germans got it right. (Of course, since 2002 the population of San Antonio has grown so dramatically that in the 2010 census it actually passed San Diego in population.) So do Germans just know more about American geography than Americans? Is this yet another example of how poorly Americans understand the world?

Actually, no. In fact, for this example it's quite the opposite. The Germans did a lot better because they knew a lot less. Most Germans didn't know whether San Diego had sports teams or particularly nice beaches. They just barely recognized the name. But they didn't know San Antonio at all (it's not that they didn't remember the Alamo—they probably never knew about it to begin with). So while Americans were puzzling over whether a famous zoo or a famous battle is more indicative of a large population, Germans were just trying to decide whether a city that they've heard of is bigger than a city that they hadn't. That's a much easier question. We typically think that more information is better, but sometimes knowing less actually helps us make better decisions.

Crystal Hall, a professor at the University of Washington, and her colleagues have done a number of studies on situations in which knowledge leads people to be less successful. In one study she told people a used car's original value and the age of the car and asked them to guess the value of the car according to *Kelley Blue Book*. Then she also told the same people the mileage on the car and had them make a new guess. People were much more accurate when they knew less: Knowing the mileage made people less accurate by an average of nearly $2,000. The same thing happened with guessing runs allowed by a pitcher in a given baseball game: People did fairly well when they knew the number of hits allowed and walks issued, but when they were also told the number of strikeouts their guesses became worse. And basketball fans did better at predicting the outcomes of games when they only knew the records of the teams and the halftime score than when they were also told the names of the teams. Sometimes having more information only distracts us from what is actually important.

Earlier we learned that voters don't know very much. But sometimes more information is actually a bad thing. In an episode of the television series *King of the Hill*, Hank Hill was determined to vote for George W. Bush for president because Hank thought that Bush was a superb governor. That was until Hank found out that Bush had a bad handshake, which caused him to strongly consider voting for "the other guy" instead. Clearly a candidate's resume is more important than the strength of his grip; more information in this case led Hank to question what (for him) was the right choice—not unlike how knowing about the Spurs made people less likely to guess that San Diego was a larger city than San Antonio.

Voters may not regularly read the newspaper, watch the cable news networks, or listen to National Public Radio, and that will certainly cause them to sometimes ignore important information. Conversely, it also might be helping them to ignore unimportant information. Voters who fail to watch a televised debate might misunderstand the candidates' positions, but they also might not realize that one candidate is significantly taller than the other. Voters may not know much about Guinean bauxite tariffs, but there are very few voters for whom this issue ought to play an important role in their voting decisions. It is an issue that will only serve to distract them. Yes, most of the time, more information is better. Most of the time—but not all the time. Although ignorance may not actually be bliss, there is reason to believe that voter ignorance may not be quite as bad as it may seem.

We have previously discussed how voters are uninformed and irrational, neither of which is traditionally associated with good decision making. But there are several factors that can help to reduce the damage. Or to put it another way, our craziness may not harm democracy quite as much as one might think.

Bioflavonoids for Congress

Which of the following is the healthiest food: broccoli, pretzels, fried eggs, Swiss cheese, raw oysters, or diet soda?

The Yale University Overall Nutritional Quality Index (ONQI) is one of the most comprehensive rating systems for determining how healthy foods are. The ONQI is thorough, taking into account fiber, folate, vitamin A, vitamin C, vitamin D, vitamin E, vitamin B12, vitamin B6, potassium, calcium, zinc, omega-3 fatty acids, bioflavonoids, carotenoids, magnesium, iron, saturated fat, trans fat, sodium, sugar, and cholesterol. And based on this data, the ONQI would tell you that broccoli is, in fact, the healthiest food on that list.

And you correctly chose broccoli, didn't you?

Of course, most of you probably guessed broccoli without knowing how much cholesterol was in an oyster or understanding the carotenoid content of a pretzel. Most people don't know the relevant information (most people don't even know what a carotenoid is), and yet when the time comes to make a decision, most people get the answer right. How is this possible? It turns out that you don't have to know everything to make good choices. People have all sorts of tricks and shortcuts (known to social scientists as *heuristics*) that we use to simplify decisions when the task is overwhelming. In the above case, you may have noted that broccoli is a vegetable and chosen broccoli based on the fact that fruits and vegetables are supposed to be good for you. This fruit and vegetable heuristic sometimes will lead you astray—for example, olives are not as healthy as oysters—but it would give you the right answer over 90 percent of the time.

Political decision making isn't all that different from choosing what to eat. We may not know a lot of the specific policy details, but we make the right mental shortcuts to make reasonably good decisions most of the time. Political scientists Richard Lau and David Redlawsk have shown that despite our ignorance and all the crazy things that influence our votes, our craziness does not cause us to make poor choices nearly as often as we might think. Lau and Redlawsk compared actual votes in five presidential elections from 1972 to 1988 with the candidate that those same voters "should" have voted for based solely on each voter's policy preferences. They discovered that individual voters made the right choice (for them) well over half the time.[1] In other words, we aren't perfect, but heuristics seem to help. Below are descriptions of just a few of the most commonly used heuristics that voters use to improve their decision making.

Forget Me Not

Korsakoff's syndrome is a dreadful illness that leads to severe, specific memory deficits. Patients suffering from Korsakoff's can remember enough words and rules of grammar to carry on a conversation, but shortly thereafter they cannot remember whom they talked to or what was said. They can learn skills, but minutes later will be totally unaware of their new abilities. If they read a funny story, they'll quickly forget the details of the story, or even that they read a story at all, but the positive mood may linger for hours.

In the mid-1980s, SUNY Stony Brook psychologist Marcia Johnson and her colleagues ran an intriguing study on these patients. The patients were shown pictures of two young men and were told events that had supposedly occurred in the young men's lives (although in reality all the events were fictional). One man was described as a rather unsavory character—he stole a car, flunked out of school, and abused his wife. The other man was an upstanding citizen—he got good grades, saved a friend's life, and was a hard worker. Unsurprisingly, three days later the Korsakoff's patients didn't remember much; only 1 in 9 patients reported that they remembered any of the information about the two men. Even when the patients were asked specific questions about the young men (e.g., "Did he ever

---

1. Lau and Redlawsk estimate that people vote "correctly" about 75 percent of the time—which is much higher than the 50 percent one would expect by chance alone.

steal anything?") the patients recalled only around 10 percent of the information.

But despite recalling almost nothing about the two men, when shown the two pictures and asked which person they liked better, they chose the good guy more than 75 percent of the time. That is, even though they couldn't tell you why they preferred the good guy, their positive impression persisted.

Other researchers have since replicated these basic findings with healthy adults. Of course, healthy adults don't forget the facts quite so quickly, but given enough time and distraction, everybody's memory is fallible. Yet even after people forget the details that led to their positive or negative evaluations, the impression lingers on. It turns out that our memory for specific facts isn't great, but those facts influence our emotional reactions, and our emotional reactions persist long after we've forgotten the facts that led us there in the first place. People use these emotional reactions to make decisions about everything from car dealerships to political candidates—a strategy known to psychologists as the *affect heuristic*.

As we've already discussed, people are generally uninformed about the issues and where the candidates stand on those issues—and even when we learn things about those candidates, we quickly forget them. But because of the affect heuristic we do not need to remember all of the specific facts. If Bob McVoter watches a candidate's speech and doesn't like what the candidate has to say about education, then he'll develop a negative view of the candidate. A week later, Bob may have forgotten why he doesn't like the candidate, or where the candidate stands on education, but his emotions still provide an accurate gauge of his preferences. When we follow an affect heuristic, we will actually be basing our decisions on a great deal of information that we've otherwise forgotten.

Of course, this affect heuristic can certainly lead us astray. Many things lead us to develop positive and negative emotional responses to candidates, from music in a campaign ad to physical attractiveness. But although the heuristic isn't perfect it can still allow us to make fairly good decisions without having to keep too much information in mind.

It's My Party, I Can Vote if I Want To

If you ever go to Albertson's grocery store cereal aisle, you'll see Albertson's brand cereals on the shelf right next to their brand-name counterparts.

Kellogg's Rice Krispies sit next to Albertson's Crispy Rice. General Mills' Lucky Charms can be found adjacent to Albertson's Magic Stars. The brand-name cereals and the generic cereals are very similar in appearance, with the most obvious difference being the price. For example, Kellogg's Apple Jacks cost 250 percent more than Albertson's brilliantly named Apple Dapple Cereal.

In 2010, personal finance blogger Len Penzo wondered whether that price difference was reflected in the taste. He put together a blind taste test for a panel of neighborhood kids (and, for some reason, a dog) and tested which cereal was preferred. For the most part, the kids' preferences were split about evenly; that is, the kids didn't like the national brand more than the generic. In fact, Apple Dapple actually beat Apple Jacks. (This result holds even if you exclude the results from the dog, who was apparently excited to eat anything except for Quaker Cinnamon Life.)

If the generic is just as good (or better), why would anybody pay for the more expensive product? Because the more expensive product has a brand name. In the early 1990s, New York University Business School professor Durairaj Maheswaran and his colleagues investigated the *brand name heuristic*. It turns out that when decisions are complicated or people are unmotivated, people will often use positive evaluations of a brand as a proxy for the quality of the product. This reliance on brands has led companies to devote large amounts of resources to branding their products and measuring brand equity (how much the brand itself is worth in sales).

Although the brand name heuristic can lead us astray at times (such as in the case of Apple Dapple), it turns out that brands can contain a great deal of information. Take, for example, the brands "Republican" and "Democrat." Merely knowing which party a politician is from will tell you a great deal about him or her. Republicans tend to oppose corporate regulations. Democrats tend to support welfare for the poor. Of course, there are notable exceptions, but it isn't uncommon to see votes in the U.S. Senate split along party lines. Voters don't need to know all that much about a candidate in most elections; merely knowing which party the candidate belongs to will allow a fairly informed decision.

But are voters actually responding to the political party brand? Or are conservatives simply always picking the most conservative candidate, who is almost always Republican? Although the data is preliminary, several different researchers have found evidence that the brand itself is very important. For instance, Lau and Redlawsk have examined this question using what social scientists call *process-tracing methods*. The basic idea is that for voters to use a heuristic they first have to seek out the information relevant to that heuristic. If you are bothering to track down a piece of information, then it must be important. By monitoring the information about candidates that voters seek out, it is possible to indirectly evaluate which information they are using to make their decisions. Lau and Redlawsk found that almost all voters (98 percent) were interested in the political party that candidates came from even when they already knew the important information about that candidate's positions. This suggests that political party is indeed a central way that people make decisions.[2] In other words, people don't need to know all that much about a particular candidate because they can get the bulk of what they need to know from party affiliation.

Being Judged by the Company You Keep

The Breast Cancer Society of Canada (BCSC) is a prominent and effective organization dedicated to fighting breast cancer in Canada. In 2007, when a group of women approached the BCSC with a large donation, the BCSC refused to accept the money. The reason? The money was from Exotic Dancers for Cancer; BCSC was concerned that other donors would be offended by the connection to exotic dancers and thus withdraw support.

In fact, organizations frequently turn down money that they could have put to good use. In October 2001, New York City Mayor Rudy Giuliani rejected, on behalf of the City of New York, a $10 million donation for 9/11 disaster relief from Saudi Prince Alwaleed bin Talal because of a statement bin Talal made suggesting that U.S. policies in the Middle East contributed to the 9/11 attacks. Giuliani argued that such statements could

---

2. Of course, it is always possible that people seek out party information but don't use it. However, as Lau and Redlawsk note, other researchers have used different techniques to try and get around this problem. For example, researchers can tell voters about hypothetical candidates and measure how voter opinions change depending on what voters are told about the candidate's party affiliation. Alternatively, researchers can use complex statistical techniques to try and parse out the impact of party affiliation in actual elections. Although none of these approaches is without its flaws, the fact that they all produce similar results suggests that the effect is real.

not be tolerated because they imply that terrorist actions are justifiable. Thus, he rejected the donation so as to distance himself from the person who made that statement.

These were both large donations to groups that could have certainly used the money, and yet it is very possible that, in both of these cases, rejecting the money was the right thing to do. Kevin Arceneaux and Robin Kolodny from Temple University did a field experiment in two swing districts during the 2006 Pennsylvania House elections. The researchers teamed up with a well-known liberal interest group and randomly assigned nearly 20,000 households to either be contacted by the group or not. Subsequently, the researchers contacted all of the households to find out whom they voted for. It turned out that when a candidate received an endorsement from a liberal group, Republicans had significantly lower opinions of the candidate; the endorsement from a liberal group made Republicans as much as 10 percent less likely to vote for a candidate. In other words, it can be dangerous to accept the support of the wrong people.

Of course, the opposite holds true as well. University of Washington professor Mark Forehand and his colleagues have found evidence for an *endorsement heuristic*, or the idea that being endorsed by a positively regarded organization leads to more positive evaluations. There's a reason that politicians (and marketers in general) try to get well-liked celebrities to be part of their campaigns, and why organizations like the Sierra Club and the National Rifle Association produce "voter guides." The idea here is that a voter doesn't have to know all that much about a candidate. Voters can "outsource" the work to a trusted source. People who know very little about particular policy issues can still make pretty good decisions by relying on others who do.

And the List Goes On . . .

The affect heuristic, the brand name heuristic, and the endorsement heuristic are just three of many different strategies and shortcuts that voters use to overcome their ignorance and biases. It would be impossible to describe them all, because there are as many heuristics as there are ways to distinguish between candidates. For example, one-issue voters might construct the abortion heuristic, the no new taxes heuristic, or even the Guinean bauxite tariffs heuristic (although we fear the last of these has probably never been used prior to this book). The important point is that although "We the People" may not know much about the issues or the candidates, we are capable of overcoming our ignorance, or at least minimizing the damage, by using heuristics.

Of course, no shortcut is perfect; these heuristics break down under predictable circumstances, and will not transform uninformed voters into wise and rational rulers. We are still crazy, even with (or sometimes because of) these heuristics. Fortunately for democracy, there are several other factors that help make us a bit more sane.

Crowding Out Ignorance

On September 4, 2010, a small airplane crashed near Fox Glacier in New Zealand killing all nine people on board. The Transport Accident Investigation Commission of New Zealand determined that the plane was unbalanced because of where the passengers were seated in the cabin. Indeed, having the wrong center of gravity can cause serious safety problems. The United States Federal Aviation Administration aircraft safety manual "The Aircraft Weight and Balance Handbook" notes that if the center of gravity of the plane is too far aft (toward the back of the plane) the plane will be unstable, and recovery from a stall becomes difficult. On the other hand, the weight being too far forward will increase drag, make the plane less efficient, and make takeoffs and landings more challenging. If the weight isn't distributed equally across the lateral axis of the aircraft (i.e., if the left or right side is heavier than the other) then planes fly inefficiently, and some aircraft become unsafe.

If you've ever purchased a ticket on a small commuter jet, you've seen the implications of this in action. After everyone boards the plane, a member of the flight crew will come through and make sure that the passenger weight is evenly distributed. If the weight on the airplane is not balanced appropriately, the crew will ask people to switch seats. Only when the weight of the airplane is evenly distributed can the plane take off.

This sort of seat swapping doesn't happen on larger planes. Partly this is because the passengers make up a smaller proportion of the overall weight of the plane. But partly this is because there are many more passengers on the plane. When there are only ten passengers, it is possible that the five heaviest passengers will end up on the same side of the plane—assuming random seating assignments it would happen about one time in 63 flights.[3] Such a seating arrangement would unbalance the plane and lead to problems. When there are 100 passengers on a plane, the odds of all of the heaviest passengers sitting on the same side of the plane drop dramatically—only one time in 50,000,000,000,000,000,000,000,000,000,000 flights. This extreme difference is due to a basic principle of statistics: As the size of the sample increases, the likelihood of random events all occurring in the same direction decreases dramatically. There is, in fact, safety in large numbers.

In fact, not only is there safety in large numbers, there is also intelligence. When people make judgments based on imperfect knowledge (the usual state of affairs), there will be some amount of randomness in those judgments, not unlike the randomness of where people sit on an airplane. When the judgments of many people are pooled or aggregated, the randomness tends to cancel out. Just like some people will end up on the left side of an airplane and some people will end up on the right side, some guesses will be too high and some guesses will be too low. But the combination of all of those estimates will tend to be close to correct. First noted by Sir Francis Galton and recently popularized by James Surowiecki, this so-called *wisdom of crowds* is really quite common. Surowiecki describes numerous demonstrations of this phenomenon: Times Square tourists correctly guessing the number of jellybeans in a jar, guests on a cruise ship correctly identifying Surowiecki's bodyweight, and even radio show listeners correctly predicting the number of books on his shelves (a piece of information that even he didn't know off the top of his head). In each case, none of the particular guesses was correct, and yet the average of all of the guesses was almost perfect.

The wisdom of crowds can extend to democratic elections as well; after all, an election is just a way of pooling the guesses of a large number of people. We've talked about how the average voter doesn't know all that much about the candidates or the issues. But so long as there are enough people voting, that ignorance will tend to cancel itself out. Imagine a race

---

3. The heaviest person who gets on the plane sits on one side of the plane. The odds of the next four heaviest people also sitting on the same side are $4/9 \times 3/8 \times 2/7 \times 1/6$. Multiply by 2, because it works for front–back and left–right axes. This assumes a ten-person plane—in a plane with "extra seats" you could end up with all ten people (both heavy and light) on the same side of the plane, which would only exacerbate the problem.

for county judge between two candidates. Neither candidate is particularly famous or influential, neither candidate is campaigning hard for the position, they both have generic names, and state law forbids the judges from running with a party endorsement. As far as most of the voters are concerned, there is really nothing to distinguish these two people; most voters will just pick randomly between them. Of course, a few people do know the two candidates, and will not be selecting randomly. Those voters know that Judge A is monumentally incompetent, whereas Judge B will do a pretty decent job. So what happens? The large number of random votes will tend to split evenly, but the few people who know something about the two candidates will all vote for Judge B. So in the end Judge B wins. The individual voters were uninformed, but collectively the voters were pretty smart.

Aggregation can also allow biases to cancel each other out. For instance, we previously discussed how polling location can affect votes; in other words, people who vote in a school are more likely to vote in favor of educational issues, whereas people who vote in firehouses are more likely to vote in favor of public safety issues. So imagine a presidential election in which one candidate has done a good job of positioning himself as the "education" candidate, and the other has done a good job of positioning himself as the "public safety" candidate. One would tend to do better among people who vote in schools, the other among people who vote in firehouses. But in a presidential election where there is a widely diverse set of places that people go to vote, any bias based on polling location will likely be averaged out.

In short, even when most individual voters are ignorant and making random or biased decisions, the electorate as a whole might actually have a good chance of making an informed, intelligent decision. The ignorance will tend to cause people to act randomly, but with enough voters, all of that randomness cancels itself out. As a result, the voters whose opinions are actually informed can drive the course of an election. Of course, canceling out random ignorance isn't the only benefit that aggregating the judgments of a crowd can provide.

Get a Clue
In the classic board game Clue, the players attempt to solve a murder by determining the perpetrator, location, and weapon. Each of the players

knows that some of the suspects are innocent, some of the locations were not the scene of the crime, and some of the weapons were definitely not used. Distributed among the group is enough evidence to solve the crime. The problem is that this information is spread out across the players—no one person has all the relevant information. The goal of the game is to find out what everybody else knows—the mystery cannot be solved until somebody has accumulated enough of the evidence to be able to pinpoint the details of the crime.

In modern society, as in Clue, the information needed to make good decisions is spread across many people. Democracies have the ability to aggregate all of that knowledge. By adding up all of the information across many individuals, not only do we reduce error, but we can also take all of those little bits of information and put together a fairly accurate picture of reality.

In the 1990s, psychologists Daniel Gigone and Reid Hastie did a series of studies on how the accuracy of small groups compares to the accuracy of individuals. For example, in one study participants were asked to guess how well various students had performed in an introductory psychology course. Some participants (the know-it-alls) were given a bunch of helpful information, such as class attendance and SAT scores. Other participants (the know-somethings) were only given a subset of that information. Unsurprisingly, the know-it-alls outperformed the know-somethings.

But what the researchers were really interested in was the effectiveness of groups, not individuals. So the researchers had all those individuals form groups and do the task again. Groups of know-it-alls improved their performance, relative to what they had done as individuals. Groups of know-somethings also improved their performance relative to what they had done as individuals and, more importantly, know-something groups outperformed know-it-all individuals as well.[4] Gigone and Hastie concluded that "the group judgment process seems to overcome the obstacle of unshared information that affects the individual judgments."

Other studies have confirmed these findings. For example, Purdue University psychologist Rebecca Henry had people work together to answer general knowledge questions (e.g., the length of the Nile). On over 80 percent of the questions, the group answer was better than the average of

---

4. This difference was not always statistically significant.

its constituent members. Moreover, the group outperformed its best member on over 40 percent of the questions. Henry later showed that instructing groups to share relevant information made them even better.

In democracies, decisions are often made by diverse groups of individuals. For instance, the U.S. Congress at any given moment contains doctors, lawyers, engineers, and small business owners; parents, grandparents, aunts, and uncles; people from wealthy and privileged backgrounds, people from middle-class backgrounds, and people who grew up in poverty. This wide diversity of knowledge, backgrounds, and experience gives Congress the potential to make extremely informed decisions, even though most legislators lack direct experience with most of the issues they discuss. For example, although Congress does not have many experts in the complexities of international adoptions in particular, it does contain former family lawyers, parents and grandparents who have direct experience with non-traditional families, and immigration law experts. All of the information necessary to make a good decision about those policies is present.

But as diverse as the U.S. Congress is, the general population is even more diverse. While each individual citizen has incomplete knowledge, the electorate as a whole has a more complete picture. One of the benefits of a democracy is that it allows society to reap the benefits of the knowledge of all of its citizens, not just the political elite. Once again, the crowd is a lot smarter than its individual members.

In Search of Stability

In 1964, political scientist Philip Converse shocked the political science establishment by demonstrating that voters don't have stable policy preferences; they believe different things about different policies on different days. He interviewed the same voters about the same issues repeatedly over a long period of time. What people said in one interview bore very little resemblance to what they said in another interview. Large portions of the electorate appeared to be responding randomly.

But while individuals have very unstable policy preferences, it turns out that society as a whole has extremely stable policy preferences. Political scientists Benjamin Page and Robert Shapiro looked at a broad array of survey and polling data from the past fifty years, and found that public opinion really doesn't change very often at all—and when it does change, it is usually in response to a particular event. For instance, during the last six months that George W. Bush was president of the United States, his lowest approval rating was 24 percent, registered in early October 2008. His highest approval rating was 33 percent, registered in late August 2008. Although there was some change in Bush's approval ratings, these data are not nearly as unstable as what one might expect given Converse's findings.

Individuals change their minds all the time, but when you add up all of those opinion changes into a poll, it turns out that most of them average out. So Bob may decide that he doesn't like the president because Bob just got laid off, while Mary just got hired and thinks that therefore the economy is on the right track. Meanwhile, Sue's arthritis is acting up, causing her to be in a bad mood and evaluate everybody and everything negatively (including the president), while Joe had a great date last night, and is pleased with the world and all that's in it (including the president). All of those individuals have unstable opinions about the president. But collectively? On any given day about the same number of people will be having unexpectedly good days as unexpectedly bad days; the Joes and the Sues will cancel each other out. On the other hand, if the unemployment rate goes up, the president's job approval goes down because there are more people like Bob, who lost a job, than people like Mary, who got hired. All of the irrational and biased behavior adds up to a crowd that acts quite reasonably.

An Afternoon's Walk along Old Man River

Danny Oppenheimer has run a number of experiments asking people to make estimations. Unsurprisingly, many of the individual responses have been pretty absurd. In one study, a participant guessed that the Mississippi River was only seven miles long, a guess that was off by a factor of over 300. Another time a participant estimated that the distance between Sydney, Australia, and London, England, was less than 100 miles, a guess that was off by over 10,000 miles. But despite the horrible guesses by particular individuals, in both cases the groups' estimates were still pretty good.

Individuals can believe some pretty extreme things. Some people believe that you can take an afternoon stroll from Minnesota to the Gulf of Mexico. Some people believe that the distance from Australia to Britain is less than the distance from Washington, D.C., to New York City. In politics, some people believe that the United States should invade China, while others believe that the United States should have no military at all. Some people believe that governments should maintain almost 100 percent tax rates and redistribute all income, while others believe that governments shouldn't raise any taxes at all and should pay their bills only through criminal fines and voluntary donations. But as extreme as individual candidates can be, the crowd is usually pretty moderate.

For instance, there are plenty of extremists who run for president, and some of them are even well known. Lyndon LaRouche, a former Communist who believes that the 9/11 attacks were a failed military coup and has pushed for mandatory quarantines for anyone with HIV, has run for president every four years since 1976, including in 1990 when he was serving a jail sentence for mail fraud. He's never come close to winning. Socialist Eugene Debs ran for president five times between 1900 and 1920, the last time while in prison for espionage. In his best showing, he received about 6 percent of the vote. The crowd tends to like moderates and dislike extremists.

Of course, there are a couple of examples of times when a democracy supposedly elected some extreme radicals. Adolf Hitler's Nazi Party did manage to achieve a stranglehold on Germany in part through the ballot box. In that sense, Hitler was (for a brief period of time) the chancellor of a democratic government. Of course, Hitler's victory did not exactly come in a free and fair election. The Nazi Party used widespread voter intimidation, including violence at the polls; they fed off of a culture of fear that was sparked by the destruction of the German capital building; and they benefited from the fact that one of Germany's largest political parties had been outlawed. Even then the Nazis still won less than half of the vote; Hitler took power as leader of the single largest political party, but not as the preferred candidate of a majority of Germans. Another commonly cited example is the French election that we described earlier in which the anti-immigrant candidate Jean-Marie Le Pen qualified for the runoff election in 2002 by finishing second in the first round of voting with just under 17 percent of the vote. Yet despite that early success, Le Pen lost the runoff election, receiving 18 percent of the vote to incumbent Jacques Chirac's 82 percent.

So, yes, every once in a while an extremist candidate can appeal to a large number of voters. But in general, crowds like moderates and extreme candidates rarely find themselves at the top for long.[5]

The Alternatives

To recap our argument to this point: When you aggregate the opinions of large groups of people, it turns out that those group opinions are a lot more knowledgeable, a lot less prone to error, a lot more stable, and a lot less prone to extremism than the opinions of any particular individual. The wisdom of crowds is a huge advantage for democracies.

Most nondemocratic systems of government rely on the wisdom of a small number of extremely powerful individuals to determine the course of a country's policies. Most obviously, monarchs and totalitarian dictators exercise extreme personal control over their countries. As a result, these countries are at the whims of their leaders in many areas. Saddam Hussein's need to project a feeling of strength caused him to encourage the West to believe that he was developing chemical, biological, and nuclear weapons—even though that belief ultimately led to the American invasion of his country. Adolf Hitler's personal hatred caused Germany to prioritize spending limited resources on killing Jews and Gypsies instead of spending those resources to fight the war against the countries that would ultimately

---

5. Of course, the people outside of the mainstream have figured this out, and a couple of groups of Libertarians have found an innovative solution to this "problem." One group has decided to encourage their members to move to New Hampshire, in a so-called Free State Project. The idea is that you move enough people who all have outside-the-mainstream ideals to one place, then in that place those ideals become mainstream. So far, it seems that they have successfully encouraged about a thousand people to move to New Hampshire, although it is unclear if this will actually have any impact on a state of 1.3 million people. Another group with similar aims has set their sights on Loving County, Texas. In 2006, the county sheriff estimated that there were 71 residents who lived on the county's 645 square miles of land. And so a small group of Libertarians from Arizona thought that it would be a good idea to move to Loving County "to control the local Government and remove oppressive Regulations (such as Planning and Zoning, and Building Code requirements) and stop enforcement of Laws prohibiting Victimless Acts among Consenting Adults such as Dueling, Gambling, Incest, Price-Gouging, Cannibalism and Drug Handling." Unfortunately for them, resistance from the locals and a dispute with the county sheriff over the validity of their purchase of property has prevented them from living out their utopian dream.

destroy his regime. Monarchs and dictators can easily find themselves acting out their own whims, to the detriment of their people, their own countries, and even themselves.

Even countries ruled by small groups can find themselves at the mercy of similar forces. In the People's Republic of China and the Soviet Union, a premium on party loyalty led to a culture that valued conformity over independence. If everyone in the group is trying to conform, then the country loses the benefits of diversity, which is necessary for a crowd to make wiser decisions than its individual members. Democracies have an advantage because the input of a large number of people from different perspectives can help prevent disastrous mistakes. Of course, before we get too excited about the power of the wisdom of crowds to overcome the flaws with democracy, it is important to note that there are times when it doesn't work all that well.

Beware of Political Scientists Bearing Candy

Andrew Gelman, a political scientist at Columbia University, regularly runs a demonstration in which he asks school kids to estimate the weight of a bag of assorted candies. First, he fills the bag with a variety of candy, of all different sizes and weights. Then he passes the bag around the room with the scale, and tells kids to pick five individual pieces of candy out of the bag, weigh those pieces, and then use that knowledge to estimate how much the bag weighs. It turns out that the estimates are always too high; and of course, the average of those estimates is way off too.

If Times Square tourists can guess the number of jellybeans in a jar, surely kids can guess the weight of a bag of candy. What's the problem? Essentially, the kids are biasing themselves. The kids' natural tendency is to grab the bulkier, heavier candies on top, and not the smaller candies that find their way to the bottom. In other words, by weighing the candy the kids outsmart themselves. They are all given a piece of information that drives up their guesses in a predictable, systematic way. As a result, no one guesses too low; all the guesses are too high.

This example demonstrates an important caveat: For the wisdom of crowds to work, errors need to be random. There need to be just as many people guessing things that are too high as there are guessing things that are too low. In many cases, like the weight of a cow or the population of Kazakhstan, this condition takes care of itself. Problems can arise, however, in the presence of misleading information or natural biases.

Let's look back at the data we cited in chapter 1. Remember that people tended to drastically overestimate things like the number of Americans in prison, the immigration rate, and the number of people executed. Why was the crowd so off in these cases? Crime, immigration, and the death penalty are all controversial, highly publicized, and highly politicized issues. Cable news programs and newspaper op-ed pages are full of frequent references to America's out-of-control immigration rate and its crowded prisons. Not unlike the students with the bag of candy, in each of these cases voters all possess the same biased information that encourages them to guess high. So instead of random guesses around the true value, the crowd systematically overestimates the true value.

In short, combining the choices of many people does provide democracy with an advantage, but it is not a perfect one. The voting public can still make plenty of errors. Thankfully, there are still other factors that help mitigate those mistakes.

The Idiot's Guide to Effective Governance

With 31 wins and only 5 losses, the 1992–1993 University of Michigan men's basketball team was one of the best in the country. And the best player on that team was Chris Webber, an All-American who would be the first player selected in the subsequent NBA draft. During the 1993 NCAA championship game, Michigan was playing the University of North Carolina (UNC). With only twenty seconds remaining on the clock, North Carolina had a two-point lead. A UNC player missed a free throw, Chris Webber grabbed the rebound, and after a brief moment's hesitation he ran down the court. Unfortunately, he ran right into a UNC double-team, and with eleven seconds remaining he found himself pinned next to the sideline. So Webber called a timeout. The problem was that his team was out of timeouts; his attempted timeout resulted in a technical foul, effectively handing UNC the game. One of the best college basketball players in the country, in the biggest game of his college career, and he forgot how many timeouts his team had left.

Garry Kasparov is one of the greatest chess players of all time. In 1985, at a mere 22 years of age, he became the youngest ever World Champion. He went on to hold the highest ranking in chess for a total of 255 months, three times longer than anyone else has held it. So in a match in 1988, it came as no surprise that Kasparov had the upper hand over Grandmaster Kiril Georgiev. Georgiev had only his king remaining, while Kasparov was attacking him with both a queen and a bishop. Kasparov was only two moves away from winning, when he did the unthinkable; he placed his queen in a position that prevented Georgiev from moving, thereby forcing a draw. The greatest chess player in the world, in a position where even a novice should have been able to win, and he accidentally forced a draw.

As the saying goes, "to err is human." Everybody makes mistakes, even the best and the brightest. So when the decisions are made by an individual or small group, it's not surprising that occasionally really big mistakes are made. Even people who aren't experts could have told Chris Webber that he was out of timeouts or Garry Kasparov that he was about to give away certain victory.

One way to avoid these mistakes is by having what political scientists call *veto players*. A veto player is simply a person or group who has the authority to prevent change. In the case of the United States government, the House of Representatives, the Senate, the president, and the Supreme Court are all veto players because each of them can stop new legislation or policies from taking effect. In California, tax increases often have to pass a popular referendum to become law, which makes the people of California a veto player (although given California's budgetary problems, perhaps not a very wise one). And all Australian laws are technically subject to the veto of Queen Elizabeth II (as Australia is still a member of the British Commonwealth and therefore under the Queen's sovereignty), although this power has never been used. Political scientist George Tsebelis has demonstrated that one of the most important ways of comparing different countries is by their number of veto players.

Unsurprisingly, democracies tend to have more veto players than non-democracies. In Iran, for instance, there is only one veto player: the clerical council that runs the country. In China, there is only one veto player: the leadership of the Chinese Communist Party. In Nazi Germany, there was one veto player: Adolf Hitler. Democracies, meanwhile, tend to have multiple houses in their legislatures; they often have independent executive branches and constitutional courts; and some of them further rely on popular referenda for certain important decisions, and sometimes even political parties and other groups that can exert enough control to effectively veto change.

Countries with more veto players have significant advantages. No matter how clever, wise, and educated a leader or small group of leaders are, they will still make errors. The more veto players, the more likely that one of them will prevent disastrous mistakes. For instance, in 1958 Mao Zedong had complete control over the Chinese Communist Party. He wanted China to become a Great Power, which meant that they were going to need a lot of heavy industry, and heavy industry requires steel. At that point China was not trading with the United States or Europe, and their main ally, the Soviet Union, was already sending them whatever steel the USSR could spare. So Mao thought that it would be a good idea to force peasants to turn in metal to be melted down into steel.

Mao's mandate was a bad idea for several reasons. First of all, most of the metal that Chinese peasants had lying around the house was of such poor quality as to be worthless to a steel mill. Second, most of that metal was in the form of vital tools needed for life on a farm. In other words, Mao had effectively ordered Chinese farmers to destroy their farming implements. The result was a massive famine that killed tens of millions of people. The problem was that China had only one veto player, Mao. When Mao came up with the Great Leap Forward there was nobody to prevent it from coming to fruition.

When people in democracies come up with catastrophically idiotic ideas there are usually people to tell them "no." Yes, democracies sometimes do some stupid things with the consent of all veto players. The Trail of Tears (the forced relocation of thousands of Native Americans to Oklahoma) was just one of many disastrous ideas implemented by America's democratic government. There are also times when too many veto players can cause government inaction on important issues. But in general, having more veto players has allowed democracies to avoid many of the more horrific acts that other countries have inflicted upon themselves.

In other words, the very fact that power is shared helps prevent foolish errors in policy. And in democracy, power is shared more than in other forms of government.

Agents of Intelligence and Mystery

We should note that there is one other factor that mitigates ignorance and stupidity in all forms of government: professional bureaucracies. As we discussed earlier, there is simply no practical way for voters or political leaders to be well educated on each and every policy that a modern country has to deal with. So legislators, presidents, and dictators alike hire professional bureaucrats to manage different areas and to provide expertise in those areas. Presidents do not have to be brilliant military minds; they have generals to fight their wars for them. Congressmen don't need to know the ins and outs of Guinean bauxite; they have diplomats and economists to help them set appropriate trade policies. Dictators don't need to understand the many nuances of running an effective space program; they can hire scientists and engineers to make sure that the satellites stay in orbit.

Of course, there is a pretty large caveat here: the *principal–agent problem*. To understand a principal–agent problem, imagine that you hire a mechanic to fix your car. In this case you are the "principal" and the mechanic is the "agent." The mechanic calls you up to tell you that your car is fixed and says, "I fixed your problem. You had a [*insert unintelligible explanation here*]. With parts and labor, that comes to $800." Now, you are left with several questions:

1. Did the mechanic actually fix your car permanently, or will you have this same problem in the future?

2. Did the mechanic actually put $800 worth of parts and labor into your car?

3. Did the mechanic actually need to put $800 worth of parts and labor into your car in order to fix your problem?

Chances are good that you will never be able to answer those questions; you simply have to pay the mechanic and hope for the best. In other words, as the principal, you hired the agent to do a job. However, because the agent has expertise that you do not have, and because the agent has different incentives than you, there exists the possibility that the agent could have taken advantage of you.

In the same way, bureaucrats have quite a bit of leeway in interpreting and enforcing the laws that they are supposed to enact. Sometimes this leeway can actually be a good thing, because it allows the bureaucrats to react to unforeseen or exceptional circumstances. But the principal–agent problem can also lead to corruption and inefficiency. Ultimately (for better or worse), all laws are at the mercy of the experts who enforce them.

Summary

Citizens in democracies don't know very much about their candidates and the issues, so it would be easy to think that by putting the power into the hands of the ignorant, we are courting disaster. But it turns out that voters can do surprisingly well at making sensible decisions despite their lack of knowledge by using adaptive mental shortcuts. These heuristics can lead voters astray, but often they help citizens vote wisely. When heuristics break down, combining the opinions of many people causes random error to cancel out, aggregates expertise, creates stability, and mitigates extremism. The fact that democracies have more veto players reduces the odds of a catastrophically bad decision being made, and professional bureaucrats provide expertise in policymaking that ensures a smoothly functioning society even when our bad decisions might otherwise cause problems.

In other words, the weaknesses of "We the People" really aren't that bad in the grand scheme of things. Sure, we wish that the average citizen were a bit more educated about the issues and a little less influenced by a candidate's appearance or campaign theme song. But dictators are people too. They are just as irrational and biased as everyone else, only they have the individual authority to make decisions all by themselves. All governments struggle with how to prevent the ignorance and irrationality that plague humanity from harming society. Democracies simply have more natural safeguards in place to prevent catastrophe, encourage growth, and maintain stability.

References

Lead Quote
Forster, E. M. 1951. What I believe. In *Two Cheers for Democracy*. Orlando: Harcourt Brace.

Ignorance Isn't So Bad After All
Goldstein, D. G., and G. Gigerenzer. 2002. Models of ecological rationality: The recognition heuristic. *Psychological Review* 109:75–90.

Hall, C. C., and D. M. Oppenheimer. Under revision. Error parsing: An alternative method of implementing social judgment theory. *Journal of Behavioral Decision Making*.

King of the Hill. 2001. The Perils of Polling. Season 5, Episode 1. Original air date October 1, 2001.

What Is a Heuristic?

Katz, D. L., V. Y. Njike, D. Kennedy, J. Treu, and L. Q. Rhee. 2007. *Overall Nutritional Quality Index (ONQI).* Retrieved June 30, 2011, from http://www.nuval.com/images/upload/file/ONQI%20Manual%205_5_09.pdf.

Lau, R. R., and D. P. Redlawsk. 2006. *How Voters Decide: Information Processing during Election Campaigns.* New York: Cambridge University Press.

Affect Heuristic

Johnson, M. K., J. K. Kim, and G. Risse. 1985. Do alcoholic Korsakoff's syndrome patients acquire affective reactions? *Journal of Experimental Psychology: Learning, Memory, and Cognition* 11:22–36.

Sherman, D. K., and H. S. Kim. 2002. Affective perseverance: The resistance of affect to cognitive invalidation. *Personality and Social Psychology Bulletin* 28 (2):224–237.

Slovic, P., M. L. Finucane, E. Peters, and D. G. MacGregor. 2002. The affect heuristic. In *Intuitive Judgment: Heuristics and Biases,* ed. T. Gilovich, D. Griffin, and D. Kahneman, 397–420. New York: Cambridge University Press.

Party Heuristic

Penzo, L. N.d. Taste-test experiment: An all-kid panel evaluates name-brand vs. store-brand cereals. Retrieved April 17, 2011, from http://lenpenzo.com/blog/id1040-taste-test-experiment-an-all-kid-panel-evaluates-name-brand-vs-store-brand-cereals.html.

Maheswaran, D., D. M. Mackie, and S. Chaiken. 1992. Brand name as a heuristic cue: The effects of task importance and expectancy confirmation on consumer judgments. *Journal of Consumer Psychology* 1:317–336.

Lau, R. R., and D. P. Redlawsk. 2001. Advantages and disadvantages of cognitive heuristics in political decision making. *American Journal of Political Science* 45 (4): 951–971.

Endorsement Heuristic

Arceneaux, K., and R. Kolodny. 2006. Educating the least informed: Group endorsements in a grassroots campaign. *American Journal of Political Science* 53 (4): 755–770.

Forehand, M. R., J. Gastil, and M. A. Smith. 2004. Endorsements as voting cues: Heuristic and systematic processing in initiative elections. *Journal of Applied Social Psychology* 34 (11):2215–2233.

Steinhower, J. 2001. A nation challenged: The donations; Citing comments on attack, Giuliani rejects Saudi's gift. *New York Times*, October 12. Retrieved April 17, 2011, from http://www.nytimes.com/2001/10/12/nyregion/nation-challenged -donations-citing-comments-attack-giuliani-rejects-saudi-s-gift.html.

Waterloo Region Record, February 10, 2007, p. A3. Breast cancer society snubs exotic dancers' donation.

Aggregation Cancels Random Error

AFP. 2010. NZ tourist plane unbalanced before crash. Retrieved on April 17, 2011, from http://www.bangkokpost.com/news/asia/205843/nzealand-tourist-plane -unbalanced-before-crash-report.

Berger, J., M. Marc, and S. C. Wheeler. 2008. Contextual priming: Where people vote affects how they vote. *Proceedings of the National Academy of Sciences of the United States of America* 105 (26):8846–8849.

Federal Aviation Administration. 2007. Aircraft Weight and Balance Handbook. Retrieved on April 17, 2011, from http://www.faa.gov/library/manuals/aircraft/ media/faa-h-8083-1a.pdf.

Galton, F. 1907. Vox populi. *Nature* 1949 (75):450–451.

Surowiecki, James. 2004. *The Wisdom of Crowds: Why the Many Are Smarter Than the Few and How Collective Wisdom Shapes Business, Economies, Societies, and Nations.* Norwall, MA: Anchor Press.

Aggregation Combines Knowledge

Gigone, D., and R. Hastie. 1993. The common knowledge effect: Information sharing and group judgment. *Journal of Personality and Social Psychology* 65:959–974.

Gigone, D., and R. Hastie. 1996. The impact of information on group judgment: A model and computer simulation. In *Understanding Group Behavior*, vol. 1: *Consensual Action by Small Groups*, ed. E. Witte and J. H. Davis, 221–251. Hillsdale, NJ: Lawrence Erlbaum.

Gigone, D., and R. Hastie. 1997. Proper analysis of the accuracy of group judgments. *Psychological Bulletin* 121 (1):149–167.

Henry, R. A. 1993. Group judgment accuracy: Reliability and validity of postdiscussion confidence judgments. *Organizational Behavior and Human Decision Processes* 56:11–27.

Henry, R. A. 1995. Improving group judgment accuracy: Information sharing and determining the best member. *Organizational Behavior and Human Decision Processes* 62:190–197.

Stability of Crowds

Converse, P. 1964. The nature of belief systems in mass publics. In *Ideology and Discontent*, ed. D. Apter, 206–261. Glencoe, IL: Free Press.

Page, R., and B. Shapiro. 1992. *The Rational Public: Fifty Years of Trends in Americans' Policy Preferences*. Chicago: University of Chicago Press.

Ruggles, S. 2008. Historical Bush approval ratings. June 20. Retrieved April 17, 2011, from http://www.hist.umn.edu/~ruggles/Approval.htm.

Crowds Don't Like Extremes

Blumenthal, R. 2006. Loving County low on people but still full of controversy/ Sheriff keeps eye on outside group with dubious goals. *Houston Chronicle*, March 5, section B, p. 5.

Freestateproject.org. N.d. Free State Project website. Retrieved May 1, 2011.

Oppenheimer, D. M., R. A. Leboeuf, and N. T. Brewer. 2008. Anchors aweigh: A demonstration of cross-modality anchoring and magnitude priming. *Cognition* 106 (1):13–26.

Oppenheimer, D. M., and A. A. Alter. N.d. Estimates of distances (unpublished dataset). Collected in 2007.

Witt, A. 2004. No joke: Eight-time presidential candidate Lyndon LaRouche may be a punchline on 'The Simpsons,' but his organization—and the effect it has on young recruits—is dead serious. *Washington Post*, October 24, p. W12.

Alternatives to Democracy

Chang, J., and J. Halliday. 2005. *Mao: The Unknown Story*. New York: Anchor Books.

Fairbank, J. K., and M. Goldman. 1992. *China: A New History*. Cambridge: Harvard University Press.

Gordon, M. R., and B. E. Trainor. 2006. Even as U.S. invaded, Hussein saw Iraqi unrest as top threat. *New York Times*, March 12. Retrieved April 17, 2011, from http://www.nytimes.com/2006/03/12/international/middleeast/12saddam.html?_r=1.

Kershaw, I., and M. Lewin, eds. 1997. *Stalinism and Nazism: Dictatorships in Comparison*. Cambridge: Cambridge University Press.

Riasanovsky, N. V. 2000. *A History of Russia*, 6th ed. Oxford: Oxford University Press.

Caveats on Wisdom of Crowds

Gelman, A. and Nolan, D. 2002. *Teaching Statistics: A Bag of Tricks*. Oxford: Oxford University Press.

Veto Players

Garry Kasparov vs. Kiril D Georgiev. N.d. Retrieved April 17, 2011, from http://www
.chessgames.com/perl/chessgame?gid=1258478.

Grubel, J. 2008. Australia swears in first woman Governor-General. Reuters, September 5. Retrieved April 17, 2011, from http://uk.reuters.com/article/2008/09/05/
uk-australia-governor-idUKSYD5995520080905.

Renolds, P. 1988. Referendum fever sweeps California: "A terrible way to run our
government," says critic. *Boston Globe*, October 16, p. A28.

Tsebelis, G. 2002. *Veto Players: How Political Institutions Work*. Princeton: Princeton
University Press.

Wolff, A. 1993. Technical knockout: When Chris Webber called a timeout his team
didn't have, Michigan was hit with a technical foul that clinched the national title
for North Carolina. *Sports Illustrated*, April 12. Retrieved June 30, 3011, from http://
sportsillustrated.cnn.com/vault/article/magazine/MAG1138253/1/index.htm.

Principal–Agent Problem

McCubbins, M. D., R. G. Noll, and B. R. Weingast. 1987. Administrative procedures
as instruments of political control. *Journal of Law Economics and Organization*
3:243–277.

Miller, G. 2005. The political evolution of principal–agent models. *Annual Review of
Political Science* 8:203–225.

8 Throwing the Bums Out

The only way I can lose this election is if I'm caught in bed with either a dead girl or a live boy.

—Edwin Edwards (no relation to the author)

The Best of Times and the Worst of Times

At the beginning of 1929, the Republican Party was at the pinnacle of American politics. They maintained large majorities in both houses of Congress and had for decades. In fact, the Republican Party had controlled the Senate for sixty of the previous seventy years, and the House for twenty four of the previous thirty years. They also controlled the White House; there had only been two Democratic presidents (Grover Cleveland and Woodrow Wilson) in the previous sixty years. Outside of the South, the Republican Party had dominated the American political landscape since Abraham Lincoln.

Moreover, the Republicans had just elected Herbert Hoover president. At the time, Hoover was well known for organizing humanitarian relief for civilians during and after World War I. Then he had been appointed Commerce Secretary and proceeded to revolutionize that department, making it much more responsive to the needs of the business community while also encouraging those corporations to increase their charitable activities and be more responsible public citizens. When Mississippi was hit by major flooding in 1927, the year before he ran for president, Hoover gained widespread renown for leading the humanitarian and cleanup efforts. Hoover was a reasonably young and fit 54 years of age at his inauguration, he was popular with the press, he had extremely close ties with the business community, and he was widely considered to be one of the great philanthropists of his day. The GOP seemed unbeatable.

Four years later, Franklin Delano Roosevelt was moving into the White House and the Democratic Party controlled over 70 percent of the House seats and over 60 percent of Senate seats. Sixty years of Republican Party dominance had come to a screeching halt. What happened?

The Great Depression. A massive economic collapse caused widespread dissatisfaction with the ruling party. A majority of voters had repeatedly expressed a preference for Republican candidates over Democratic candidates for the previous two generations. But when the Depression hit, the people seemed to change their minds.

Based on all of the data about voter irrationality, voter ignorance, the incumbency effect, and our flawed elections, it would be easy to conclude that issues just don't matter. The logical conclusion would be that the will of the people is simply a myth that we have been told to make us behave, a Santa Claus for responsible citizenship. Politicians, it would seem, have free rein to do whatever they want, as long as they can relate to voters and manipulate the system. But if that were true, then Herbert Hoover should have been reelected president in 1932.

In fact, every once in a while issues do seem to matter. The voters occasionally give stark reminders to their leaders about who is actually in charge. And even if it only happens occasionally, it has the long-term effect of encouraging politicians to work in the public's best interest.

Pretty in Pink Slips

Think about what you would do, or not do, to keep your job. Americans willingly give up free time, change their clothes, rearrange their schedules, travel extensively, regularly sit through tedious meetings, deal with annoying coworkers, and endure back-breaking physical labor. In some cases, people are even willing to do unethical, immoral, or illegal things just to keep from being fired.

If your boss has actually fired an employee recently, it creates all that much more motivation to toe the line. For example, many employers have policies that forbid playing games, watching videos, or viewing pornography on company computers during office hours. Now, imagine that you are a huge fan of Minesweeper. You know that it is against the rules to play games at work, but you also know that if your boss doesn't actually see you play and you get your work done on time, then you should be safe. So you often play Minesweeper against company policy. Then one day a coworker is fired for playing a Facebook game on the job. Are you likely to keep playing Minesweeper at work? Not if you like your job. Even if there is only a very small chance that you will be caught and fired, the penalty for breaking the rule is simply too high to risk it.

Politicians may be powerful men and women, but they are also workers who want to keep their jobs. The difference is that instead of going through an annual review process, they have to run for reelection. Just like the rest of us, politicians will do many things to keep their jobs—including sometimes trying to be responsive to their constituents' needs.

As we will demonstrate, politicians don't know what issue or event might lead to their downfall. They can lose an election by upsetting only a minority of their district. And no politician is ever completely safe from the wrath of the electorate. In other words, all politicians are vulnerable to electoral defeat—to being fired from their jobs by their bosses (us). Moreover, politicians tend to overestimate their chances of being fired for ignoring the voters. You can see why politicians might be somewhat reluctant to violate the public's trust too blatantly.

Of course, sometimes politicians do ignore their constituents, take bribes, and give lackadaisical responses in times of crisis with full confidence that the voters are not paying attention—just like sometimes you might play Minesweeper when you know that your boss isn't paying attention. But most of the time, politicians cannot be certain that the public isn't paying attention, just like most of the time you cannot be exactly certain that your boss will not walk by your office. This uncertainty makes politicians less corrupt and more attentive than they would otherwise be.

So think back to the story of Mobutu at the beginning of Part II, the dictator of Zaire who let his countrymen starve while he built special runways near his palaces so that his family could go on shopping excursions to Paris. That level of corruption and sheer disregard of his population was possible because he maintained the firm support of the army and the bureaucracy. He was well aware of the groups that he needed to bribe to stay in power, he took care of them, and he completely ignored the needs of the rest of the country.

Politicians in democracies may be self-serving and corrupt. Yet an elected official who was as corrupt and disdainful as Mobutu would have found himself out of a job long before he did so much damage to his country.

What We Know and What We Don't

Of course, the Minesweeper analogy is not perfect. If your boss fires you for playing Minesweeper, then there is a clear cause and effect. You played Minesweeper. The boss caught you. You were fired as a result. Elections are much more complicated; for example, Franklin Roosevelt's demeanor, public speaking ability, facial features, campaign strategies, and name recognition all certainly played a factor in his election. In that sense, the 1932 election was not entirely about the Great Depression. The Great Depression almost certainly played a part, although as we will see, there is no way of determining just how large a part it actually played. Moreover, it would be wrong to conclude that voters who ousted Herbert Hoover were making rational decisions based on which party had the better policies to help the country recover from the Great Depression. Eighty years later, economists still disagree on which government policies are best suited to pull a country out of an economic slump, and historians remain starkly divided over how successful the New Deal actually was. Roosevelt's triumph was therefore not a clear-cut case of a wise population choosing Democratic ideas over Republican ideas.

More likely, people were out of work, they were struggling to feed their families and hold onto their homes, and they were upset at a perceived lack of governmental response. They were angry, and in that anger they lashed out at the ruling party. As a result of that anger, there were any number of dedicated public servants and skilled legislators who were kicked out of Washington in 1930 and 1932. This was hardly an anomaly: According to the Pew Research Center, high unemployment rates have often predated dramatic changes in government control. Many of those fired politicians had little or nothing to do with the high unemployment rates; in some cases, they may have even taken the proper steps to get people back to work. Voter anger may be understandable, but it is hardly rational.

Moreover, we don't actually know why people voted for Franklin Roosevelt in 1932. Scientifically proving causal relationships between a particular issue and a particular election result is extremely difficult. However, a number of political scientists have shown that in democracies, the laws tend to mirror public opinion.

For example, Columbia University professors Jeffrey Lax and Justin Phillips have found a strong relationship between public support for gay rights in different American states and the enactment of gay rights policies. States whose populations express greater friendliness and acceptance toward homosexual behavior in surveys also tend to have laws that are more gay-friendly. Unfortunately, as useful and interesting as these findings are, they are somewhat difficult to interpret. That correlation could indicate any number of different things; the three most obvious explanations are:

1. Politicians survey public opinion and modify their own stances to suit the public's interest. That is, politicians are influenced by the will of the people.

2. As politicians change the laws to reflect their own wishes, public opinion changes to match. That is, the will of the people is influenced by the laws (or by the campaigning that accompanies those changes to the law).

3. Politicians just do what they want to do, but as public opinion changes, so do the opinions of the particular members of the public who are responsible for passing laws. In other words, whatever influences the will of the people also influences politicians.

Additionally, studies like this one cannot yet tell us why public opinion changes. It cannot yet tell us why the public sometimes votes politicians out of office. And it cannot yet tell us why public opinion correlates with policy on some issues—but why at other times politicians are able to ignore voters for long periods of time with no penalty.

Nonetheless, as in the case of the Great Depression, there have been several other notable cases where otherwise popular politicians quickly lost favor with the electorate. For the most part, these are situations where the public seemed to quickly change its mind about a candidate whom it had previously loved, in a way that seemed to clearly stem from that politician's policy stance or scandal. From these examples, we can learn four lessons:

• It is easy to overestimate the impact of issues on an election.

• It is hard to predict which issues will cause politicians to actually lose their jobs; they range from issues of great national importance to local scandals.

• An issue only has to change the votes of a minority of the population in order to substantially influence an election.

• Even exceptionally popular politicians are vulnerable, no matter how "safe" their seats may appear.

As we will see, these four factors combine to create a powerful incentive for politicians to pay attention to the will of the people—however flawed, irrational, and hard to understand the people's will may be. Even if issues rarely matter, if a politician doesn't know which issues *do* matter, then a politician who wants to keep her job cannot afford to neglect any of them. This uncertainty, in turn, forces politicians to try to develop policies that benefit all voters and not just themselves.

Positive Paranoia

After every election, the media rallies around particular story lines to explain why one candidate won and the other lost, and these story lines almost always focus on issues. When Obama beat McCain in the 2008 presidential election, the *New York Times* declared that the election was "a repudiation of a historically unpopular Republican president and his economic and foreign policies, and an embrace of Mr. Obama's call for a change in the direction and the tone of the country." In the 2006 midterm election, a different *New York Times* reporter declared that "The election was a negative referendum on President Bush and the Republican Congress, specifically their mismanagement of Iraq, their ethical problems, and their inability to balance the federal budget or refrain from trying to distract Americans [sic] public with noisy wedge issues rather than provide solutions to more pressing problems." In 2004, when George W. Bush beat John Kerry, much of the credit was given to the high turnout of "values voters" because of high-profile antigay marriage ballot initiatives in many battleground states.

But were these elections really about the War in Iraq, the budget, or gay marriage? Probably not. As we explained in Part I of the book, most voters don't really have strong and informed opinions about issues. In most cases, a candidate's behavior or stance will change some minds in one direction and other minds in the other direction. This is why you'll find that no matter what the press says about an election, the incumbents still win most of the time; that when the incumbent lost, he or she was usually facing off against an opponent who appeared taller, friendlier, and more "competent"; and that the voters in all of these races were just as confused about the candidates and issues as always.

The truth is that our search for logical explanations can often lead us to find patterns where none actually exist. For instance, if you've ever watched a basketball game, you've probably seen a player make several shots in a row. Players often refer to that as a "hot hand" or being "on fire," and common knowledge in basketball says that when a player has a hot hand, he should take as many shots as possible. But the "hot hand" is a myth. In the mid-1980s, psychologists Thomas Gilovich, Robert Vallone, and Amos Tversky studied jump shots by Philadelphia 76ers, free throws by the Boston Celtics, and controlled shooting-experiments by the Cornell University men's and women's varsity basketball teams. The probability of hitting a shot in basketball has absolutely nothing to do with whether or not the shooter made his or her previous shot. In other words, if a 50 percent shooter makes five shots in a row, her chances of hitting shot number six are 50 percent; if a 50 percent shooter misses five shots in a row, the chances that she hits shot number six are also 50 percent. And yet we challenge you to find a basketball analyst who does not frequently refer to "hot hands" or "streak shooters." Simply put, we like to find patterns in the events around us, even when those patterns don't actually exist.

Similarly, we like to think of ourselves as rational and intelligent human beings who are not prone to subconscious manipulation. University of Michigan psychologists Richard Nisbett and Timothy Wilson once asked shoppers in a store to judge between four pairs of identical nylon stockings and pick which one they preferred. Regardless of what the stockings looked like, the majority of respondents chose the right-most pair as "the best." When asked why, the respondents inevitably came up with some reason that had to do with the quality of that particular pair of stocking—even though all four pairs were identical. Almost none of the participants were even open to the idea that the position of the stockings might have affected their choice.

These same human nature trends apply to pundits and politicians. If you are a political analyst, you want to be able to identify the key issue that can explain why twenty Republicans just won reelection while a dozen others were defeated. In the same way, if you are a politician then you want to feel like your stance on some issue or your superior campaign strategy resulted in your victory. Of course, as we have demonstrated, most elections really aren't about those things at all; they are about name recognition, irrational biases, and a host of other mostly random factors. But a politician is unlikely to admit that he won an election because he was taller than his opponent, just like the shoppers at the department store were unlikely to admit that they chose a pair of stockings because it was on the right. It is simply a lot more satisfying for everyone involved if an election was about the public's stance on gay marriage than if it was about which candidate had the best jaw line.

Take for instance the 2010 special election that saw a Republican, Scott Brown, defeat a Democrat, Martha Coakley, for the Massachusetts Senate seat left open by Ted Kennedy's death. When Scott Brown was elected to the U.S. Senate, many in the media trumpeted that the election had been a referendum on the Obama administration. This argument says that citizen discontent with a massive budget deficit and a controversial health care reform plan led large numbers of moderate and liberal voters to rally around a conservative candidate. This basic theme could be seen in the postelection analysis from a diverse group including Senators Jim Webb (D-VA) and Mitch McConnell (R-KT), Representatives John Boehner (R-OH) and Steny Hoyer (D-MD), and a wide range of pundits, from Fox News host Glenn Beck to *New York Times* columnist Charles Blow.

But is it true? Were the issues of "stalling health care reform" and "conservative fiscal policy" really responsible for Scott Brown's election? The argument in favor of these "Big Issues" rests on three factors. First, Brown's victory took away the Democrat's filibuster-proof majority in the Senate, thereby decreasing the chance that the Democrats would be able to pass health care reform. Second, Scott Brown's campaign repeatedly mentioned the basic themes of lower taxes, balancing the budget, and stopping health care reform. And third, postelection polling indicated that the people who supported Scott Brown were generally opposed to Obama's health care plan.

It doesn't sound like a bad argument. Unfortunately, that logic is seriously flawed. First, when you compare Massachusetts voter turnout when Scott Brown won, relative to the 2008 presidential election, it just so happens that voter turnout in 2010 was extremely high in places that McCain won and extremely low in places that Obama won. Now consider that exit polling indicated that Martha Coakley won the people who thought that health care was the most important issue in the election. That same polling indicated that even among people who voted for Scott Brown, those voters still distrusted Republican handling of the economy and wanted Brown to work with Obama on the economy and on health care. The media story line does not seem to stand up to close scrutiny: Liberal and moderate voters did not flock to Brown because they wanted him to take a stand against taxes and health care. Instead, liberal voters stayed home, while the moderates and conservatives who voted for Brown seemed largely to want him to compromise.

Of course, we can't know for certain exactly why Brown beat Coakley, any more than we can be sure why Roosevelt beat Hoover. But given that Brown's voters disagreed with many of Brown's policy positions, and considering what we know about voter ignorance and irrationality, it seems probable that Brown's victory owed more to his physical stature and his engaging personality than to his stances on the issues.

After all, Scott Brown was the husband of a local celebrity, the father of an *American Idol* contestant, and looked good driving around in his beat-up pickup truck in his campaign ads. In their debates and respective ad campaigns, Coakley came across as the kind of person you'd want to hire as your lawyer. Brown looked like the kind of person you'd want to have over for dinner. Brown trumpeted his desire to meet and talk to every person in Massachusetts. Coakley was reluctant to campaign outside during the cold winter. In short, Brown was a more appealing candidate than Coakley when it came to many of the most important irrational factors that contribute to candidate success.

Thankfully, the myth that issues regularly drive electoral outcomes works to our advantage. Politicians are more scared of voter anger than they really should be. Policy positions don't seem to really change all that many votes. But as long as politicians believe that they can change voters' minds, then politicians will continue to make an effort to do what they think their constituents want. Scott Brown may have actually won because of his looks and personality, but the people of Massachusetts will have a better senator if he believes that his election was due to his policy stances.

Ain't No Issue Small Enough

At noon on August 9, 1974, Gerald Ford was officially sworn in as president of the United States, taking over after the Watergate scandal had driven Richard Nixon from office. President Ford initially had very good approval ratings. Gallup estimates that Ford's initial approval rating was about 71 percent; no incoming president has started with approval ratings that high since. But less than two months later, Ford decided to pardon Richard Nixon and all others associated with the Watergate scandal. The decision was extremely controversial, and Ford's approval ratings immediately dropped to 51 percent. Ford's popularity never recovered, and two years later he lost a close election to Jimmy Carter.

Unlike the Great Depression, Nixon's pardon did not negatively affect the everyday lives of most Americans. However, Ford's decision did seem to anger the voters. In other words, it doesn't matter how many people are directly affected by the issue at hand. Displeasing the voters can be dangerous to a politician's career—even when the "issue" really isn't about public policy at all.

In the case of Don Sherwood (R-PA), the collapse of his political career had nothing at all to do with his actions as a representative of his constituents. Sherwood's downfall appears to have been the result of voter disapproval of his personal life.

Representative Sherwood first won election to the House of Representatives in 1998 from the 10th district in Northeast Pennsylvania. In both 1998 and 2000, he narrowly defeated a well-known Democrat, Patrick Casey. But after 2000, the lines of his district were redrawn, making it extremely safe. In 2002 and 2004, the Democrats did not even bother to run a candidate against Sherwood. Sherwood beat third-party candidates in both elections, taking over 90 percent of the vote. But then in 2006, Democrat Chris Carney defeated Sherwood 53 percent to 47 percent.

What issue derailed Sherwood's political career? It was revealed before the 2006 election that Sherwood had had a five-year extramarital affair with a young woman, and that their relationship had ended with accusations of abuse. That year, a Democrat won an election in the Pennsylvania Tenth Congressional District for the first time since John F. Kennedy was in office.

Both Gerald Ford and Don Sherwood did things as incumbents that cost them votes in their next election. In the one case, it was by intervening in a criminal investigation; in the other it was by making poor choices in his personal life. There's a lesson to be learned here: All sorts of issues could potentially resonate with the public, even issues like Ford's and Sherwood's, which did not affect the daily lives of their constituents. As it happened, enough voters were paying attention, and disapproved of their actions, that it cost those men their jobs. And because it is so hard to predict what voters will take note of, politicians have to consider the likely public reaction to almost everything that they do. Otherwise, they could end up unemployed.

Enough Is Enough

It would be hard to overestimate Senator Ted Stevens's (R-AK) popularity in Alaska before his sudden downfall. He was first sent to the U.S. Senate in 1970, having been appointed by the governor, and he had since won reelection on eight different occasions. During that time, he never failed to win at least 55 percent of the vote in any primary or general election. He was so popular and widely respected that in 2000 he was named Alaskan of the Century and had the largest airport in the state named after him. No candidate could have hoped to match the election funds or name recognition of Ted Stevens in Alaska, and Stevens certainly knew how to win elections.

When Stevens ran for reelection during a presidential election year in 1996 he won 76 percent of the vote. Bob Dole won Alaska for the Republicans that year, and Dole won just over 50 percent of the vote. In other words, in that election about half of the people who didn't vote Republican for president still voted for Ted Stevens as senator. In 2008, with popular Alaskan Governor Sarah Palin on the presidential ticket pushing Republican turnout, John McCain won Alaska with 59 percent of the vote. One might have thought that this would have paved the way for yet another Ted Stevens landslide. It would seem that he should have at least been able to match the 76 percent that he won in 1996. Instead, Stevens lost to Mark Begich, the Democratic mayor of Anchorage, 48 percent to 47 percent.

So why did Ted Stevens lose? Before the election it was revealed that an oil company had paid for significant renovations to Ted Stevens's home, and then charged him only a fraction of what those renovations actually cost. He was convicted by a jury for failure to properly report gifts, although it was largely reported in the press as a bribery investigation. Although the

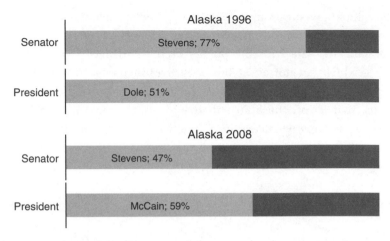

Figure 8.1
Comparing votes received by Republican candidates for Senator and president in
Alaska during the 1996 and 2008 elections.

conviction would eventually be overturned because of prosecutorial mis-
conduct, the allegations that Stevens took a bribe from an oil company
did not sit well with the voters. That corruption scandal seemed to negate
his monumental advantages in terms of money and name recognition.

Of course, keep in mind that when we talk about "the voters" here, we
are really talking about only a small percentage of the electorate. Mark
Begich defeated Ted Stevens in that race by a mere 4,000 votes. Was corruption a big issue—big enough to swing the election result? Absolutely.
But how many votes did the corruption scandal actually change?

In 2008, Stevens won 47 percent of the vote. Given his performance in
the 1996 election, Stevens could have reasonably won 70 percent of the
vote, which means that being convicted of corruption cost him at most
23 percent of the vote—and probably a lot less than that. In other words,
the majority of people who were going to vote for Stevens before the corruption conviction continued to support him after that conviction. Only
a minority of voters might have had their votes changed by the scandal;
it just happened to be a large enough minority to swing the election.

This same basic principle applies to all of the other races that we have
discussed. The people voted against Herbert Hoover in 1932, but he still
won almost 40 percent of the vote. Don Sherwood's constituents may have
been very upset at him for his promiscuity, but he won 47 percent of the

vote in his 2006 house race. In both cases, a sizable portion of the electorate continued to support the incumbent. Once again, elections are affected by many different factors. Issues may only play a small part, but sometimes even a small part may be enough to change the outcome of an election.

Even in a modern-day United States presidential election, in which millions of people vote, it can take only a fairly small group of angry voters to change the outcome. The United States Census Bureau estimated that there were just over 300 million people in the United States in 2008. About 208 million of those were eligible voters. About 131 million of those people actually voted—that's about 64 percent of eligible voters or 43 percent of the population. Barack Obama received 69 million votes; that is 52 percent of people who voted, 33 percent of eligible voters, and 23 percent of the total U.S. population. He beat John McCain in the popular vote by fewer than 10 million votes, which means that if 5 million people had changed their minds, McCain would have won the popular vote. Five million people may sound like a lot, but remember: That is less than 1.6 percent of the population. In fact, because of the Electoral College, if only 2 million voters (less than 1 percent of the population) spread across the right states had changed their minds, John McCain would have become president.

In fact, most presidential election results would have been different if only a small percentage of the voters had changed their minds. The average margin of victory among the popular vote for United States presidential elections since 1900 is 13.5 percent. So on average, a swing of 7 percent of actual voters could have changed the winner of the popular vote in more than half of the elections in the last century. If we apply this same math to a congressional election—where the average congressional district in the United States has fewer than 600,000 people and the person with the most votes actually wins the election—you can quickly see how it only takes a few thousand changed minds to fire a member of the House of Representatives. An issue doesn't have to matter to most of the people in order to change the outcome of an election. It only has to change the votes of a minority of voters—as long as it changes their minds in the same way.

If politicians only had to worry about upsetting all of their supporters, there would be very few issues that they would have to be concerned about. However, their task is much more difficult; they have to worry about maintaining the support of relatively small groups of citizens. If a politician upsets even a small minority of their constituency, because of personal behavior, particular policy stances, or anything else, he or she could be fired. This vulnerability forces politicians to be responsive to the needs of the people.

No One Is Safe

Of course, there are politicians who feel so safe that they start to take their positions for granted. And yet voter wrath can touch them too. In fact, if there was a politician in the country who was safer than Ted Stevens, Alaskan of the Century, it should have been Representative William Jefferson (D-LA).

William Jefferson was the representative of Louisiana's Second Congressional District, which contains almost the entire City of New Orleans. The district is 64 percent African American, and according to the Cook Political Report, it is one of the most liberal congressional districts in the country. Jefferson was the first African American to represent that district, having won election to Congress in 1990. In that election, he won with only 52 percent of the vote, but between 1992 and 2004 he never failed to win at least 60 percent of the vote. We should also note that the second-place finisher in most of those elections was also a Democrat, and that during that time no Republican won more than 20 percent of the vote.[1] He was a liberal African American from a liberal African American district, and a skilled politician to boot.

But in 2005, the FBI raided Jefferson's home and found that he had bribe money stuffed in a freezer. The following year, Jefferson ran for reelection again; he still managed to win, although he was forced into a runoff election and his vote total dropped considerably. Eventually, the Justice Department decided to press charges against him for repeatedly taking bribes. So when Jefferson ran for reelection in 2008, he did so while under indictment on federal bribery and corruption charges.

Except for the corruption charges, Jefferson should have won easily. First of all, Jefferson was running against a conservative Republican in an over-

1. Up through 2006, there were no primaries in Louisiana. There was one election in which all candidates put their names on the ballots; if no candidate received more than 50 percent of the vote, there was then a runoff election between the top two candidates. In the 2008 elections, the state changed to have traditional party primaries and a single winner-take-all general election.

whelmingly Democratic district, in an election in which the Republican Party lost ground in virtually every state. Meanwhile, the turnout of both liberal Democrats and African Americans was extremely high across the country owing to Barack Obama's candidacy, which should have benefited the liberal Jefferson. Jefferson also had all the normal advantages that a powerful, long-serving incumbent has, including name recognition, connections with powerful local leaders, and the ability to raise large amounts of cash.

But all of those advantages could not ultimately outweigh those pesky corruption charges: Jefferson lost to a conservative Republican, Anh "Joseph" Quang Cao, 49 percent to 47 percent. The people overcame their biases and voted a Republican into office. As a result, in 2009 William Jefferson was out of politics and the Louisiana second district was, according to the Cook Report, the only one of the 100 most liberal congressional districts in the country to be represented by a Republican.

Of course, remember that all elections are complicated events. In particular, voter turnout in 2008 was less than half of what it was in 2004. The corruption charges may have had an effect there; certainly many Democrats would have found both candidates distasteful and simply not bothered to vote as a result. But by far the more important consideration in this particular drop in voter turnout was Hurricane Katrina: The City of New Orleans was dramatically smaller in 2008 than in 2004. In this case, we can still be confident that the corruption issue did play a role. In particular, more than twice as many people voted Republican in 2008, despite the hurricane, than voted Republican four years earlier. And two years later a different Democrat easily defeated Cao. Katrina might have influenced the 2008 elections, but it seems most likely that Jefferson lost because of the corruption charges.

No politician is ever completely safe from the public's wrath. Voters can turn against anyone. Just look at how the South turned on Lyndon Johnson and the Democratic Party in the 1960s. The American South had been voting for Democrats, and only Democrats, for the previous eighty years. At that time no former Confederate State had elected a Republican to the United States Senate since 1880. And yet, legend has it that when President Lyndon Johnson signed the Civil Rights Act in July 1964, he remarked to an aide that "We [the Democrats] have lost the South for a generation." Johnson's alleged remark was an exaggeration, but the Democrats certainly paid a price in Southern votes for the Civil Rights Act. Most notably, in the presidential election later that same year, Johnson's opponent, Republican Senator Barry Goldwater of Arizona, won only six states. Goldwater, who was a popular senator in his home state, won by only 1 percent of the vote in Arizona: He defeated Johnson 50.5 percent to 49.5 percent. Goldwater won exactly five other states: Mississippi, South Carolina, Louisiana, Alabama, and Georgia, and all with at least 54 percent of the vote.

LBJ was a Southerner who won over 60 percent of the nationwide vote. Yet Johnson's opponent, Goldwater, did better in the Deep South than in his home state. How can that be?

Simply put, those were the five states that were most resistant to civil rights. LBJ in 1964 was wildly popular across the rest of the country, and before 1960 he had been popular in the Deep South as well. But those Southerners felt betrayed by the Texan President who pushed through the Civil Rights Act.

On a moral and ethical level, those voters did the wrong thing. The Civil Rights Act is one of the most important pieces of legislation in the history of the United States. That piece of legislation outlawed discrimination based on race, ethnicity, gender, or religion by any government body or in any public accommodation, it authorized the United States Attorney General to fight for school desegregation, and it required that any and all voting restrictions be applied equally regardless of race. In a very real sense, the 1964 Civil Rights Act was the first step toward giving black Americans real, permanent political power for the first time. The Southerners who voted to punish LBJ for his support of that act were just plain wrong. The people may be powerful, but they are not always wise.

And yet even when voters are wrong, our periodic punishment of unresponsive politicians is still a positive thing. Those Southerners who punished the Democrats for the Civil Rights Act did a morally reprehensible thing, and their continued support of segregationist candidates harmed the country. We should laud those politicians who stood up to the people by doing the morally right but politically unpopular thing. But in the long run, having a government that is responsive to the public's demands is better than having a government that is unresponsive to the public's demands—even if the public sometimes fires the wrong people for the wrong reasons.

Summary

When politicians lose their jobs, it's often for reasons that have nothing to do with the quality of their leadership—things like their physical attractiveness, their last name, the weather, or the structure of the ballot. But sometimes politicians lose their jobs because of personal moral failings. Sometimes they lose their jobs because of their own greed and corruption. Sometimes they lose their jobs because they miscalculate how much the public will actually care about an issue. And sometimes they even lose their jobs because they do the right thing instead of the popular thing.

Yes, election results are usually driven by factors that have nothing to do with a leader's actual job performance. But at least democracy gives us some ability to punish wayward politicians, short of the outright revolution and chaos that we described in chapter 6. Democracy is effective because our leaders fear that if they are not responsive to the needs of the people, then they will lose their jobs.

References

Lead Quote
Thomas, E., and D. S. Jackson. 1985. Taking a Louisiana Mudbath. *Time*, March 11. Retrieved April 18, 2011, from http://www.time.com/time/magazine/article/0,9171,962609-2,00.html.

Great Depression
Herbert Hoover Presidential Library. N.d. Herbert Hoover biographical sketch. Retrieved March 25, 2011, from http://hoover.archives.gov/info/HooverBio.html.

Hofstadter, R. 1948. *The American Political Tradition*. New York: Alfred Knopf.

Kohut, A., J. Allen, and R. Auxier. 2010. It's all about jobs, except when it's not: Unemployment and presidential approval ratings 1981–2009. Pew Research Center for the People and the Press, January 26. Retrieved March 25, 2011, from http://pewresearch.org/pubs/1476/unemployment-presidential-approval-ratings-1981-2009-reagan-obama.

Policy Responsiveness to Public Opinion
Lax, J., and J. Phillips. 2009. Gay rights in the states: Public opinion and policy responsiveness. *American Political Science Review* 103 (3):367–386.

Burstein, P. 2003. The impact of public opinion on policy: A review of an agenda. *Political Research Quarterly* 56 (1):29–40.

Politician Paranoia

Bumiller, E., D. Halbfinger, and D. Rosenbaum. 2004. The 2004 elections: A look back–The campaign; Turnout effort and Kerry, too, were GOP's keys to victory. *New York Times*, November 4. Retrieved March 25, 2011, from http://query.nytimes.com/gst/fullpage.html?res=9F07E6D7173CF937A35752C1A9629C8B63.

Jones, E. E., and V. A. Harris. 1967. The attribution of attitudes. *Journal of Experimental Social Psychology* 3 (1):1–24.

Gilovich, T., R. Vallone, and A. Tversky. 1985. The hot hand in basketball: On the misperception of random sequences. *Cognitive Psychology* 17:295–314.

Malkiel, B. 1973. *A Random Walk Down Wall Street*. New York: W. W. Norton.

Nagourney, A. 2008. Obama elected president as racial barrier falls. *New York Times*, November 5.

Nisbit, R., and T. Wilson. 1977. Telling more than we can know: Verbal reports on mental process. *Psychological Review* 84 (3):231–259.

Schaller, T. F. 2006. The (fictional) triumph of conservative Democrats. Midterm Madness blog at NYTimes.com. Retrieved March 25, 2011, from http://midtermmadness.blogs.nytimes.com/2006/11/14/the-fictional-triumph-of-the-conservative-democrats/.

Scott Brown vs. Martha Coakley

Alarkon, W. 2010. Hoyer: Voter anger should worry both parties; Dems to focus on health, jobs. *The Hill*, January 20. Retrieved March 25, 2010, from http://thehill.com/homenews/senate/77067-hoyer-voter-anger-should-worry-both-parties.

Beck, G. 2010. Beck: We'll be watching, Scott Brown. FOX News, January 20. Retrieved March 25, 2011, from http://www.foxnews.com/story/0,2933,583568,00.html

Blow, C. M. 2010. Mobs rule. *New York Times*, January 22. Retrieved March 25, 2011, from http://www.nytimes.com/2010/01/23/opinion/23blow.html.

McConnell, M. 2010. The message of Massachusetts: We need to move in a new direction. Press release, January 20. Retrieved March 25, 2011, from http://mcconnell.senate.gov/public/index.cfm?p=PressReleases&ContentRecord_id=860c654b-4eb3-4295-a574-e64f18d6ae4f.

Payne, D. 2010. What voters were saying at the polls. *Boston Globe*, January 27. Retrieved March 25, 2011, from http://www.boston.com/bostonglobe/editorial_opinion/oped/articles/2010/01/27/what_voters_were_saying_at_the_polls.

Steel, M., and K. Smith. 2010. GOP leader comments on Scott Brown's victory and the future of the health care debate. Standard Newswire, January 20. Retrieved March 25, 2011, from http://www.standardnewswire.com/news/400054875.html.

Webb, J. 2010. Statement of Senator Webb on the election results in Massachusetts. Press Release, January 19. Retrieved March 25, 2011, from http://webb.senate.gov/newsroom/pressreleases/2010-01-19-01.cfm.

Gerald Ford

Jones, J. M. 2006. Gerald Ford retrospective: Approval ratings low by historical standards. Gallup News Service, December 29. Retrieved March 25, 2011, from http://www.gallup.com/poll/23995/gerald-ford-retrospective.aspx.

Don Sherwood

Townhall.com Election Center. N.d. Pennsylvania—District 10. Retrieved March 25, 2011, from http://election.townhall.com/election-2010/state/PA/district/10.

Vlahos, K. B. 2006. Don Sherwood tries to shake scandal in Pennsylvania. FOX News, June 12. Retrieved March 25, 2011, from http://www.foxnews.com/story/0,2933,199050,00.html.

Ted Stevens

CBS News. 2010. Ted Stevens, Longest-Serving GOP Senator Dead. CBSNews.com, August 10. Retrieved March 25, 2011, from http://www.cbsnews.com/stories/2010/08/10/national/main6760221.shtml.

Yardley, W. 2008. Election results 2008: Alaska. *The New York Times*, November 18. Retrieved March 25, 2011, from http://elections.nytimes.com/2008/results/states/alaska.html.

William Jefferson

CNN.com. 2008. Indicted Louisiana congressman loses reelection bid. CNN.com, December 6. Retrieved March 25, 2011, from http://articles.cnn.com/2008-12-06/politics/louisiana.congress_1_election-gop-seat-turnout?_s=PM:POLITICS.

New York Times. 2010. Election 2010: Louisiana 2nd District profile. Retrieved March 25, 2011, from http://elections.nytimes.com/2010/house/louisiana/2.

Lyndon B. Johnson vs. Barry Goldwater

Gibson, C., and Jung, K. 2002. Historical census statistics on population totals by race, 1790 to 1990, and by Hispanic origin, 1970 to 1990, For the United States, Regions, Divisions, and States. Working Paper No. 56. Population Division, U.S.

Census Bureau, September. Retrieved March 25, 2011, http://www.census.gov/population/www/documentation/twps0056/twps0056.html.

Leip, D. 2005. US election atlas: 1964 presidential general election results. Retrieved March 25, 2008, from http://www.uselectionatlas.org/RESULTS/national.php?year=1964&f=0&off=0&elect=0.

Mayer, J. D. 2001. LBJ fights the white backlash: The racial politics of the 1964 presidential campaign. *Prologue Magazine*, 33 (1). Retrieved March 25, 2011, from   http://www.archives.gov/publications/prologue/2001/spring/lbj-and-white-backlash-1.html.

Conclusion: The Means Justify the Ends

How wonderful that we have met with a paradox. Now we have some hope of making progress.

—Niels Bohr

Success Where We Least Expect It

At 6′8″, Shane Battier is on the short side for a forward in the NBA. His career shooting percentage is about league average. He's never made an NBA All-Star Game, won a three-point shooting contest, or received any votes for the league's Most Valuable Player. You won't see him making spectacular dunks on ESPN. By NBA standards he is described as "at best, a marginal athlete." If you were trying to identify the source of his team's success on the basketball court, you wouldn't point to Shane Battier.

But you'd be wrong.

As author Michael Lewis noted in the *New York Times Magazine*, if you measure by how well his team performs when he is on the court, Battier has consistently been one of the best players in the league. When Battier is on the floor, his team plays better, while the other team plays worse. Basketball isn't just about being the best scorer or the best athlete; it's about your *team* playing better than the other team. And Shane Battier does many little things to make his team better, even though most of those things never show up on a highlight reel or stat sheet.

Often the true causes of success are not the most obvious ones. Pundits and politicians like to talk about the success or failure of democracy hinging on the wisdom of an informed populace and on their ability to elect intelligent and capable leaders. But just like the pundits who underestimate Shane Battier, they've got it wrong. The brilliance of democracy does not lie in the people's ability to pick superior leaders. It lies in the many ways that it subtly encourages the flawed people and their flawed leaders to continually work toward building a better society.

Means and Ends

Of course, many of democracy's critics *are* actually right about its problems. Voters are driven more by snap judgments and gut feelings than by a rational consideration of the merits of the arguments. We are fed misleading information by the media and the polls, and then told to use that information to go and vote in elections that are subtly manipulated by the very people whose names appear on our ballots. Then we expect our politicians to understand what we want and come up with coherent policies to faithfully represent the popular will. It's all a bit absurd, if you really think about it.

And you know the most absurd thing about the system? It works really well. It works because we believe that the system is fair. It works because the most extreme and bizarre voices tend to cancel each other out, while the rest of us rely on simple shortcuts that tend to stabilize our decisions. It works because the people who have the most power in our society want it to continue to work. And it works because every once in a while the voters step up to remind the powerful who is really in charge. In short, democracies do a better job at providing for the needs and liberties of their citizens because of the processes that spread power among the many—not because of policies created by a wise and benevolent populace.

Democracy is an extremely successful form of government, yet despite that success it isn't hard to come up with long litanies of stupid and even evil things that democratic nations have done. Among other things, the collective American conscience is burdened with slavery, Jim Crow, the Japanese-American internment camps in World War II, forced migration of Native Americans, and the periodic imprisonment and harassment of political dissenters (stretching from the Alien and Sedition Acts of 1789 through the Red Scare and the McCarthy era).

If you try to judge American democracy by individual policies, it is easy to fall into the trap of fuming at the "obvious" stupidity, irrationality, or backwardness of the American voter. But this misses the key point: Yes, the American people are crazy. *All* people are crazy. Democracy works anyway, because democracy allows all of those crazy people to work together.

Don't get us wrong: It is important to have a well-functioning government that does the right things. Policies do matter, but they don't matter nearly as much as the simple fact that we are all working together to create them. After all, even though democracies (like all other governments) do some pretty stupid and horrible things, in the long run their citizens will be better off because they live in one. A democracy doing the "wrong" thing will be ultimately more successful than any other government doing the "right" thing. The means justify the ends.

Being Better Citizens

But as well as American democracy works right now, it could work even better.

As individual voters, there are a few things that we can do to at least mitigate some of our irrational tendencies. For instance, we need to be more fully aware of our ignorance and bias. Everyone believes that he or she is right. You believe your political opinions are obviously correct—but so does the person who disagrees with you. Although there is a strong temptation to ignore the opinions of people who think differently from you, democracy functions more effectively when diverse opinions are considered. So try to keep an open mind and really listen to other points of view.

Besides, the world is too complicated to know everything about everything. For the issues that matter most to you, try to find out what the facts really are and where the candidates really stand. And for the rest, it is okay to acknowledge your ignorance and to rely on the opinions of trusted sources.

Imagine that you believe that the protection of the Alaskan National Wildlife Reserve (ANWR) against oil drilling is the big issue of our time. In that case, it should not be too much to ask that you spend a few minutes before every election to do a little research on that issue. You may discover that your senators do not conform to their party platforms; there are Democrats who support drilling in ANWR and Republicans who oppose it. You might discover that there isn't as much oil up there as you had initially believed and that drilling is therefore less attractive. Or you might find that the drilling will only affect a small amount of land, making drilling much more attractive. You might even find that legislation regarding drilling isn't going to be discussed in Congress this year, and it might be worth voting on a different issue altogether. Who knows what you'll find, but if you keep an open mind, you just might learn some surprising information.

In the same way, when you develop an opinion about a candidate, take a moment to ask yourself if you really like what he or she is saying—for that matter, take a moment to ask yourself if you even know what he or she is saying. We'd all be better off if we listened to what the candidates actually stand for, instead of allowing our decisions to be dominated by our first impressions. If we all do a little research maybe we can prevent good candidates from losing because they have a weak jawline or are listed second on the ballot.

You can also demand more from your news media. Audiences have an unprecedented ability to talk back to reporters. Every major news network now runs frequent segments in which viewer e-mails are read on the air. Newspapers maintain blogs and Twitter feeds that allow their readers to comment on stories. This feedback gives the audience power, so we might as well use that power to try to get better news.

If you see a reporter misrepresenting or overinterpreting polling data, say something. If you want to see stories on a particular topic or about a particular politician, say something. If you found the expert opinion in a story to be unconvincing or unsatisfying, say something. And when all is said and done, vote with your remote and your pocketbook. If you don't like a show, don't watch it. The problem with the news isn't that journalists don't know what they are doing; it's that the networks appear to think that the viewers prefer doom-and-gloom and gossip to real news. If you don't like that assumption, then prove them wrong by changing the channel.

Citizens can also improve democracy by participating in it. As we discussed in chapter 5, when citizens vote they become invested in democracy and more likely to engage in other behaviors that benefit society. Moreover, large voter turnouts help to add legitimacy to the electoral process and increase the procedural justice of the system. Other forms of citizen participation (writing letters to representatives, serving on juries, volunteering to work at the polls, etc.) can also build on the self-fulfilling belief that our democracy is healthy and successful. Therefore, policies that increase voter turnout will lead democratic societies to function more effectively. While there is a great deal of controversy about the effectiveness of various "get out the vote" campaigns, increasing participation is a goal worth striving for.

Another way to increase participation is for government to make laws, regulations, and paperwork easier to understand. Citizens befuddled by arcane and complex prose in government documents will be less likely to take part in the sorts of behaviors that strengthen democracies. Moreover, people who cannot understand regulations may be suspicious of those regulations, and feel that the process is unfair. Currently, many government documents are full of unnecessary jargon and complexity. For example, Calvin Woodward of the Associated Press identified a winter weather advisory which read:

> Timely preparation, including structural and non-structural mitigation measures to avoid the impacts of severe winter weather, can avert heavy personal, business and government expenditures. Experts agree that the following measures can be effective in dealing with the challenges of severe winter weather.

He notes that this advisory could have been written much more simply:

> Severe winter weather can be extremely dangerous. Consider these safety tips to protect your property and yourself.

Inscrutable writing has led to the development of the plain language movement, a grassroots effort to reduce needless complexity in government documents, legal contracts, and other official communications. In our opinion, the goals of this movement are laudable not just because they can improve the efficiency of government, but because they help support the processes that make democracy successful.

Power and Corruption

There are many ways to make democracy more effective, and not all of them require changes in behavior from individual citizens. So far, we've focused on ways to overcome the weaknesses inherent in democracy. But there are also a number of ways that we can bolster democracy by playing to its strengths. And some of these methods are quite counterintuitive.

For example, in chapter 6 we discussed how a well-functioning democracy requires that those in power be willing to lose that power should they lose elections, while those who aren't in power need to be patient enough to wait until the next election. In general, American democracy manages both of those concerns remarkably well. Of course, as Watergate demonstrated, sometimes the people in power do abuse their power—and when that happens, it is perfectly reasonable for society to have the means to keep that abuse in check and to punish the abusers. But there is a problem: An overzealous prosecution of these abuses can destroy a president's willingness to cooperate with his or her successor.

Think back to the incentives for a president to leave office when his or her time is up. One of the key things that separates democratic leaders from autocratic leaders is that democratic leaders can count on having a decent retirement. Retired autocrats end up dead or in prison, so they do everything they can to hold on to power, to the detriment of their people. Retired presidents and prime ministers end up as rich and influential citizens, which makes giving up power much easier. If we start throwing ex-presidents in jail, they will be more resistant to giving up power when the voters tell them to.

Prosecuting ex-presidents also encourages cover-ups that are potentially damaging to the country's future. Simply put, presidents need to know what their predecessors did. If presidents expect to face a criminal investigation upon retirement, then they will try to get rid of any potentially damning evidence: Destroy any documents, bribe or threaten any potential witnesses, and so on. If presidents start repeatedly destroying information that their successors might need, it could be very detrimental to the long-term health of the country.

So it would be best for us all to put a stop to the recent fad of calling for major investigations of outgoing presidents. In the last thirty-five years it has become commonplace for new administrations to have to deal with demands to prosecute the members of previous administrations. Virtually every president since Richard Nixon has faced these demands. Every time one of these issues comes up, there are widespread calls to set an example of the outgoing president in the name of justice, lest the abuse of presidential power become commonplace. But here's the problem: Imprisoning former presidents creates the wrong incentives for the current president.

Yes, we fully appreciate the need to curtail abuses of power, and we agree with the principle that presidents are citizens who must abide by the same laws as everyone else. But we also need to be aware of the damage that we're doing to our democracy as a result of such investigations. Criminal investigations of former presidents can end up doing a lot more harm than good.

Toward a Fairer Society

Another way to ensure that our democracy functions as effectively as possible would be to design the rules governing elections so that they promote both fairness and the perception of fairness. Think back to what happened in Texas in 2003. We mentioned previously how the Republican-controlled Texas legislature took the unusual step of redistricting between censuses, arguing that the previous districts did not do a good job of representing a right-leaning state. When the Republicans first tried to announce the redistricting plan, the Democratic legislators responded by deciding as a group not to show up for the vote. This refusal to participate prevented a quorum from forming—in other words, there weren't enough legislators present to legally start the session. In Texas, the governor can call the Texas Rangers (the law enforcement agency, not the baseball team) to come and force legislators to attend the session, which is exactly what Governor Rick Perry did. So how did the Democrats respond? They fled to Oklahoma, outside of the Texas Rangers' jurisdiction.

After a prolonged stand-off, the Democrats came back to Texas under the promise that the GOP would not bring up redistricting again during that session. So when that session was ended, Governor Perry called a special session of the legislature to pass the new redistricting plan. At that point, another group of Democrats fled the state to prevent a quorum—this time going to New Mexico. A month later, one of those Democrats finally returned to Texas, attended the session, and allowed the GOP to pass the redistricting plan. But of course the story doesn't end there. A citizens group immediately sued the state, arguing that the legislature, in their zeal to seat as many Republicans as possible, had effectively disenfranchised black and Hispanic voters. That suit ended up in front of the Supreme Court in 2006, which upheld one of the complaints and forced Texas to produce its third district map in a decade. It is a completely absurd chain of events, but it was all fully legal. Legal—just not fair.

As much as we might wish that everyone would take the time to educate themselves, realistically even if every American took a week out of every year to study the positions of their candidates, our democracy might only improve marginally. The more substantial improvements can only come by eliminating some of the most unfair or antidemocratic rules that still mar our system of government. After all, one of the key reasons that democracy works is because people believe that the rules that govern our elections are more or less fair. What happened in Texas had the potential to undermine that belief.

But the Texas fiasco could have been avoided. A small number of states, most notably Iowa, have started using bipartisan or nonpartisan councils to draw district maps. As a result, district maps cannot be taken hostage by partisan legislatures; the system becomes a little more fair, and we avoid the kind of embarrassments to our democracy that stem from partisan redistricting.

Gerrymandering is not the only little piece of unfairness that we can eliminate from our democracy. In Ohio, names appear on ballots in a random order that is different in each county. This system, or one like it, ought to be put in place everywhere. This will minimize the unfair advantage given to any candidate whose name appears first on a ballot.

Speaking of ballots, we should take the advice of the Caltech/MIT Voting Technology Project: Districts should move to optical scan voting in the short run, while we need better research into voting machine improvements in the long term. It's worth a few dollars to ensure that voters have faith that their votes will be counted.

Additionally, all states should take steps to ensure that their election officials are unbiased and nonpartisan (or bipartisan) whenever possible. Elected or appointed secretaries of state shouldn't be in charge of counting ballots, managing voter registration rolls, or declaring winners. Even if most secretaries of state do a good job most of the time, this kind of biased officiating violates basic norms of procedural justice. Processes need to look fair, and that means that all election decisions ought to be determined by neutral bipartisan or apolitical councils.

After all, some elections will always be so close that they are virtually tied. Besides the 2000 *Bush v. Gore* Florida recount, recent years have also given us the 2008 Minnesota Senate election and the 2004 Washington Gubernatorial election in which the recount and following lawsuits went on for months, and the 2006 Vermont Auditor of Accounts election in which a winner was actually certified only to be declared the loser after a recount. But these elections need to be decided in ways that leave everyone satisfied that the process for determining a winner was fair. Remember back to what we said about procedural justice: When we believe that elections are fair and that our votes count, we are more likely to be civically engaged and less likely to participate in antisocial behavior. In other words, *Bush v. Gore* may not have caused the downfall of American democracy, but it probably did suppress voter turnout in subsequent elections and may have even decreased the number of people who paid their taxes on time.[1]

Power to the People

Another improvement that we could make to the perceived fairness of democracy would be to eliminate the Electoral College. Again, one of the key reasons that democracy works is because people believe that their votes matter. The Electoral College was designed specifically to take the decision of who should be president out of the hands of the people. Twice in American history, the winner of the popular vote has not won the presidency, and each time it led to widespread disaffection with American democracy. The election of 1824, in which John Quincy Adams won the presidency over Andrew Jackson, came to be called the "Corrupt Bargain." And of course there is the election of 2000, when Al Gore won more votes than George W. Bush but lost the presidency owing to the disputed Florida result. Many Democrats still refer to that election as "stolen."

In practice, the only role that the Electoral College plays is to undermine the fairness of presidential elections. After all, when it does anything

---

1. Many theorists have expressed worry about other threats to the fairness (real or perceived) of American society. Some people fear that income inequality, low voter turnout, and/or diminished citizen participation in government will undermine democracy. Some have even expressed this concern over a drop in participation in various social clubs or community organizations. Any of these fears could be realized, if the general perception of these problems causes people to lose faith in government and in society. In that sense, the bigger problem isn't income inequality or low voter turnout; it is that the fear of income inequality or low voter turnout might cause people to believe that our democracy is no longer working properly.

besides rubber-stamping the popular vote total, the result is political turmoil and the widespread questioning of the legitimacy of our electoral system. Democratic fairness relies on a simple rule: The candidate who wins the most votes wins the election. The Electoral College undermines that rule.

Yes, we appreciate the profound practical and political difficulties of this. First of all, to eliminate the Electoral College would require a Constitutional amendment, which would in turn require the consent of most of the states. That isn't likely to happen. The Electoral College effectively makes the voters in small states more powerful than the voters in large states. For instance, in 2008 California had 55 electoral votes for almost 37 million people; that's one elector for every 670,000 people. Wyoming's 544,000 people got three electoral votes. That effectively made a vote for president in Wyoming almost four times more powerful than a vote for president in California. Those small states are unlikely to want to give up that power voluntarily.

Yet despite these difficulties, American democracy would be better off if we could eliminate the Electoral College.

"That Government of the People, by the People, for the People, Shall Not Perish from the Earth"

As he stood over the battlefield at Gettysburg, Pennsylvania, Abraham Lincoln pleaded with his audience to remember the sacrifices that the soldiers had made on that battlefield in defense of democracy: "that we here highly resolve that these dead shall not have died in vain—that this nation, under God, shall have a new birth of freedom— and that government of the people, by the people, for the people, shall not perish from the earth." Democracy certainly is of the people, by the people, and for the people. It reflects what the people truly are: irrational, biased, and capable of monumental acts of both genius and stupidity. Such is the nature of the human condition: We're all a bit crazy, and it would be unreasonable to expect our government to be any less so. But that central craziness of humanity has helped us to fly to the moon, to dive to the bottom of the oceans, to split the atom, to beat back famine, and to cure the plague. The people's government is certainly capable of great evil, but it is also capable of great good. And most importantly, as the people's government, democracy is as resilient as we are. Democracy is crazy; we shouldn't want it any other way.

References

Lead Quote
Bohr, N. N.d. BrainyQuote.com. Retrieved April 18, 2011, from http://www.brainyquote.com/quotes/quotes/n/nielsbohr124673.html.

Shane Battier
Lewis, M. 2009. The no-stats All-Star. *New York Times Magazine*, February 13. Retrieved March 25, 2011, from http://www.nytimes.com/2009/02/15/magazine/15Battier-t.html.

Suggestions for Improved Voting
Caltech/MIT Voting Technology Project. 2001. Voting: What is and what could be. Retrieved March 23, 2011, from http://vote.caltech.edu/drupal/files/report/voting_what_is_what_could_be.pdf.

Woodward, C. 2011. Feds must stop writing gibberish under new law. Yahoo News, May 19, reprinted from the Associated Press. Retrieved July 25, 2011, from http://old.news.yahoo.com/s/ap/20110519/ap_on_re_us/us_no_more_gobbledygook.

Texas Redistricting Chaos
Abrams, J. 2003. Texas Democrats relent on boycott; Session to debate redistricting plan. *Boston Globe*, September 10, reprinted from the Associated Press. Retrieved March 25, 2011, from http://www.boston.com/news/nation/washington/articles/2003/09/10/texas_democrats_relent_on_boycott.

Lavandera, E., J. Meserve, and M. Ahlers. 2003. Texas Democrats return home. CNN, May 16. Retrieved March 25, 2011, from http://articles.cnn.com/2003-05-16/politics/texas.legislature_1_house-speaker-tom-craddick-texas-democrats-texas-house?_s=PM:ALLPOLITICS.

Index

Note: Page numbers followed by "f," "t," or "n" refer to figures, tables, and footnotes, respectively.